Education for Professional Librarians

·edited by Herbert S. White·

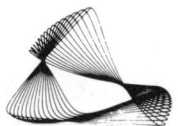

Knowledge Industry Publications, Inc.
White Plains, NY   London

Professional Librarian Series

Education for Professional Librarians

Library of Congress Cataloging-in-Publication Data

Education for professional librarians.

    (Professional librarian series)
    Bibliography: p.
    Includes index.
    1. Library education. 2. Librarians--Education.
3. Library science--Vocational guidance. 4. Information science--Vocational guidance. I. White, Herbert S.
II. Series.
Z668.E42   1986   020'.7'15   86-7250
ISBN 0-86729-197-4
ISBN 0-86729-196-6 (pbk.)

Printed in the United States of America

Copyright © 1986 by Knowledge Industry Publications, Inc., 701 Westchester Ave., White Plains, NY 10604. Not to be reproduced in any form whatever without written permission from the publisher.

          10 9 8 7 6 5 4 3 2 1

Table of Contents

List of Tables and Figures iv
Preface v
About the Authors ix

PART I: PRACTITIONER EXPECTATIONS AND NEEDS

1. University Research Libraries, *by Sheila D. Creth* 3
2. Large Public Libraries, *by Donald J. Sager*...............27
3. College Libraries, *by Evan Ira Farber* 49
4. Small Public Libraries, *by Sara Laughlin* 67
5. Corporate Libraries, *by Elin B. Christianson* 89
6. Medical Libraries, *by Erika Love* 105
7. School Libraries and Media Centers,
   by Karen K. Niemeyer 123
8. Federal Government Libraries and Information Centers,
   by Patricia W. Berger.................................141
9. The Information Industry, *by Dr. Herbert R. Brinberg*....155

PART II: EDUCATIONAL PREPARATION PROGRAMS

10. Graduate Education for the Library Profession,
    by Herbert S. White 173
11. The Role of the Undergraduate Library Education
    Program, *by Ronald Bryson* 201
12. Continuing Education Programs and Activities,
    by Darlene E. Weingand 223
13. The View of the Student, *by Louise D. Schlesinger* 237
14. Summary and Conclusions, *by Herbert S. White* 251
Bibliography...271
Index 283

List of Tables and Figures

Table 6.1: Clientele Served and Total Budget 112
Table 6.2: Knowledge and Skills 113
Table 6.3: Other Knowledge and Skills 113
Table 6.4: Personal Attributes, Attitude Toward Profession .. 113
Table 6.5: Total Staff vs. Total Professional Staff 113
Table 6.6: Staff Development Funds........................ 114
Figure 9.1: Information Business Map 157

Preface

No issue so consistently captures and holds the attention of professionals in any field as that of the educational preparation for work in the field. Inevitably each profession strikes out on its own and charts its own course in its own way. For the field of librarianship and information science, there are several widely recognized milestones. Before the turn of the century, there was the establishment of library training programs carried out in universities, as well as in libraries, by Melvil Dewey. The Williamson Report in 1923 set our sights on a higher level of preparation, which involved education as well as training. The shift from undergraduate to graduate-level preparation took shape with the development of accreditation standards for graduate education and with the insistence by some libraries and groups of libraries on this level of educational achievement as prima facie evidence to be supplied by job applicants. During the last 20 years the profession has seen the rapid development of doctoral programs that have presumably changed the chief characteristic of library school educators from practitioners to researchers, a trend common in other educational disciplines as well. Some employers have been sorry to see this change and long for what they consider a more practical curriculum. Others have applauded it, but most have their own ideas which, dictated by their own operating environments, may fall somewhere in between.

We have seen in the last 10 years a renewed, possibly cyclical, interest in what students learn before their first jobs. An increasing insistence that educators ought to teach what potential employers tell them to teach is countered by the argument that library education in a university setting must adhere to value systems imposed by the academic community. Furthermore, studies in which I have participated clearly indicate not only that the expectations of practitioners are narrow and oriented toward specific jobs in specific libraries, but also that expectations accumulate into a curriculum of staggering dimensions and contain contradictions between one group and another. Efforts to implement these models inevitably lead to fragmentation into a number of different noninterchangeable preparation models. While we might at some point have to give up the idea of librarianship as a unified profession with a common core, we should certainly not do so rashly.

And yet the search for "solutions" continues headlong. It includes lists of skills developed in a variety of settings, and belligerent letters from round tables, task forces and other special-interest groups demanding to know why library schools aren't offering more courses in their own areas of interest. In one sense these remind the recipient of the lists of nonnegotiable demands so popular with student groups in the 1960s. And yet negotiation and discussion are absolutely essential if we are to find workable and meaningful solutions.

Educators are also trapped—by the already-mentioned requirements of an academic value system; by the characteristics of their own small units (because, in addition to specialization in courses, employers want candidates available locally and without a need to pay relocation expenses; students want the ability to attend part-time at a location within easy driving distance). In addition, starting salaries make it difficult to compete with other disciplines for the high-quality students we all want to attract.

Healthy and vigorous internal discussion can be a positive force in any profession, but when it spills to the outside it increases our vulnerability. Even if we could agree on educational preparation we would continue to have difficulty enforcing our standards in the face of government agencies and private employers who do not understand what librarians are supposed to know and would rather not pay for that knowledge. Efforts by the federal Office of Personnel Management (OPM), various state agencies and some library boards to seek relief from the "expense" (laughable as such a term may be) of hiring professional librarians, can be expected to exploit any apparent divisiveness in our profession. For proof, we need only note the OPM suggestion of an inherent difference between so-called one-year and two-year graduate programs, a difference clearly invented for the OPM's own purposes and without support from the educators who administer the programs.

Certainly our profession needs solutions to continuing problems of educational preparation. However, this book is not an attempt to seek them, because such an action would be premature. There is no shortage of articles proposing specific programs, but these must be prioritized within each group, with at least some examination of alternative mechanisms of education, training and continuing education. The proposals must also be examined within the context of the whole profession—and it is clearly my preference to continue to look at it as one profession, even though it is a changing profession and even though specialization within the framework of information work does continue to develop.

The issue presents more questions than answers at this stage of discussion. Can we find a common denominator for graduate library and information science education? Should there be an undergraduate component? For some or for everyone? Should there be a postgraduate component? There would appear to be some consensus on this last question, but no clear agreement on what it is to contain, who is to do it, when it is to take place, and who is to pay for it.

The idea for this book came from the realization that we were talking about solutions without identifying what the problems were and why they existed. We were talking about "educators" and "practitioners" without realizing first of all that there are great diversities within each of those two categories and, secondly that these boxes are not hermetically sealed. Finally, we have totally ignored the third ingredient, the student. This we do at our peril, because it is students who pay for the educational process, and only their availability makes any sort of selection possible for the employer. Where there are no interested graduates, additional concerns may even eclipse those of educational content, as those now trying to hire children's librarians and catalogers well know. The students' influence is perhaps more subtle because they don't speak with an organized voice. Nevertheless, it is they who decide whether or not to attend at all, where to attend and at least what electives to take or to ignore.

My task as editor has been to find leaders in the various communities—individuals with stature and recognition, concerned about these issues, and able to write. While they visibly and actively represent the constituencies about which they write, as the brief biographical sketches that follow this preface clearly demonstrate, in another sense, they cannot really be considered representative, because both their backgrounds and the level of their concern stamp them as leaders. However, leadership is exactly what the process requires at this point.

That there is no common format or writing style was a conscious decision. Any effort to impose such restrictions would have been counter-productive to the main purpose—to identify issues for dialogue and investigation. In the final chapter, I endeavor to pull together some of the agreement, divergences, issues and alternatives that emerge through this process. This book is not an end. It is an attempt at a rational professional beginning. That may disappoint some readers, because it is more satisfying to deal with conclusions and concrete proposals. Conclusions are already plentiful in our literature, but they are narrowly self-serving and they don't help the process. Every journey starts with the first step, and I hope that this book will take us part of the way down a difficult but essential road.

Herbert S. White

ACKNOWLEDGMENTS

There are many individuals who should be thanked, and not enough space to thank them or a good enough memory to include them all. The most direct appreciation must go to the authors of the specific chapters. It is an impressive group of junior and senior professionals who think seriously about our field, and this alone should give us optimism for the future. As always, my wife, Virginia, has served as a sounding board, evaluator, and highly objective and perceptive reactor, and I am very grateful to her. My own career in librarianship, in which time as a practitioner and manager still exceeds that as an educator by more than two to one, has put me in contact with thousands of individuals, and their beliefs and hopes have helped to shape my own approach to this issue and to this book.

About the Authors

Patricia Berger has been active in Washington on the federal library scene for many years and is currently chief of the Information Resources and Services Division of the National Bureau of Standards. She has served both as president of the Washington, DC, chapter of the Special Libraries Association and as a member of the American Library Association council and executive board. She is a member of the Federal Library Committee and deeply involved in its activities regarding government standards for librarians. She has received numerous awards, including the Department of Commerce Outstanding Administrative Management Award.

Herbert R. Brinberg is president and chief executive officer of Wolters-Samson U.S. Corporation, an organization that includes among its subsidiaries the Aspen Systems Corporation and three publishing organizations. Prior to this assignment, he was vice president of the Information Technology Group of American Can Company. In the private information sector he has served as board chairman of the Information Industry Association and as chairman of the Associated Information Managers (AIM). He has written and spoken extensively on information resource management and the organizational implications of new technology.

Ronald Bryson is chairman of the Department of Library Science at Spalding University in Louisville, KY, a post he has held for 13 years. Prior to that he served as head librarian for two college libraries and as a school librarian. He is active in the American Library Association, the Kentucky Library Association and the Association of Library and Information Science Education.

Elin Christianson is a library consultant serving corporations, associations, networks, and various types of libraries, as well as a part-time faculty member in two library education programs. She served as head librarian of the J. Walter Thompson advertising agency in Chicago, and is coauthor of many journal articles and monographs, including *Special Libraries: A Guide for Management*. Particularly active in the Special Libraries Association, she has chaired its advertising and marketing division.

Sheila Creth is assistant director for administrative services at the University of Michigan Library, where she has spearheaded many innovative personnel management practices. Prior to her present assignment, she served as assistant director for personnel of the University of Connecticut Library, and she is a frequent speaker and consultant on manpower planning and personnel administration. A contributor to the professional literature, she is coeditor of the highly acclaimed book, *Personnel Administration in Libraries*.

Evan Farber has served as librarian at Earlham College since 1962. In a long and distinguished career in college librarianship, he has numerous publications and consultant assignments to his credit and has edited a number of major research volumes, including *Combined Retrospective Index to Book Reviews in Scholarly Journals*. With a particular interest in bibliographic instruction for college students, he has been active as a member of the Council of the American Library Association and served as president of the Association of College and Research Libraries.

Sara Laughlin is coordinator of the Stone Hills Area Library Services Authority, a ten-county network of small public libraries for which she manages grant, staff and contract functions. Active in both the Association of Specialized and Cooperative Library Agencies and the Public Libraries Association, she is also the recipient of two citizen participation awards from the governor of Indiana.

Erika Love is professor and director of the University of New Mexico Medical Center Library. She previously served in a variety of important medical library administrative posts, including that of deputy associate director for library operations of the National Library of Medicine. She has been particularly active as speaker, writer, and consultant in continuing education for medical librarians and has written extensively on this topic. She has held numerous offices in the Medical Library Association, including the presidency.

Karen Niemeyer serves as director of Media Services of Carmel Clay Schools in Indiana, after serving as both a school and public librarian. She has spoken and written on topics of concern to school and media librarians, particularly those dealing with copyright and the application of computers. Very active in the American Association of School Librarians, she has also served as president of the Association of Indiana Media Educators.

Donald Sager is currently city librarian of the Milwaukee Public Library and director of the Milwaukee County Federated Library System. His distinguished career has included the post of commissioner of the Chicago Public Library and an assignment as distinguished visiting scholar at OCLC. A long list of publications includes the recent work *Managing the Public Library,* and he has been a frequent speaker and consultant. His activities at the state and national level include major offices in the American Library Association and the Public Libraries Association, including the presidency.

Louise Schlesinger is a recent graduate of a dual master's degree program with degrees in Library Science and Public and Environmental Affairs. She currently serves as reference program director of the Southeastern Indiana Area Library Services Authority. She was winner of the 1984 Student Essay Competition of the Special Libraries Association Library Management Division.

Darlene Weingand has a dual appointment from the School of Library and Information Studies and the Extension Communications Program of the University of Wisconsin at Madison, with responsibility for the development and administration of statewide professional continuing education programs in the field. She has written numerous articles and several monographs, including

The Organic Public Library and *Women and Library Management.* Her many professional activities include chairing the 1985 conference of the Association for Library and Information Science Education.

Herbert S. White is dean and professor at the Indiana University School of Library and Information Science. Prior to that he worked extensively in the administration of industrial and government libraries and information centers and in the information industry. A prolific writer, guest speaker and consultant, he is the author of two recent monographs, *Managing the Special Library* and *Library Personnel Management,* and serves as a regular columnist in *Library Journal.* He has been president of both the Special Libraries Association and the American Society for Information Science.

I
Practitioner Expectations and Needs

1

University Research Libraries

Sheila D. Creth

As we hurtle toward the year 2000, librarians must assess and reassess the constantly changing university library environment. We cannot talk about the future as if it were far away, shrouded in mystery. The future is as close as tomorrow, and we must deal with it every day, with every decision we make or avoid. Individually and collectively, librarians cannot afford to ignore the changing shape of information services that is emerging. Nor should they hesitate to take pride in and use the traditions and values that have served libraries and users so well in the past. The primary objective of university libraries—to organize and provide access to information—will not alter, though the format and methods will change dramatically, providing new opportunities and challenges.

TRADITION AND TRANSITION: THE UNIVERSITY AND THE LIBRARY

To understand the needs of university libraries we must first understand the major factors that influence higher education: scholarship, technology and economics—all of which are interrelated. The dynamics and demands of the scholarly community continue to shift, with an increasing focus on interdisciplinary studies, an increased use by scholars of information sources outside the library, and stiff competition for academics to conduct and publish research in a timely manner. These aspects coupled with the continuing explosion of published and unpublished materials needed by scholars have intensified the demands on information organization and access.

University librarians, as they have in the past, will have to be comfortable and conversant with the world of scholarship and research, understanding the research process generally as well as maintaining knowledge about the subject disciplines they serve. They will also need to work with the growing number of non-library research sources (some of which will be scholar-generated) and in some situations be prepared to develop the databases to provide access to such materials.

Librarians in the research library system must recognize the support of instruction and research beyond their own department or clientele, and they must consider the needs of the broader university community as well as the scholarly community outside of their own university. University libraries support some collections because of their national or international scholarly value whether or not they serve a significant group on the local campus. As the multiple and diverse needs of scholars emerge, choices related to collections and services will have to be made based on a number of factors involving local as well as national research considerations.

The Impact of Technology

Technology is having a growing impact on higher education specifically related to instruction and research. Indeed, universities with highly publicized "computer czar" positions and talk of "wiring" the campus are rapidly becoming high-tech environments. The library, which has often been at the forefront in using automation and proclaiming its virtues to university administrators and faculty, will now find it imperative to play a central role in planning for campus-wide automation as a tool for information access.

As the use of technology expands on campuses with resulting new services, users and expectations, tensions and strains between university libraries and computer centers are likely to increase over issues of information design, control and management. Battin sees the library and the computer center joining together to provide an "information infrastructure to stimulate the continuing autonomous use of information sources." Referring to Columbia University, she says that "the integration of Libraries and the Computer Center, each with its specific strengths and expertise, will provide one-stop shopping for the University community as well as a stabilizing planning mechanism for effective and flexible response to rapidly changing technologies."[1] Veaner suggests that a new relationship is needed and that "if the library and the computer center should somehow be unified, or at least drawn closer together, staff in both areas will realize how complementary are their different expertise and how together they can create superior products and services."[2] While these views represent a desirable goal, it is not likely to come about smoothly or comfortably on most campuses since information will increasingly be seen as a valuable and political commodity. An uneasy truce may be the more likely relationship to exist during the next decade.

Clearly university librarians cannot afford to be either ignorant or passive about technology and its implications within the university environment. University librarians will have to be imaginative and innovative in working with technology, to maintain a familiarity with campus automation developments, and to involve themselves whenever possible in campus telecommunications as a way of creating new contacts and opportunities for library services. A view of technology as a tool for scholars in the information age is best depicted by the concept of the scholar's workstation, consisting of a microcomputer that provides a single environment from which a researcher will be able to gain access to a variety of bibliographic resources.

Battin describes activities that will be possible for the scholar in this setting:[3]

- Downloading capacities and local interactive manipulation of all files
- Full-text access to databases, data files and published works also preserved on optical disk
- High resolution graphics
- Capacity to order offline prints of machine-readable text, facsimile transmission of journal articles and/or delivery of printed publications

- Links to printed works through online indexes and tables of contents
- Access to current scholarly output through author-supplied subject access
- Access to online preprint exchange, with papers maintained online for six months
- Online access to education, training and consulting services

In this setting, faculty or their surrogates will no longer have to physically come to the library for information about or receipt of materials. Such an approach to information services suggests that researchers are going to expect more in the way of access to information not all of which will be located at their university library or even within a library. De Gennaro says that "Users will no longer be limited to what a library has, but to what it can provide."[4] To achieve this projected level and diversity of services, librarians will need to be knowledgeable, skilled and innovative enough to integrate all information sources and respond to new services the electronic scholar will expect.

The Impact of Economics

Economics continues to be a primary contributing factor in making decisions and planning directions in higher education and will continue to do so for the foreseeable future. Costs continue to rise for all university functions but most particularly for salaries and fringe benefits, automation, energy, equipment and building maintenance. (Libraries are major consumers in each of these areas.) Universities have instituted measures to trim expenditures by demanding greater fiscal accountability, limiting new programs and reducing existing programs, or simply making cuts in staff without any corresponding reduction in services or numbers of people served. A conservative economic picture has a direct impact on the library's budget. A static or reduced budget is onerous when research libraries are faced with increasing costs of materials and staff, and particularly after a decade of erosion of library budgets.

In this economic climate, library managers have to be more

accountable for how they use their funds—making selection decisions, offering services, establishing staffing levels—and they will have to explore new ways to accomplish work and provide services in order to contain costs without diminishing the quality of services or the role of the library in the university. What is not affordable is for libraries to reject innovation and change when budgets are tight. An attitude of holding the line could spell disaster for the library. Instead, innovation—new thinking—in times of fiscal retrenchment is what is needed in order to identify new opportunities for increasing the vitality of the library.

The University Environment

Clearly, the university library cannot stand isolated or aloof from the internal and external forces that shape the university. Librarians must understand university politics and governance as well as scholarship, economics and technology. They should seek ways to take an active role in the governance of the university both to educate themselves and to provide visibility for librarians on the campus. If librarians have not formerly been keenly aware of and actively involved in their institutions, they will need to be in the future. An active interest and informed view of the university will allow librarians to define their role in the university rather than having it defined by others.

The university library is in a transition period with traditional functions and services beginning to evidence dramatic changes as a new concept and role for libraries and librarians emerges. A number of the changes that have been forecast have already begun to occur, such as a shift from a production to a managerial role for librarians with a concurrent shift of traditional librarian tasks to support staff. This has certainly occurred in cataloging, where automation has been commonplace for over a decade. Now the issue of the librarians' role, and therefore that of the support staff, will be increasingly reviewed and rethought in every function.

Already considerable discussion has taken place about the reference function, specifically the role of nonlibrarians at the reference desk. The issue for the future, though, will probably not be centered on the reference desk. Librarians will increasingly provide reference service and research support through electronic means—bulletin boards, electronic mail and conferencing—as well as reference by appointment and through instruction in classes. They will be teaching researchers to access databases independently while also developing databases to provide access to materials otherwise not organized. The question will not necessarily be who will sit at the reference desk but whether there will be a reference desk as we currently understand it and, if so, how that service will relate to the new services.

University librarians will need to think about functions and services in a completely different way to consider what opportunities technology will offer to provide traditional services in different ways as well as the means to develop different services. They will also need to identify what to relinquish—even activities they may have cultivated and refined over the years—in order to provide the new and more effective services. De Gennaro states that research libraries are moving into a "major transition from the collection-centered institutions that they are today to the access and service-oriented institutions that they must . . . become in the next two decades."[5]

This period of transition will probably last for a long time; indeed, we may come to see that university libraries are in perpetual transition, moving gradually from one environment to another. This condition will require that librarians develop a new understanding and expectation of working in a library. While most people have long since ceased to believe that libraries are quiet places to work, libraries are not perceived as dynamically changing and shifting organizations; and yet, this may be the reality for the future. There will be tensions and strains between the traditional and the transitional, with staff and users who prefer one over the other. This should be expected. The tensions are not necessarily unhealthy but they need to be recognized and addressed. It should be expected that the pace of acceptance and change will vary among individuals, functions and activities, and the receptiveness to change among faculty and students also will vary by individual and discipline.

The transitional phase will also be marked by the need to maintain parallel systems in two aspects. On the one hand, the library will change dramatically but also remain the same. Collections in printed form will continue to be important along with electronic publications and software; individual assistance to users in use of printed indexes and online databases will continue and coexist with new and yet unknown services. So traditional library activities, with all of the attendant knowledge and skills required of librarians, will exist alongside the emerging activities requiring new knowledge and skills. In addition, as technologies change, university libraries will upgrade a system and in doing so have to run two systems in parallel, maintaining operations on the old while implementing the new. These situations will make considerable demands on staff and require a vast range of knowledge as well as a high degree of flexibility.

ORGANIZATIONAL CHANGES: BUREAUCRATIC VS. ENTREPRENEURIAL

New technologies may call for organizational changes in the traditional library. Will it always be prudent to maintain separate divisions for public and technical services? Do the current and future technologies suggest different ways to organize collections and services?

Writing about the centralization or decentralization of library collections, Stevens says that "the issue has reemerged but is framed in different considerations. Centralization or decentralization must now be considered in relation to such factors as new technology, resource sharing, and other information services and sources. The administrative control of information, not its physical location, is the crux of the issue today."[6] Technology offers the possibility of maintaining centralized collections and services in a distributed online information environment, or distributing a variety of services among library locations and maintaining administrative control through the central online system. Decisions will hinge on the current university climate and the costs for either approach rather than on the past issue of access. It will also be possible in the online environment to expedite selection, acquisitions, cataloging and reference by means of library teams organized in clusters of related disciplines. The entire organizational structure of research libraries should be rethought and possibly reconstituted as technology provides opportunities for delivery of services in unique ways.

The Librarian as Entrepreneur

How will the hierarchical, bureaucratic structure of the library be affected by technology, and will it serve the emerging new needs of the university community well?

Veaner says that microcomputers and networks are "already fostering the growth of a new kind of librarian—the entrepreneur who seeks out clients in an active 'marketing' mode rather than waiting for patrons to come to the institution."[7] Robbins-Carter says that "it will be extremely difficult, if not impossible, to foster productive competition and entrepreneurial attitudes if we maintain our present functional structure." She feels that discipline-focused organizational structures are required but goes on to say that it is "ironic that the radical change in organizational structure that is required can be facilitated by the hierarchical bureaucracy that now permeates our libraries."[8]

It is likely that librarians are going to have to operate for some time in a hierarchical organization while demonstrating entrepreneurial behavior.

People in the Information-Age Library

Beyond the issue of organizational structure, which would, of course, affect the jobs and roles of librarians, the organizational characteristics most likely to be affected by the integration of technology into all aspects of the work place include employee attitudes, management processes, interpersonal relations, interdepartmental relations, and organizational structure, with additional changes in location of work, shifts in mode and timing of communication and changes in the work product itself.[9]

If supervisors rely more extensively on technology to interact with staff, will libraries become increasingly regimented? According to Giuliano, "New technology inevitably affects the organization of work." He defines three evolutionary stages of office organization as preindustrial, industrial and information age. "Each stage is characterized not only by its technology but also by its style of management, personnel policies, hierarchy of supervisory and managerial staff, standards of performance and human relations among office workers and between the workers and their clients or customers."[10] Giuliano feels that the "information-age office exploits new technology to preserve the best aspects of the earlier stages and avoid their failings." He feels that the information-age office combines high efficiency through access to a continuously updated database with a people-centered rather than machine-centered environment.[11]

One could draw a parallel between the industrial stage, assembly-line approach to work found in many industries and certain operations in a library. Malinconico indicates that electronic data-processing technologies have allowed information work to take on "the characteristics of mass production jobs: mechanical pacing of work, repetitiveness, minimal skill requirements, predetermined use of tools and techniques, surface mental attention, and minute subdivision of labor."[12] The challenge for librarians will be to use the technology to move into the information stage effectively and efficiently and avoid the assembly-line environment with the all-too-familiar problems.

The traditional university library has certain attributes that make it an attractive place to work despite low salaries. Libraries are viewed as people organizations both because they are labor-intensive (there are a lot of people) and because they are service organizations. The library is seen as a place where social contacts and relationships are the way that work is accomplished. If library work increasingly involves people interacting with terminals rather than with other people, how will that affect people's desire to work in the library? Schraml attributes the potential dehumanizing aspects of computerization to "its unrelenting pace, its intolerance of human error, and the requirement that its operators communicate in a coded language."[13] Other authors have pointed out the potential for alienation from work in environments where work is checked by machines rather than by supervisors who would then provide assistance and encouragement.[14] Library management will need to identify positive qualities of the high-tech environment which can be introduced into the library.

Fringe Benefits

There are indications that organizations that offer employees access to the benefits of technology may reap benefits in return. As libraries are increasingly automated, library staff at all levels will be acquiring new knowledge and skills and ones that will be very marketable. This can help people perceive the library as an attractive place to work. Libraries that make telecommunications systems (electronic mail, bulletin boards and conferencing) available to staff are likely to see increased communication between people throughout the organization with less regard for position, department, role, status or social position.[15] This increased and diversified communication serves to establish in the organization new links and relationships that can help to mitigate the negative impact of a machine-centered work place. While it is not yet clear exactly how communication in a computer-mediated environment will develop, it is clear that dramatic changes will occur and these, in turn, will contribute to further organizational change.

Another attraction of the high-tech research library will be the possibility for staff to work at home and access their work and co-workers via online systems. Supervisors can monitor work products for many jobs via the online system. A new breed of library employees may emerge: "telecommuters." Home employment via telecommunications would offer many people employment who might otherwise be unable to work because of family obligations or physical handicaps. It could offer flexibility in work schedules and cut the costs of transportation, meals, child-care arrangements and clothes for the work setting.

For the organization, home work can increase productivity without increasing the demand for space and furniture and with minimal added expense for terminal and communication charges. The disadvantages may include a loss of interaction with supervisor and co-workers which could create a sense of alienation, and a lack of commitment and interest in the work and the library. Atkinson points out that "out of sight, out of mind" may affect the telecommuter who is interested in promotional opportunities.[16]

Not everyone is convinced that there will be a big rush for home work. Naisbitt asserts that "people want to go to the office. People want to be with people, and the more technology we pump into society, the more people will want to be with people."[17] It is likely that both situations will coexist; home workers will become a reality in the near future though they may represent a small percentage of library employees. Librarians will have to be able to supervise work and workers in the library and at home as well as establish a bridge between these two groups of employees.

All of these issues will need to be addressed as the university library shifts and changes its services, organizational structure, priorities and role in the information age. Many of these shifts will result as technology continues to evolve. The challenge for librarians will be to identify the negative effects of technology and seek ways to minimize them and to find ways to use technology to improve the quality of work life, not only the efficiency of the organization; they will need to create a people-oriented organization in an increasingly machine-oriented environment, and develop management and leadership skills to operate effectively in both; and librarians will need to visualize and put into effect new services to take advantage of existing and emerging technologies. Technology is only the tool; it is librarians who will provide the vision and energy to make use of this powerful tool.

THE UNIVERSITY LIBRARIAN

In the context of the issues facing higher education and university libraries, what are the expectations and requirements for university librarians? In general, librarians will be responsible for activities that are both familiar and quite different. Management responsibilities will be a primary activity but with a new set of demands. To manage work, people and services in an increasingly automated environment will require more sophistication in management techniques and facility with multiple management approaches and strategies. Furthermore, management will in time involve more, if not all, librarians.

The provision of reference services is likely to change considerably in character and scope. More online reference service will be provided both in response to specific requests and in anticipation of faculty and student needs. Librarians will participate in teleconferencing and message systems and establish databases for otherwise unavailable research materials held by faculty or others. Analytical and technological skills will be essential for these types of activities. The concept of who is a reference librarian should begin to shift, as catalogers and collection development librarians become involved in providing assistance to users through online reference service. These librarians have considerable understanding of collections and are thus far a largely untapped resource for assisting library users directly.

Selection will continue to be a primary focus for research librarians though the complexity will increase as multiple formats become the norm. Software purchased for the library collection may have to be replaced more often, and unpublished or published materials available in an electronic format may be kept online for only a brief period of time. Copyright problems and guidelines for circulation and use will also occupy librarians' thinking. In addition to the subject and language knowledge required and the ability to work with faculty, they will also need to understand how to develop a budget request (taking into account a variety of factors such as collection use, inflation, value of the dollar, etc.) and how to manage a budget.

Catalogers will increasingly become project managers, training and supervising support staff who will then handle all but the most complicated cataloging. Librarians will be involved in resolving the relationship between local needs and standards and national utilities, and resolving complex bibliographic issues bound by specific technological requirements. In addition, as indicated previously, librarians with knowledge of the collection should be more actively involved in providing research assistance to users.

In general, university libraries have the potential to unlock a wealth of expertise by using librarians in activities and services based on their talents rather than adhering to the traditional department or division organizational structure. Technology will facilitate this transition. While many professional activities will remain familiar and stable in the near future, new activities will evolve and require correspondingly new knowledge, skill and ability. Librarians—new and experienced—will need to recognize what will be expected of them currently and over the next decade in each of these components.

The Research Librarian of the Future

Battin has described the characteristics she feels are essential for research librarians:

- A first-rate mind with problem-solving abilities
- A solid undergraduate education in which the rigor of the undergraduate education and training is critical, not the subject matter
- Concrete evidence of managerial abilities (even the beginning librarian will have to supervise)
- An intellectual commitment to research librarianship[18]

Hoadley describes the ideal academic librarian as a person who has the following attributes:

- The ability to think and reason
- The ability to communicate clearly—both in writing and orally
- Good interpersonal skills
- The ability to function in an automated environment
- Strong research capabilities
- Basic knowledge of library operations and principles[19]

Veaner describes the following requirements in his two-part paper on academic librarianship in the next decade:

- Knowledge and currency in higher education developments
- High-level skills in oral and written expression
- Solid grasp of mechanical skills and tools
- Strong intellectual abilities
- Skills for the management of institutional time and money[20]

Veaner specifically points out the need for librarians to possess typing skills, among other mechanical skills, in order for them to operate with ease in the online environment. Typing has often been viewed as a valuable skill for clerical staff only.

Powell and Creth found that university librarians with up to

10 years of experience already ranked management skills (specifically planning, personnel and training) as very high in importance but also ranked it very low in knowledge already possessed.[21] The same results were found on the knowledge base of automation: librarians ranked it high in importance but low in the knowledge they possessed. In addition, certain areas of knowledge were perceived by these university librarians as relevant only when associated with specific positions, when indeed they are critical to all professional positions. These knowledge bases include writing skills, systems analysis, program evaluation techniques and inferential statistics. This is a troubling response from university librarians. How can a librarian be effective without the ability to think analytically or write well? How can professionals be effective if they are unable to evaluate services and activities using program evaluation techniques, or to conduct operational studies using statistics?

The research by Powell and Creth suggests that librarians recognize gaps or deficiencies in the knowledge and skills they will need to be prepared for in the future. These deficiencies can be addressed through appropriate education and training programs. The research, though, also suggests that university librarians may not always be taking a sufficiently broad view of what is and will be expected of them in the increasingly complex university library environment. This will require a different effort to overcome.

Taken together, the variety of expectations for university librarians presents something of a paradox. The ideal university librarian should be

- An entrepreneurial risk taker—who is adept at working in a hierarchical structure
- An independent worker—but also a team player
- Excellent at fulfilling the requirements of a specific assignment—while also able to contribute to the library system, the university and the profession as a whole
- Competitive and assertive—and cooperative and willing to compromise
- Intellectually committed—but also equipped with technical and managerial competencies
- Enthusiastic in response to new technologies—without becoming emotionally attached to any one system

Other requirements for research librarians imply a paradox but in truth represent the diversity of talent that will be needed and the degree of flexibility required. These expectations represent current reality not some futuristic picture. Librarians will have to be able to operate on many levels, within many different—sometimes conflicting—situations and with many constituencies representing different views and demands. Rather than developing a managerial style or a personal approach to all situations and people, librarians will need to recognize and develop strategies that can be used to fit the situation in which they are working at the moment.

How will librarians acquire all of the necessary requirements for the university library, which is so clearly in flux and for which a broad range and depth of experience are expected?

EDUCATION: WHO IS RESPONSIBLE?

The expected requirements for present and future research librarians are quite impressive if not staggering. There is no way that this level of expertise can be achieved without serious attention to the process of education. This education must be ongoing, with responsibility being shared by the faculty in the graduate programs, research library administrators and managers, and the individual librarians themselves. Each should approach the topic of education with a global and integrative view.

Graduate Programs

Certainly graduate library schools must be far more aggressive in attracting to their programs a student body diversified enough to reflect a wide range of personal attributes and educational preparation. Faculty should be rigorous in establishing curriculum and placing demands on the students; library schools cannot afford to be seen as offering an easy master's program or as supplying the union card for obtaining a professional position. To remain viable in the information age, the master's degree in library science should be valued as highly as the MBA, a computer science degree or a degree in organizational psychology.

The curriculum should reflect—indeed anticipate—changes in

the profession and in library organization. This requires that the faculty keep up to date on issues and trends as well as practices. No less important in establishing the models required for the new librarian are enthusiasm and taking an active role in research and professional matters. The graduate library science program should draw on appropriate courses in other academic departments, while not watering down a core curriculum designed for information specialists. While library schools cannot necessarily cater to university libraries—or any specific library for that matter—they do need to be cognizant of the needs of different library organizations and attract into their programs people who will meet these needs, and then provide the relevant curriculum. If they ignore either aspect, they will be failing in part of their mission and university libraries will have to look elsewhere to find the professional talent they need. As Battin says, "If the choice is between credentials and talent, I think we must opt for the talent."[22]

The Library

The graduate library school program cannot be expected to provide all of the knowledge, skill and ability that university librarians will need as they begin their careers, much less over careers that may span 20, 30 or 40 years. Therefore, the university library must accept as a primary responsibility and objective the continual development and training of its staff. University librarians must demand as much from their libraries in training and development as they demand from library schools; they must turn the same critical eye on internal staff development programs and opportunities as they use to scrutinize the library school curriculum. University libraries do not currently enjoy a reputation for offering well-planned, organized staff development programs; indeed, libraries that have such programs are the exception not the rule. Too often supervisors fail to support staff development programs, claiming that staff are too busy to attend or, worse, they resist change when an employee returns from a workshop with new ideas.

Supervisors should demand more from the organization to support their own internal job training. Without a planned program of training and development, chaos tends to result as change is continually introduced. This in turn can lead to inadequate services, poor staff morale and high turnover, and eventually a diminished view of the library by faculty, students and administrators. Research libraries cannot be successful without knowledgeable and enthusiastic staff, and this is even more critical as libraries face the quiet revolution of technological change.[23] Substantial resources should therefore be allocated to provide numerous opportunities for learning and development—even during tight budget times.

Librarians

Finally, of course, librarians have a responsibility for their own learning and development. They cannot wait patiently to see what others will do for them but must be aggressive in identifying areas they need to strengthen and developing the methods for doing so. Even when a solid library education has been acquired, and the library organization provides learning opportunities, the librarian must be responsible for his or her own growth and development. Professionals should attend and participate in local, regional and national conferences as well as enrolling in workshops and taking formal courses. While not all university libraries require a second master's degree, certainly any librarian in the research environment benefits from acquiring a subject master's. Librarians must also be willing to spend their own money to support their continued education and professional participation.

Librarians will need new knowledge, skills and abilities as change occurs; they will also have to relinquish some old outlooks, attitudes and behaviors in the new environment.

RECRUITMENT: OPPORTUNITIES AND OBSTACLES

University library managers must recognize the need to conduct recruitment for professional positions in a sophisticated manner. Recruitment is one of the most important public relations functions for a library. University libraries must market themselves; they must be able to describe the opportunities for contribution, learning and advancement that are available in the research library environment. While it is possible that smaller academic libraries or special libraries may offer new librarians more immediate involvement in a full range of organizational activities, university libraries offer greater variety and opportunity over a period of time. There is room for expansion and change and very real opportunity to contribute to education and research.

To be successful in recruiting new and experienced staff, library managers must recognize the potential obstacles that exist in attracting "the best and the brightest" so that these can be overcome or minimized. The obstacles include salaries; the diminished mobility of librarians, particularly the two-career couple; the scarcity of professionals with management experience to fill middle- and upper-level positions; and tenure/promotional requirements.

Salaries

Salaries are affected by the fact that librarianship is a female-dominated profession and library work and librarians have historically been undervalued. In addition, higher education institutions have never been likely to provide substantial monetary rewards. The first factor presents a problem in attracting the widest range of talent to graduate library schools. The second factor—university salaries in general—makes it difficult for university libraries to compete with special or corporate libraries or with public libraries that benefit from civil service or union negotiated salary structures.

While we cannot make absolute statements about a group as diverse as university libraries, there was some improvement in librarian salaries during the early 1980s. Unfortunately, however, university libraries tend to try to improve local salaries by comparing only with peer libraries where salaries are higher. Real improvements in librarian salaries will occur when they are compared with those of teaching faculty and other professional groups on campus, as well as with those of comparable information professionals in industry. Even when such comparisons receive support from university administration, improvements in salaries require a commitment of funds from the university, and progress is therefore likely to be slow as long as the economic conditions remain relatively static. Library administrators naturally will keep trying to improve the overall salary situation and to reward librarians who make the most significant contributions to the library and its users. But since it is not likely that dramatic change will occur in the salary situation, library managers and librarians will have to establish other rewards and means of recognition for professional staff, and to ensure that professional assignments are challenging and satisfying.

Mobility

The library profession is a potentially mobile one and yet over the past five years it has become more difficult to persuade librarians to relocate. Two major factors appear to be influencing this reluctance to relocate. One is the phenomenon of the two-career couple, in which both members are seeking a position that will reflect advancement and a satisfying career choice. As a result, university libraries may lose qualified candidates because of the lack of opportunity for the spouses.

The second factor which has contributed to a diminished interest in relocating is the national economic climate. Individuals who already own homes, for instance, are likely to experience real financial losses if they have to refinance to purchase a new home. Quite often the salary differential between the current position and the offered position is not great enough to make the move financially attractive, particularly if there is a considerable difference in the cost of living between the two locations. University libraries are also handicapped when it comes to providing employees with other benefits, such as moving expenses, assistance with financing a new home or locating low-cost rental accommodations, and other nontaxable benefits, such as tuition assistance for the librarian and family members. Libraries that can offer such benefits beyond the salary are clearly in a more competitive position. To offset these limitations, library managers will have to make the career opportunities provided by positions more apparent to potential candidates.

Finally, many librarians have very strong ties to a community or a geographic region of the country and are not willing to relocate without a compelling reason.

Middle Management

Middle management positions in university libraries often remain vacant for long periods of time, with searches being repeated. While the relocation problem contributes to this situation, there is often a shortage of candidates with the appropriate management experience. This is an increasing problem and university library administrators must evolve ways to close the gap between requirements and qualified candidates. For some positions is may be necessary to seek candidates whose experience is outside of the library profession, such as personnel administrators, systems staff and financial managers. But increasingly candidates without library experience may be hired for other roles in the research library. Individuals who have university management experience, research or teaching experience, or technological experience may be sought for a variety of positions if qualified librarians are not available.

Library administrators must decide how to prepare more librarians to assume not only upper-level management positions but also the many new positions that will emerge. Industry long ago recognized the need to provide training and development to attract and retain good people and thus assure the success of their organizations. This has not been a responsibility readily assumed within university libraries but if the gap between needs and available qualified candidates is to be closed, the library will have to play a role in that effort. Indeed, this may be the major mechanism available to university libraries to address the multiple problems of recruitment.

Tenure and Promotion

A final reason for recruitment becoming difficult for many

university libraries is that the requirements for tenure and promotion are rigorous. For libraries whose staffs have faculty status, the requirements for obtaining tenure are especially stringent. Librarians considering positions with faculty status should therefore weigh whether they want to expend the time, energy and money to attempt to achieve tenure. As tenure requirements become more rigorous some librarians will choose to avoid institutions with faculty status. University libraries that do not have faculty status and its attendant requirements may have promotional systems which also contain requirements for performance and contributions outside of the primary job assignment. In some libraries, there may be a requirement to promote from the entry level to the next level or be terminated (the "up or out" practice).

Promotional systems less rigorous and thus less frightening than the tenure process may also discourage librarians from seeking otherwise attractive positions if considerable additional activities are required beyond the position requirements. When librarians are discouraged by such requirements, it is often because they see low salaries in conjunction with high demands for job performance as well as other professional contributions.

This is not to suggest that requirements attached to tenure and promotion systems do not benefit the individual librarian. Indeed, the activities in which librarians involve themselves beyond their specific assignments is what adds a critical dimension to the role of the professional. Librarians should be interested in opportunities for contribution beyond their position within the university and in the profession as they consider a specific position and library. Librarians have to assess all aspects of a position and an organization—salary and benefits, career growth and potential, the reputation of the institution, which may add to their strength for later positions—and not simply look at the short-term salary picture. There is no question, though, that salary will continue to be the dominant consideration for most individuals.

Library managers will need to be increasingly sophisticated in the recruitment function but, more important, they will need to be sure that professional positions do offer sound opportunities for growth and development, participation and contribution.

SUMMARY

Changes within university libraries regarding requirements, responsibilities and roles for librarians will vary by library and university though the pace and direction of change is clear.

More will be expected of university librarians. Their role and activities will become increasingly sophisticated and more diverse. They will be expected to strengthen certain traditional areas of expertise, such as subject knowledge and knowledge of organizing collections, while expanding into the technological and management areas and integrating these to bring about new services, new products and potentially a new concept of the research library.

NOTES

1. Patricia Battin, "The Electronic Library: A Vision for the Future," *EDUCOM Bulletin* 19: 12-34 (Summer 1984), p. 17.
2. Allen B. Veaner, "1985 to 1995: The Next Decade in Academic Librarianship, Part II," *College and Research Libraries* 46:295-308 (July 1985), p. 297.
3. Battin, p. 17.
4. Richard De Gennaro, "Shifting Gears: Information Technology and the Academic Library," *Library Journal* 109:1204-1209 (June 15, 1984), p. 1206.
5. *Ibid*, p. 1204.
6. Norman Stevens, "Centralization/Decentralization: New Views on an Old Issue," *Library Issues* 4 (May 1984), p. 1.
7. Veaner, p. 296.
8. Jane B. Robbins-Carter, "Reaction to '1985 to 1995: The Next Decade in Academic Librarianship, Parts I & II,'" *College and Research Libraries* 46: 295-308 (July 1985), p. 310.
9. Margrethe H. Olson and Henry C. Lucas, Jr., "The Impact of Office Automation on the Organization: Some Implications for Research and Practice," *Communications of the ACM* 25: 838-847 (November 1982), p. 83.
10. Vincent E. Giuliano, "The Mechanization of Office Work," *Scientific American* 247:149-164 (September 1982), p. 158.
11. *Ibid*, p. 162.
12. S. Michael Malinconico, "People and Machines: Changing Relationships?", *Library Journal* 108: 2222-2224 (December 1, 1983), p. 2222.

13. Mary L. Schraml, "The Psychological Impact of Automation on Library and Office Workers," *Special Libraries* 72: 149-156 (April 1981), p. 152.

14. Shoshana Zuboff, "New Worlds of Computer-Mediated Work," *Harvard Business Review* 60: 142-152 (September-October 1982); F. Frendan Loughridge, "Against the Self-Image of the Trade: Some Arguments Against Computers in Libraries," *Assistant Librarian* 72: 114-116 (September 1979); S. Michael Malinconico, "People and Machines: Changing Relationships," *Library Journal* 108: 2222-2224 (December 1, 1983).

15. Sara Kiesler, "The Hidden Messages in Computer Networks," *Harvard Business Review* 64:.1: 46-60 (January-February 1986), p. 15.

16. William Atkinson, "Home Work," *Personnel Journal* 64: 105-109 (November 1985), p. 107.

17. John Naisbitt, *Megatrends: Ten New Directions Transforming Our Lives* (New York: Warner Books, Inc., 1984), p. 43.

18. Patricia Battin, "Developing University and Research Library Professionals: A Director's Perspective," *American Libraries* 14: 22-25 (January 1983), p. 23.

19. Irene B. Hoadley, "Reactions to 'Defining the Academic Librarian,'" *College and Research Libraries* 46: 469-471 (November 1985), p. 470.

20. Veaner, pp. 298-300.

21. Ronald Powell and Sheila Creth, "Knowledge Bases and Library Education," *College and Research Libraries* 47: 16-27 (January 1986).

22. Battin, "Developing University and Research Library Professionals," p. 22.

23. De Gennaro, p. 1204.

ADDITIONAL READINGS

Abell, Millicent D. "The Changing Role of the Academic Librarian: Drift and Mastery." *College and Research Libraries* 40:154-164 (March 1979).

Bearman, Toni Carbo. "The Changing Role of the Information Professional." *Library Trends* 32:255-260 (Winter 1984).

Bok, Derek. "Looking into Education's High-Tech Future." *EDUCOM Bulletin* 20.3:2-10 (Fall 1985).

Conroy, Barbara. "The Human Element: Staff Development in the Electronic Library." *Drexel Library Quarterly* 17:91-106 (Fall 1981).

Cronin, Blaise. "Post-Industrial Society: Some Manpower Issues for the Library/Information Profession." *Journal of Information Science* 7:1-14 (1983).

Drake, Miriam. "Managing Innovation in Academic Libraries." *College and Research Libraries* 40.6:503-510 (November 1979).

Lancaster, F. Wilfrid. *Libraries and Librarians in an Age of Electronics.* Arlington: Information Resources Press, 1982.

Leonard-Barton, Dorothy and William A. Kraus. "Implementing New Technology." *Harvard Business Review* 85:102-110 (November-December 1985).

Lynch, Beverly. "Options for the 80s: Directions in Academic and Research Libraries." *College and Research Libraries* 43.2:124-129 (March 1982).

Malinconico, S. Michael. "Managing Organizational Culture." *Library Journal* 109:791-793 (April 15, 1984).

Matheson, Nina W. and John A.D. Cooper. "Academic Information in the Academic Health Sciences Center: Roles for the Library in Information Management." *Journal of Medical Education,* October 1982, part 2.

Olsgaard, John N. "Automation as a Socio-Organizational Agent of Change: An Evaluative Literature Review." *Information Technology and Libraries* 4:19-28 (March 1985).

Rayward, W. Boyd. "Conflict, Interdependence, Mediocrity: Librarians & Library Educators." *Library Journal* 108:1313-1317 (July 1983).

White, Herbert S. "Defining Basic Competencies." *American Libraries* 14:519-525 (September 1983).

2

Large Public Libraries

Donald J. Sager

The most recent survey of U.S. public libraries, conducted by the National Center for Educational Statistics (NCES) in 1982, revealed that 52.4% of all public library expenditures went for salaries.[1] Since personnel constitutes so great a percentage of public library budgets, one would expect the public library profession to take a great interest in preparation for librarianship. Unfortunately, that does not appear to be the case, at least according to an analysis of conference programs and a review of the literature. The schedule of the first national conference of the Public Library Association (PLA) held in Baltimore in 1983, for example, contained only a single program on preparation for the profession. An online database search of the literature on education of public librarians from 1980 to the present turned up only 11 articles.

While this may be of some concern to public librarians in general, it should be of special concern to those associated with large public libraries. The 1982 NCES survey revealed that more than 20% of all professional librarians were employed in 63 large public libraries.[2] The NCES divides public libraries into various categories, using population served as a criterion. They range from 14 libraries serving more than 1 million persons to 5495 libraries serving 9999 or fewer persons, with a total universe of 8597 libraries. For this essay, I define large public libraries as those serving 500,000 or more, although I acknowledge that it is arbitrary and that institutions serving smaller populations face many of the same problems.

PERSONNEL NEEDS

Professional employment among these large public libraries has been decreasing during the past several years, according to the last 2 NCES surveys. The 1978 NCES survey reported 8828 professionals in a universe of 54 libraries serving 500,000 or more.[3] The 1982 NCES survey reported 7632 professionals among 63 libraries in that population class.[4]

No recent survey of large public libraries appears in the literature to indicate what significant changes have occurred in the type of duties assigned professionals. However, a review of advertisements for public library positions in major libraries which have appeared in the journals during the past several years, and informal discussions with the administrators of large public libraries, who meet at each midwinter and annual American Library Association (ALA) conference, reveal some obvious trends. In recent years large public libraries have experienced some difficulty in recruiting and retaining children's librarians, automation specialists and competent middle management. Some decline in extension and outreach programs has occurred, as many local governments declined to pick up innovative outreach programs directed at special user groups typically concentrated in metropolitan areas. These programs were often initiated by Library Services and Construction Act (LSCA) grants during the 1960s and early 1970s, and large portions of LSCA funds allocated to the states by the federal government went to large public libraries. For example, in 1977 30% of all LSCA funds granted to local public libraries went to the 54 largest public libraries in the U.S.[5]

Despite the continuation of LSCA, the creation of a major urban resource library component (MURLS) that earmarks funds for 140 urban areas, and the original intent of this legislation to improve library service to special users, a comparative study of recent reports prepared by U.S. Department of Education officials indicates that grants to serve special users are declining relative to grants for projects such as development of statewide bibliographic databases and other automation projects.[6]

Local governmental financial constraints have also sharply reduced the capability of large urban public libraries to develop innovative programs or extend existing services. While total income among public libraries rose from $1.5 billion in 1977-78 to $2.2 billion in 1982, an increase of 46%, they experienced a net decline when compared to a 50.3% increase in the Consumer Price Index.[7] Figures for large public libraries reveal an even greater real decline. Many administrators of large public libraries report a decrease in the number of extension agencies such as branches and bookmobiles, or a reduction in the hours of service, in order to make ends meet. While some large public libraries have experienced growth and dramatic improvement, the overall trend in terms of professional employment among large public libraries is negative. Normal turnover as a result of retirement, transfers of spouses and similar activity, leaves the large public library as a major market for new professionals, nonetheless.

FACTORS AFFECTING RECRUITMENT

Skills required among large public libraries have always been more specialized than those in the public library field as a whole. The vast special collections and the heavy emphasis on reference service require individuals who have gained advanced academic training in subject fields or who have gained extensive experience through work in special collections. While the large public libraries, unlike academic libraries, have not stressed the second master's degree in their advertisements or civil service requirements, there is an increasing tendency in that direction. Typically, many municipal and county libraries, as divisions of local government, provide some sort of tuition reimbursement as a fringe benefit, which contributes to this process.

According to the 1985 edition of the *American Library Directory*,[8] the overwhelming majority of the larger public libraries have subject departments, and many have archival, document and multimedia responsibilities. Many libraries serve the blind and physically handicapped. Many have sophisticated, independently staffed automated services and large administrative functions, often serving larger geographic areas on a cooperative or multitype library basis.

The special skills required in a large public library also reflect the diversity of the metropolitan area served. Foreign language skills representing the major ethnic mix of the region are only one element. While metropolitan areas are increasingly diverse in terms of business and industry, an area that historically based its economy on heavy industry will probably have a public library with major holdings in patents, technical specifications, engineering and related collections, and a need for personnel familiar with the literature of those fields. Local history and archival skills are also common requirements. While all public libraries need personnel with such training, needs of large public libraries are even greater because the local history and archival holdings of a large public library are typically at a research level.

The administrative requirements of a large public library are substantially more complex than those of the average public library, where the director is frequently personnel officer, business manager, purchasing agent, contract administrator, chief planner and public relations director, all rolled into one. The hierarchy of a typical large public library is generally multi-tiered and further complicated by its interrelationship with an even grander municipal or county hierarchy and myriad policies, procedures, regulations and ordinances. The budget process alone for a large metropolitan library can consume a major segment of an administrator's time for the better part of the year. While the elements of administration are the same for most public libraries, large libraries are more likely to be specialized and to need librarians with mastery of local administrative practice, procedures and politics.

Certification and Standards

While many states have certification or standards for professional librarians, these do not have great impact upon large public libraries. Many states specifically exempt large cities from regulations that affect professional services elsewhere in the state. These home-rule provisions exempt cities or counties with large populations and grant authority over personnel regulations to civil service boards in those governmental units. Where state library associations maintain certification or standards, there is not likely to be an exemption, and librarians are treated equally, regardless of the size of the institutions in which they serve. Nonetheless, academic credentials and continuing education requirements may vary with the "class" or size of the library: there are more self-educated librarians in smaller public libraries, where they are often awarded professional status through their experience rather than their formal training, than in larger ones, where the requirements are more strictly adhered to.

In 1982-83 the Public Library Association (PLA) created a special task force, chaired by R. Kathleen Molz, to study the feasibility of a national certification program to replace the hodgepodge of varied certification requirements established by individual states. While certification of public librarians is assigned to the state library agency in many states, it can be argued that the responsibility is more appropriate to a professional association, since such bodies are better equipped to determine what is acceptable in terms of professional standards, and the state's role is more properly one of licensing. But certification is a matter of high emotion, and the PLA task force stepped hurriedly back after studying the issue and left it as the province of each state library agency and state library association.

Personnel Turnover

No study of personnel turnover in large public libraries has appeared in the literature in recent years. An analysis of retirements, age levels and other forms of attrition would be useful and provide administrators and library schools with more accurate information as a basis for recruitment and counseling. Civil service regulations in many large public libraries often restrict promotional opportunities to those who have had prior service in a prerequisite civil service grade, thereby guaranteeing that promotion comes from within. Although affirmative action programs have broken down some of these barriers to opportunity, the individuals still on the panels doing the selection are usually products of the old civil service procedures. As a result, the professional personnel in a large public library system are likely to enter the system at graduation and remain in that system until retirement. That presents advantages as well as problems for large public libraries. On the positive side the institution benefits from continuity and the opportunity to develop special skills necessary for its collections and services. On the negative side is the tendency toward insularity, conservative programming and resistance to change.

Civil Service Policies

Most large public libraries are under civil service or merit system regulations and policies, and even those with greater autonomy are affected in their selection and promotion procedures by the policies of their sister municipal or county institutions. That implies competitive formal examinations, especially at the entry level, assessment panels usually recruited from other departments or libraries, and selection teams consisting of representative administrative staff from the institution. Selection is usually restricted to the top three to five persons who score highest on exams, and there is considerable agreement among administrators willing to discuss the issue that the process does not always produce the most qualified candidates, since attributes such as leadership cannot be determined through testing. The persons who score highest in civil service tests are very often those who know how to pass tests. While public library administrators are granted some input in the development of civil service tests, total control rests with the civil service agency.

Beyond the entry level, civil service policies usually place increasingly greater weight on experience and third-party panel assessment of the applicants' qualifications for positions. The implication of this process is that it becomes extremely difficult to undertake recruitment, mentoring and many of the other developmental activities on an individual basis. Top-level administrators of a large public library do not get involved in the selection and promotion process until the very last step, when they are presented with a choice of three or four candidates who have survived the earlier stages. The individual they may have thought showed the most promise may have fallen out of contention by that time because of veteran's credit or some other vagary of the scoring process.

Affirmative Action

Affirmative action programs have forced some modification in the civil service procedures, as well as in all library personnel procedures. While public libraries of all types have been stimulated to correct inequities in racial and sexual balance, as well as increasing employment of the physically impaired, it has had an even greater impact on the large public library, since the metropolitan areas they serve contain higher percentages of minorities and the handicapped. The goal of affirmative action is to establish some parity between the composition of the community at large and public employment. While libraries have done well in developing a high percentage of female administrators, compared with other departments of local government, they have not done as well in the recruitment of minorities.

Despite recent steps taken by the federal government to downgrade the importance of affirmative action, many local governments have become awakened to their responsibilities, and they are continuing to stress affirmative action. The implication for large public libraries is that they must continue to recruit minorities and the handicapped in their professional and administrative ranks, and they are experiencing difficulty in finding them. To illustrate the problem, ALA-accredited library schools graduated only 221 minority librarians in 1982, out of a total class of 3784.[9] The blame is often placed on the professional schools for failing to do more recruitment, but in fact it is a shared responsibility. The professional schools can point to the decline in public library placements and the absence of federal aid programs. Better dialogue between the graduate schools and the public library community is required before more progress can be made.

Special Skills

Earlier in this chapter, mention was made of the special skills required of professionals in large public libraries. In a recent article on preparation for public librarianship, Betty Turock pinpointed one of the technical skills required, when she noted that "for the next decade, the public library will require entering professionals who can design databases at the local level, as well as participate in planning regional and national networks."[10] Coupled with that is the ability to use the growing number of commercial databases. Again, this is a skill required of any public librarian engaged in reference service, but given the heavy demands on larger public libraries to provide research and reference service, it is of much greater importance. The 1978 NCES survey revealed that 47% of all reference service in the U.S. is rendered by large public libraries.[11] While reference skills are crucial, other special skills include advanced subject knowledge, archival and records management training, skills in serving special clientele, foreign languages, automation and advanced management ability.

These special skills would merit reconsideration of a second year program, but Turock observed that this has met with little success.[12] Edwin Gleaves, writing on library educational trends in the 1980s, agreed.[13] This flies in the face of recommendations for a two-year program made by Conant in his study of education for librarianship which appeared in 1980.[14] Gleaves stated that the two-year program has made only limited progress because of its cost and the shrinking market.[15] In actuality it may also be that a second master's degree in another subject field is a more attractive alternative for many in the public library field.

OTHER RECRUITMENT FACTORS

Beyond these factors in the selection of personnel for large public libraries, there are a number of other issues that affect the ability of these institutions to attract competent and specially qualified professionals. Among the first is salaries. Comparison of beginning and intermediate salaries listed in the biennial Allen County, IN, Public Library survey of larger public libraries (100,000+)[16], and positions advertised in the professional journals for the past several years reveal that larger public libraries have consistently maintained higher wages than their suburban or rural counterparts. This differential is usually justified by higher living expenses in the metropolitan areas. More often, the higher wages are due to city and county labor agreements, from which professional librarians benefited, whether they were part of the bargaining unit or not. The higher wages, of course, may help explain why many of the larger public libraries are also experiencing financial problems and why the personnel complement has declined. The higher wages are also justified by the working conditions which many professionals in large public libraries face, such as assignments in neighborhoods with high crime and poor public transportation. In recent years there has been increased resistance to wage demands throughout the economy and, if the trend continues, there may be greater parity of wages and benefits with suburban and rural libraries.

Municipal Policies

Municipal policies and politics also confront administrators in their efforts to recruit more competent professionals. Many cities have residency requirements, and individuals who take employment with local government are required to take up residence there within a comparatively short time. Because this limits choice, and usually imposes additional costs upon the individual, it presents another barrier for the large public library. While most large cities and counties have civil service or merit systems designed to prevent patronage, they can be bypassed by the simple expedient of making interim appointments pending the establishment of the next civil service qualifying exam. Fortunately, only a few major cities suffer from patronage abuse, but more subtle political pressures exist in every major city, and they hinder governance and administrators in recruiting competent professional personnel.

Another related problem is the increasing instability of large city governments. As more cities experience fiscal problems and public services decline, the electorate is more willing to toss incumbents out of office. In many cities and counties today, being the incumbent elected official is no longer a political advantage. As a result there is more frequent turnover at the policy-making level, and this results in uncertainty regarding long-range plans for city and county services, less willingness to take risks in financing major public improvements, and the need to reeducate each new administration regarding the services and activities of city or county departments such as the library.

Institutional Size

Yet another factor influencing the large public library in the recruitment of personnel is a limitation imposed by the sheer size of the institution. Many professionals do not want to become lost in a staff consisting of hundreds or thousands of people. In former years this fear was offset by having the opportunity to work in an institution possessing rich collections, innovative programs and a staff with a national reputation. Now the collections may have declined, the innovative programs have ended, and the renowned staff has retired and not been replaced. All that is left may be a feeling of anonymity in an institution fighting a holding action against the next fiscal crisis. Finding ways to foster professional growth is a challenge many large public libraries are facing, but it is often slow and painstaking.

The large public library may seek to improve the participation of its professional staff in decision making and may have a well-developed committee system, but it does not compare favorably with the opportunity granted many professionals in small public libraries. The literature today reflects the fact that small public libraries often have sufficient flexibility and funding to experiment with new programs and services, and their professional staffs are not bound by rigid hierarchical structures and detailed procedures.

Changing Job Descriptions

Another element likely to confront the administration of the large public library is the issue of obsolescence of job descriptions. While professional job requirements and responsibilities are continually changing in all sizes and types of libraries, the large public library is faced with less flexibility. Civil service review is generally required before a job description can be changed, and every effort is made to limit the number of unique job descriptions and titles. If the change in job description involves the possibility of a pay adjustment, which is common, the local government's budget office enters in to assess the effects this change may have on the fiscal health of the local government. If these hurdles are passed, approval by the city council or county board of supervisors and the mayor or county executive is required. It should be little wonder that job descriptions in many large public libraries are obsolete and fail to reflect actual duties and requirements.

Opportunities for Development

Training and professional development opportunities in larger public libraries are likely to be more formal and more highly developed than those available in small and medium-sized public libraries, at least on the surface. Tuition reimbursement programs are commonplace in many of these institutions. Many personnel departments have training officers and programs. Some routinely contract with local academic institutions for special training. Less common, however, are opportunities to attend professional conferences on local government time and with local government reimbursement for expenses. The reason is a continuing belief that these conferences are really junkets, and taxpayers would criticize use of public funds for this purpose. Many cities and counties tightly control conference attendance, and there is particularly intensive media coverage of who attends which conferences and where they are held. As a result, a large public library with hundreds of professionals is likely to have a disproportionately small percentage of that staff in attendance at a professional conference, unless the conference happens to be held in that city.

There may be exceptions to this, and there are certainly many small and medium-sized libraries with similar problems, coupled with staffing limitations. However, they usually have greater flexibility in allowing staff to attend professional conferences than do larger public libraries. A limitation upon conference attendance also affects professional participation in those associations, since it limits the opportunities for contact with other professionals in the field.

EDUCATIONAL EXPECTATIONS

So far, this chapter has concentrated on the personnel needs of larger public libraries and factors affecting selection and recruitment. The balance of this chapter is devoted to expectations in the preparation of the professional for service in large public libraries and the steps the professional schools and large public libraries can take to better prepare tomorrow's professionals. In a recent article on the education of library and information science professionals, James Rush reviewed the course offerings of the professional schools.[17] He observed that the courses dealt with media, but not messages, with sources, but not their content, with age groups rather than the diverse spectrum of individual information users, and with historical rather than modern techniques and technology. He then listed areas in which he felt tomorrow's professional should possess some competency, including marketing, planning, budgeting and financing, telecommunications, electronic publishing, records management, regional networking, information brokering, indexing and abstracting, computer architecture, database management, computer graphics and revenue generation. He found most of these absent from the catalogs of the library and information science programs listed in a recent edition of the *American Library Directory*.

Information Technology

In another frequently cited article, Pauline Wilson also stressed the inadequacy of information science training in the professional curriculum.[18] She went on to report that electronic technology will become the single most important influence on library science curriculum, but she also added that it would not necessarily have an impact on teaching methodology. Indeed, there is concern among many large public library administrators that newly graduating professionals lack basic computer skills. Colson observed that the typewriter was invented in 1885 and was in general use in libraries by 1900.[19] "Yet as late as 1940, the 'library hand' still was taught in some library schools." He went on to note that computers were introduced in libraries in the 1960s, yet a decade and a half later a majority of library school students graduate with no more than an introduction to computers.

Of even greater concern are thousands of today's professionals who are confronted with new technology and lack the skills to use it effectively to cope with growing public demand for reference service, and decreasing personnel to provide it. This plight will affect tomorrow's professional as well, for the skills they may be mastering in elementary programming and database design may not be of permanent value. Teaching what is permanent in the use of new technology is something that practitioners among large public libraries presume—or at least hope—that graduate schools are doing.

User Orientation

Still another expectation concerns user orientation. While large public libraries have high hopes for computers, they still expect tomorrow's graduate to possess fundamental skills in public service. Writing in Great Britain's *Journal of Librarianship,* Blaise Cronin and Irene Martin discussed the significance of social skills training.[20] They observed that more public libraries have begun to apply marketing principles to the management of public service. However, a single rude, socially inept librarian could destroy the best marketing strategy. Indeed, there is a suspicion among some library administrators that the professional schools still attract "the wrong type." They blame faculty for producing graduates who are more interested in materials than in people. In fact, it is the profession that must deal with the problem rather than just the graduate schools. While *American Libraries* may run articles on how the profession has improved its image, there is still room for improvement. If it's any consolation, librarianship is not the only field concerned with its public image.

While automation promises to substantially change how librarianship serves the community, it still comes back to a one-on-one interaction between the librarian and the client. Information scientists may theorize about the evolution of "expert systems" taking the place of the reference interview, but there will always be a need to have a knowledgeable person available for those who are not computer literate. Furthermore, the development of any expert system is dependent upon a body of theory and practice that is still in its infancy in this profession.

Social Skills

Public librarianship has long emphasized the community analysis, but it has not translated that into strategies necessary to aid individual users. Cronin and Martin propose social skills training as a logical step in this process.[21] They define social skills as behavior that facilitates human social interaction, both generated responses and perceptions of others.[22] It is concerned with the emission and perception of behavior signs—verbal and nonverbal. Library training concentrates on the teaching of technical as opposed to social skills, and there is yet to be any impact on graduate preparation. The reluctance to accept social skills training or user analysis as part of the graduate curriculum is undoubtedly due to several factors. Cronin and Martin contend that it is due to mistaken associations with group therapy and encounter sessions.[23]

The already crowded curriculum is another factor. There are just so many subjects that can be crammed into a single year's program. Another factor is the absence of library-related research on user analysis, although there is a substantial body of general knowledge in the social sciences that can be drawn upon. Perhaps the greatest reason for the absence of course work that would improve professionals' user orientation is the failure of public library administrators to articulate this need clearly. Instead, there is resigned acceptance that some professional staff have the ability to work effectively with the public while others do not, and the fault is obviously due to the professional school. In Cronin and Martin's assessment, social skills or user analysis "should not only lead to an increase in social confidence and competence, but also to an increase in an individual's ability to 'diagnose' the needs of clients."[24]

Management Ability

Large public libraries also expect that the new graduate will possess supervisory skills. The NCES surveys reveal that there is a much higher ratio of nonprofessional and paraprofessional staff to professionals in large public libraries than in medium-sized to small libraries.[25] That understood, one would suspect that large public libraries would have management development programs. Yet a survey reported by Gleniece Robinson revealed that "large public libraries do not plan systematically for the development of managerial personnel, nor do they use any deliberate process for short-term or long-term management development training."[26] The findings were based on a telephone survey of 51 libraries serving over 500,000 persons. Forty-six of the libraries responded. Presently, there are only two formal academic programs available for library management development in the U.S. One is the Executive Development Program for Library Administration offered by the Center for Management Services at the Miami University School of Business Administration in Oxford, OH, and the other is the Library Administration Development Program offered by the University of Maryland's College of Library and Information Service at College Park.

In a brief article which appeared in *Public Libraries,* Darlene Weingand identified some preliminary competencies for public librarians.[27] Interestingly, a fairly high percentage of the competencies she proposed were those normally associated with supervision, such as planning, evaluation, organization, policy development, negotiation, and budgeting. Despite the apparent need for competency in supervision, a survey of ALA-accredited library schools undertaken in the early 1980s revealed that less than 20% offered a full course in public library management.[28] The survey polled 69 schools, of which 52 responded. It could well be that elements of public library management were part of other courses developed by the schools, such as general library administration, but there is a body of theory and practice on the management of the public library that could easily justify a separate course, particularly given the high ranking this receives among many public library administrators.

Practical Experience

Public libraries also expect that incoming members of the profession will have sound insight into current trends, needs and problems in this field. At one time some graduate schools required prior experience in a library as an entrance requirement. Today that is not a requirement, and it has led some to suggest that some clinical experience be added to the program in preparation for public library service. Colson observes, however, that students may become "encumbered with biases derived from their work experiences."[29]

To underline the value of clinical training opportunities, Lukenbill cites a 1977 study conducted by Rue Bucher and Joan Stelling on the experience of students in different professional programs.[30] The programs involved internal medicine, biochemistry and psychiatry, but Lukenbill drew out the elements of the studies relevant to librarianship. The findings showed that clinical experience did have an impact on trainees in terms of policy making. The Bucher and Stelling study revealed that realistic role playing as well as role modeling, coaching and peer group reaction strengthened mastery.[31] Interestingly students became very selective in adopting attributes of admired role models, and they also used negative models to reject attributes they didn't like. Nonetheless, the study indicated that mere exposure to some part of a field, whether it be activity, theory, method, philosophy or ideology, does not ensure that students will incorporate these into their new professional identity or professional definitions. The study also showed that students gaining clinical experience often learn that the knowledge base of their field is inadequate, and because of this, they come to value the process of doing their work rather than the actual results of the process.

Although Lukenbill predicted "the adoption and widespread integration of clinical experiences into educational programs for public librarians may soon be at hand,"[32] there is room for doubt. In his conclusion, Lukenbill calls for more money for library schools, larger staff, more training time, higher academic credentials for clinical field workers and more research. Also needed is dialogue between the graduate schools and public library administration to ensure that field work is more than free labor, and to establish standards that provide more meaningful learning experiences for the student.

Other Administrative Needs

While improvements in clinical experience may help students enter the profession with more knowledge of current trends, needs and problems, there is a body of expected skills that go beyond technical knowledge and supervision. These include analytical and problem-solving ability; capacity to make a commitment to and gain involvement in the community; communications and motivational skills; financial acumen and resourcefulness; and leadership. These are the permanent personnel skills that transcend technical and supervisory ability. While they may be incorporated in the varied coursework provided by the graduate school, the student must emerge with fundamental ability to analyze not only the problems the public library confronts today, but those that are certain to emerge in the future. Librarians should know the process of selecting the best solution from an array of complex alternatives. Students must also be prepared to make a commitment not only to the profession, but to the community they serve, for the knowledge of the community and the individual users being served is surely as critical as the technical skills mastered.

Communication with that community and with the individual users being served cannot be underestimated, for whatever professional skills the student may possess become useless if potential clientele are unaware of them. In the larger urban setting, these skills become even more crucial because of the media information overload. As large public libraries are called upon to perform more services to satisfy more special-interest groups, tomorrow's professional must possess the motivational skills to draw effectively on the human resources available. A frequent complaint among the staff of many large public libraries, as reflected in staff attitudinal surveys received by the PLA, is that administration does not make effective use of staff ability.

Certainly, financial acumen is of growing concern, as the competition for available tax revenue increases and alternative sources must be found. Making optimal use of available funds is also essential, and that will be a fact of life for the public library of the future. Increasingly, professional librarians may be called on to generate revenues for their programs, just as other professions do, and this is a matter that neither the graduate schools nor the profession as a whole have confronted. It is a fact that public library service has never been free. Someone pays. What remains to be determined is who pays for what, and how.

Leadership is another permanent skill required in our profession, just as it is in all others. If the large public library is not only to survive but to flourish in the future there is a tremendous need for leadership. While the profession may take for granted the essential nature of the public library, we are on a collision course with other public services and those who must foot the bill for the maintenance of these services. Somehow, the large public library must recruit or develop leadership among its professional staff to ensure that the institution evolves, further improves its visibility and utility, and effectively fulfills its mission of educating, informing and enriching its clientele. That is a responsibility not only of the library's governance and administration, but of its entire professional staff as well.

PLANNING FOR THE FUTURE

To fulfill these expectations, there are some steps which both the professional school and the large public library must take in the future. First, there is a need for closer rapport between those who prepare the professionals and those who recruit and supervise them. The profession primarily relies on an accreditation process that can only deal with the fundamentals in preparation for librarianship. Even with representation from different aspects of the profession, too few practicing librarians participate in the process of evaluating professional training programs, and the evaluation is too infrequent. What is needed is continuing dialogue between the professional organizations concerned with public library development and those responsible for educating the professionals who serve public libraries. For large public libraries, there are the metropolitan libraries section of the PLA and the Urban Libraries Council. They should make a commitment in this matter.

The survey of ALA-accredited library schools cited previously, revealed that only 34 of 52 schools responding (65.4%) offered a full course in public library service.[33] While many included public libraries in other courses in the curriculum, there is clearly a need to make more schools aware of public library personnel needs and keeping them informed more effectively about placement opportunities.

Some need also exists to give graduate faculty more opportunity to observe on a first-hand basis the needs, trends and problems facing large public libraries. The survey conducted by Todaro reveals that of the 50 persons teaching public library courses in 1982, only 35% to 45% had had public library work experience within the previous 10 years.[34] Exchange programs between major public libraries and graduate schools can improve this situation. Betty Turock also called upon more public libraries to seek library school faculty for problem solving instead of turning to private field consultants, in order to build up a body of expertise.[35]

The administrators of large public libraries also have a personal obligation to become more aware and committed to those graduate schools upon which they rely for professional staff. They may serve as adjunct faculty or members of advisory committees, but that is often a passive role and not a substitute for developing cooperative programs that will motivate outstanding students to consider public librarianship as a career path. These same administrators can develop more meaningful clinical experiences, contribute to school developmental activities, aid faculty in forecasting placement opportunities, and contract for continuing education programs so that the library's present staff can obtain better interaction with the faculty.

Preparation for the profession is not a unilateral process, and if administrators believe that graduate schools are ivory towers, they are not blameless. While there are dangers in establishing too close a relationship between any institution and the graduate school—for the freedom exercised by the faculty in designing the curriculum and establishing standards should not be tampered with—there is a much greater risk in failing to communicate.

To ensure that high standards are maintained, both the graduate schools and the public library administrators may need to be more circumspect in the accreditation of new programs. Gleaves reported that between 1967 and 1980, the number of accredited library schools increased from 39 to 62, a growth of 59%.[36] There were 67 accredited programs in 1984.[37] During approximately the same period, public library employment was virtually unchanged, and in large public libraries, employment of professionals actually declined. The creation of a local graduate program is often a temptation visited upon academic and public library administrators. Perhaps another alternative might be to negotiate for the extension of a program from an existing accredited school, if a real need genuinely exists, thereby strengthening that institution and still providing local staff with access to professional training programs.

SUMMARY

Many of the expectations and needs of large public libraries in the preparation of librarians are common to libraries of all sizes and types. Nonetheless, large public libraries possess some unique problems in terms of special skills, employment levels, standards and turnover. Civil service and merit system regulations often hamper recruitment and development efforts, although affirmative action plans have permitted some flexibility. New technology has resulted in an increased demand for personnel competent in this area. Shortages also exist for children's librarians and competent supervisors.

While salaries and fringe benefits remain competitive among most large public libraries, competition has slowed in recent years as resistance to bargaining unit effort has increased. Municipal policies such as residency and the political and financial instability of many large cities have adversely affected recruitment of outstanding professionals, and opportunity for professional growth is often limited.

Despite these factors in selecting and recruiting professional staff, large public libraries still have high standards and expectations of the new graduate. The individual joining the large public library is expected to be technically competent in a subject field, and in the use of computers. The new professional is also expected to have supervisory ability. A user orientation with social skills is often an unstated expectation. Finally, the beginning librarian is expected to have the foundation for effective analysis and problem solving, community commitment and involvement, communications and motivational skills, financial acumen and resourcefulness, and leadership potential.

The preparation of professionals for service in the large public library requires the commitment of both the professional school and the library administration. Communication regarding needs, participation in the development of the school's program, exchange opportunity for faculty, use of faculty for research and planning needs, improvement of clinical experience and greater care in the accreditation of additional new graduate programs are factors that can lead to better preparation for the professional of the future.

Although the nation's large public libraries have experienced some financial constraints and other problems during the past several decades, they still employ a significant percentage of the nation's public librarians, and they can influence and aid the graduate schools in their responsibility for preparing tomorrow's professionals.

NOTES

1. Robert A. Heintze, "The NCES Survey of Public Libraries, 1982," in *The Bowker Annual of Library and Book Trade Information,* 30th ed. (New York: R.R. Bowker, 1985), p. 415.

2. Ibid., p. 413.

3. U.S. National Center for Educational Statistics, *Preliminary Report: Library General Information Survey, LIBGIS III: Public Libraries, 1977-78* (Washington, DC: The Center, 1982).

4. Heintze, p. 413.

5. LIBGIS III.

6. Ray M. Fry, "U.S. Department of Education Library Programs, 1984," in *The Bowker Annual of Library and Book Trade Information,* 30th ed. (New York: R.R. Bowker, 1985), p. 271.

7. Heintze, p. 414.

8. Jaques Cattell Press, ed., *American Library Directory,* 38th ed. (New York: R.R. Bowker, 1985).

9. Association for Library and Information Science Education, *Library and Information Science Educational Statistical Report* (State College, PA: The Association, 1984).

10. Betty Turock, "The Public Librarian and Library Education," *Public Library Quarterly* 4 (Fall 1983):10.

11. LIBGIS III.

12. Turock, p. 7.
13. Edwin S. Gleaves, "Library Education: Issues for the Eighties," *Journal of Education for Librarianship* 22 (Spring 1982): 268.
14. R.W. Conant, *The Conant Report: A Study of the Education of Librarians* (Cambridge, MA: MIT Press, 1980), p. 194.
15. Gleaves, p. 269.
16. Allen County (IN) Public Library, *Survey,* 1983.
17. James E. Rush, "The Challenges of Educating Library and Information Science Professionals; 1985 and Beyond," *Technical Services Quarterly* 3 (Fall 1985/Winter 1985/86): 102.
18. Pauline Wilson, "Impending Change in Library Education: Implications for Planning," *Journal of Education for Librarianship* 18 (Spring 1978): 159.
19. J.C. Colson, "Professional Ideals and Social Realities: Some Questions about the Education of Librarians," *Journal of Education for Librarianship* 21 (Fall 1980): 92.
20. Blaise Cronin and Irene Martin, "Social Skills Training in Librarianship," *Journal of Librarianship* 15 (April 1983): 105.
21. Ibid.
22. Ibid., p. 109.
23. Ibid., p. 120.
24. Ibid., p. 121.
25. Heintze, p. 413.
26. Gleniece Robinson, "Management Development Programs in Large Public Libraries in the U.S.," *Public Library Quarterly* 5 (Spring 1984): 27.
27. Darlene E. Weingand, "Competencies for Public Librarians: A Beginning," *Public Libraries* 21 (Winter 1981):104.
28. Julie Todaro, "Public Librarianship in Library Education: What Are We Doing," *Public Libraries* 21 (Winter 1982): 159.
29. Colson, p. 101.
30. W.B. Lukenbill, "Clinical Education Experiences for Librarians: Implications for Public Libraries," *Public Libraries* 19 (Summer 1980):61.
31. Rue Bucher and Joan B. Stelling, *Becoming Professional* (Beverly Hills, CA: Sage, 1977), p. 10.
32. Lukenbill, p. 62.
33. Todaro, p. 159.
34. Ibid., Idem.
35. Turock, p. 10.
36. Gleaves, p. 267.
37. Robert Wedgeworth, ed., *The ALA Yearbook of Library and Information Services,* vol. 10 (Chicago: ALA, 1985), p. 34.

3

College Libraries

Evan Ira Farber

To generalize about almost any aspect of college libraries is a risky, even dubious exercise, simply because there is such diversity within that group. There are college libraries in which one professional librarian serves a few hundred students with a collection of less than 50,000 volumes. At the other end of the spectrum are the prestigious, affluent colleges with sizable library staffs and substantial collections approaching—some even surpassing—those of many university libraries. And if one wants to include in the group the community college libraries, a number of which serve as many as 25,000 students, the range is stretched even further. The kinds of curricula, and thus the types of collections, also vary widely. At one extreme, perhaps, is St. John's College in Annapolis, MD, with a pristinely traditional liberal arts curriculum; a community college can provide the other extreme, a community college that offers many courses in a variety of applied fields as well as in the more conventional academic disciplines.

CHARACTERISTICS OF THE COLLEGE LIBRARY

If, then, college libraries are so diverse, how can one talk about them as a group? Is there any commonality that can be ascribed to them? There is one, I think, a very important one, and that is the fact that they all serve undergraduates—perhaps not exclusively, but primarily. The role, the programs, the thrust of college libraries is largely determined by this fact—and so, then, should be the kinds of librarians who work in those libraries.

Purpose

The role of the college library is very different from that of the university library. While a university library serves many purposes and types of clientele, its primary function is to support research, to build collections for the needs of scholars and graduate students. The reputations—indeed, the ranking—of university libraries are predicated on the size of their collections, or on their expenditures for acquisitions, or on a combination of quantitative factors. The purpose of a college library, on the other hand, is primarily to serve undergraduates and to do that by supporting the teaching/learning process. How well it does that, and not its size or its expenditures, should be the measure of a college library's success. There is some parallel with the difference between the roles of a university professor and a college professor. The former gains a reputation and gets tenure by research and publication; the latter, by the quality of his or her teaching, student evaluations of which have become increasingly important. Of course it is not that clear-cut, but it is a matter of emphasis, and there is no doubt that the emphasis of most colleges is on teaching. A college library may have as one of its objectives the support of faculty research, but the emphasis of its service will be on supporting the teaching/learning process.

This difference between the purposes of a university library and a college library ought be clearly kept in mind by a college's faculty, administration and library staff. When any of these groups fails to recognize the distinction between the two, the library's ability to work toward its primary mission, support of the teaching/learning process, is probably doomed to failure. With its limited resources, a college library can do just so much; to try to emulate a university library's role or practices is foolhardy and simply leads to the college library fulfilling neither role: a small-scale university library is almost a contradiction in terms, but in trying to be one the college library must sacrifice its real purpose and its true clientele, the students.*

This distinction, then, becomes important when considering almost any aspect of the college library's program, procedures or personnel. Yet, as important as the distinction is, too often it's ignored in the literature of academic librarianship, including that on the recruitment and training of academic librarians. There are, to be sure, more similarities than differences between the qualities that applicants for positions in college libraries should have and those that applicants to university libraries should have. It may be even more a matter of degree than a matter of striking differences, but that matter of degree, or those differences in particular cases ought to be kept in mind. And the difference in the purposes of the two types of libraries is often the key factor.

Staff Size

Another characteristic of college libraries that must be considered in defining their personnel needs is staff size. Most college libraries have small professional staffs. The libraries in such colleges as Oberlin (with 17 professionals) or Smith (with 21) are few and far between, and hardly representative of college libraries. For example, Austin College surveyed 16 liberal arts colleges around the country a few years ago, colleges with which it wanted to compare itself. Though 11 of the 16 are considered selective colleges, the number of professional librarians averaged slightly less than 5.[1] Another example: a survey taken last year of 22 private college libraries in Indiana showed that while they averaged 4.2 professionals, 2 of the colleges had only 1 professional, and 10 had 2 or 3.[2] These minimal staffs are not at all unusual for what have been

---

*In another essay, I have gone in more detail into the reasons and consequences of this ambivalence. "College Libraries and the University-Library Syndrome," in *The Academic Library: Essays in Honor of Guy R. Lyle,* ed. by Evan I. Farber and Ruth Walling (Metuchen, NJ: Scarecrow Press, 1974), pp. 12-23.

called the "invisible colleges," those small, private, often church-related colleges with limited resources that make up about a third of our four-year colleges.

ASPECTS OF COLLEGE LIBRARIANSHIP

The small number of professional librarians in most college libraries affects the work of the librarians in two important aspects: the *style* of work—the relative autonomy of the librarians; and the *content* of work—the need for college librarians to be generalists rather than specialists. Not only are these two aspects interrelated, each also reinforces the other.

In his recent essay, "1985 to 1995: The Next Decade in Academic Librarianship," Allen Veaner noted that "in smaller academic libraries, virtually all the major management responsibilities fall upon the chief librarian," and then went on to say that although it had been pointed out "that the autonomous professional model is not the reality in the large research library, it could be highly functional in a college library or junior/community college library."[3]

The Autonomous Librarian

What Veaner is talking about here is the librarian's professional autonomy—the freedom, the independence of judgment that derives from not being a cog in a large organization. That is certainly true in the smaller library: there are many more opportunities for professionals' individual decisions, or at least for not having to check so many other professional opinions. To anyone who has worked in a large organization, especially one beset by bureaucratic procedures, that seems like a most appealing situation, but one must recognize certain limitations.

The first is that while there may be independence of other professional judgments, there is not always a similar independence from one's clientele and/or faculty colleagues. Many small colleges appeal to a special group, and so the small college community is usually a closeknit one. Even those with a wider constituency, however, like to think of themselves as forming a community, and in such a community many voices, not always expert or even knowledgeable, often want to be heard when decisions affecting them in even the slightest way are made. The college librarian who insists on going his or her own way without listening to, or at least hearing, these voices jeopardizes the staff's working relationships, and, in the long run, the library's effectiveness. This of course does not mean that the librarians need to check every possible move with everyone; it does mean, however, that the librarians need to be aware of faculty, administration and student feelings and opinions on certain matters, and to take those into account when appropriate—and appropriate often means politically expedient. Knowing the faculty and students—their academic interests and needs, their concerns, even their likes and dislikes—is almost a requirement for running a successful library program at a small college.

The Isolated Librarian

A second limitation is the reverse side of "not having to check so many other professional opinions." That is, the disadvantage of not having many other professional opinions available, particularly in matters where specialized knowledge is needed. Because college librarians need to perform such a variety of tasks, to be such generalists (as described in the following paragraph), it is almost impossible for them to keep up with aspects of librarianship that are changing rapidly, almost any area where there is a need for much technical expertise. This disadvantage is exacerbated by the locations of many small colleges—distant from large cities or large libraries, even from each other, so that the opportunities to talk with specialists outside the college community are even more limited.

The Generalist Librarian

The third limitation is that the independence available to college librarians also demands that they be generalists. Charles

Maurer, Director of the Library at Denison University, put it this way:

> In large organizations, including large libraries, the director has assistants for some or all of these [administrative] areas and in addition is insulated by the size of the operation from day-to-day concerns; department heads or section chiefs or area supervisors handle that. . . . In any case, the [college library] director *will* sometimes be on reference, or circulation duty, and will *not* have personnel specialists or budget managers to take care of the details of those concerns. In an era of growing specialization this library head is one of the last generalists.[4]

William Moffett, Director of Libraries at Oberlin College, extended the generalist label to the rest of the college library staff as well. First, he asked that we think of the different types of academic librarians by considering them on a continuum. At one end are those "who see themselves as professional librarians employed in academia"—that is, those who work in large university libraries—"and at the other, those who tend to regard themselves as academics working in libraries"—the college librarians. And so we have, on the one hand, professional specialists "whose first loyalties are to the values of the guild; and, on the other, generalists whose professional skills are clearly subordinate to the educational function to which they are committed."[5] Moffett did not mean to imply that all college librarians are committed to the educational function any more than he would insist that all university librarians see themselves only as professional specialists. He was simply pointing out the "different tendency" between the two—the tendency of professionals in large libraries to specialize, and the tendency of those in smaller libraries to be generalists.

The Teaching Librarian

Being a generalist extends to many areas for the college librarian. In his essay "A Paradigm for College Libraries," Peter Dollard, the Library Director at Alma College, wrote that "the college librarian should keep the managerial function clearly subordinated to the major goal of maximizing the laboratory potential of the library." He went on to say:

> This leads directly to another quality academic librarians must have: they must to a large extent see their role as that of a teacher. You do not answer reference questions, you demonstrate a research methodology. . . . Technical services librarians in college libraries are commonly scheduled at the reference desk. . . . A librarian supervising student assistants often teaches more than simply how to get a job done. It is not that teaching is a major activity of all college librarians, but that college librarians must enjoy teaching when the occasion arises.
>
> Related to the service ethic, but also very much related to a particular mind-set, is the way college librarians relate to all parts of the collection they are developing. You must have enough general knowledge and curiosity and be sincerely interested in a wide enough variety of subjects in order to pursue collection development with some vigor. . . . You must have a real conviction that knowledge and learning are valuable ends in themselves to be able to develop your collection with zest.[6]

The Academic Librarian

Another aspect of being a generalist is closely related to Moffett's view of college librarians as "academics working in libraries." That is, at many small colleges, librarians play a variety of roles not closely—perhaps not at all—related to the library. There are a number of college librarians who, with their additional subject backgrounds, teach courses in a variety of disciplines. There are librarians who coach or help coach sports, librarians who serve as academic advisers, and on many college campuses librarians who participate in various aspects of the conduct of the college by serving on special and standing committees. The point is, in a small college, individuals may wear several hats because there are many more responsibilities and opportunities for service than there are people to meet those needs. As part of that small college community, the librarians wear whichever hats fit and are appropriate to their talents or inclinations.

Before going on to discuss the implications of these characteristics for the preparation of college librarians, let's review them briefly. First, college librarians are primarily concerned with undergraduates, with supporting, even enhancing their instruction. Second, most college libraries have small professional staffs, leading to a great deal of professional autonomy on the one hand, but on the other some professional isolation. Third, college librarians usually work in a community where there are close, sometimes inhibiting, working relationships. Finally, also because of the small staffs, college librarians need to be generalists within the library and often serve their colleges in capacities outside the library.

THE PREPARATION OF COLLEGE LIBRARIANS

How should the preparation of librarians for positions in libraries such as these differ from those for university or other research libraries? Or, should there be a difference? It seems appropriate to see what recent writings have had to say about the preparation of academic librarians. There are of course a variety of opinions, but even with this variety, one can come up with a certain consensus. The writings I've particularly looked at are those of Lester Asheim,[7] Patricia Battin,[8] Harold Borko,[9] John Budd,[10] Edward G. Holley,[11] Barbara Moran,[12] W. Boyd Rayward,[13] Robert Stueart,[14] Allen Veaner,[15] and reactions to Holley's paper by Irene Hoadley, Sheila Creth and Herbert White.[16]

There's surely general agreement that while technical competence is important, it's no longer enough, that there needs to be more stress on theory and on research. Some feel that academic librarians need to know more about the field of higher education, even more particularly about the type of learning or institution in which one intends to spend a career. There was a continuing stress on the importance of communication, both oral and written, and on the ability to manage. Since Patricia Battin's list of qualifications for research librarians was quoted approvingly by at least four of the above authors, they should be mentioned:

1. A first-rate mind with problem solving abilities
2. A solid, rigorous undergraduate education

3. Concrete evidence of managerial abilities
4. An intellectual commitment to research libraries[17]

To make these even more generally applicable, Veaner suggested that one should "substitute any type-of-library adjective in place of 'research.' No academic librarian anywhere can afford to lack these requirements."[18]

It would be hard to argue with any of this in spelling out the desirable preparation for a college librarian. Do college libraries want, then, their recruits to have the same training and qualifications as other academic librarians? The answer is—well, yes, but with some modifications.

Basic Training

Yes, of course college libraries need staff members who have good basic training, training based on that "identifiable 'core of knowledge' common to all types of librarianship . . . that all students, no matter what their declared eventual career aspirations might be, should be exposed to."[19] This is especially important for college librarians because they have to be generalists; the smaller the staff, the more widely spread will the librarians' knowledge have to extend.

For similar reasons, it is just as important for college librarians to have a solid educational background, and that needn't be restricted to one's formal education. What we do want are traits that one associates with a broad, rigorous education—flexibility in thought, openness to opinions and experiences, intellectual competence, a sense of values and a breadth of interests and perspectives. Because the college librarian is ultimately responsible for building the collection—a collection that is not just to support the present curriculum but also to serve future generations of students, and, as Peter Dollard noted above, must "relate to all parts of the collection" and develop the collection "with zest,"—a breadth of interests is essential. Likewise, in order to work more effectively with faculty—and thus to help integrate the library into the teaching/learning process—college librarians need to talk with, appreciate, support the interests of those faculty, whether they come from economics, music, biology or Afro-American studies.

Almost half a century ago, Harvie Branscomb, Director of Libraries at Duke University, wrote what is still one of the wisest commentaries on college libraries and librarians, *Teaching With Books, A Study of College Libraries*. [20] As opposed to a university librarian, he wrote, the position of college librarian demands

> more of the qualities of the teacher and educator. . . . One can set out three main qualifications for the college librarian besides those general ones of intelligence and integrity which would be assumed. These are (a) a knowledge of the principles of library administration, (b) scholarly interests and understanding, with which is included an interest in the education of college undergraduates, and (c) an ability to work with students and to cooperate smoothly and efficiently with those sometimes difficult individuals, the faculty.[21]

The Context of Higher Education

College librarians, even more than university librarians, should have an understanding of the field of higher education, and especially the social and political context in which the particular library operates. Again, that need is so important to college librarians because of the various roles they play and because of the small size of their institutions. A successful college librarian is one who is going to be asked to do many things on campus. In order to serve on a campus curriculum committee or on an administrative council, one must know and appreciate the institution's educational mission, its academic and administrative idiosyncrasies, and the keys to interpersonal relationships that keep it going. And to work more closely with students, as an academic adviser or as an informal adviser, as many college librarians do, knowledge of the institution and the higher educational scene in general is surely important.

First-rate minds? Of course they should be required for all prospective librarians, but again, because college librarians work closely with students, often in a teaching capacity—with both individuals and classes—that quality is especially desirable. Furthermore, because of that close working relationship, college librarians can serve as models for students and can help recruit better applicants into librarianship. Since first-rate minds attract other first-rate minds, the entire profession should benefit. Likewise, the ability to communicate is a crucial quality. The more frequent contact with faculty and students means that oral communication is especially important.

Professional Involvement

The importance of professional involvement can hardly be exaggerated for college librarians. As noted above, small libraries may be handicapped by their lack of expertise as well as by their geographical isolation, and they may not have "many other professional opinions available, particularly in matters where specialized knowledge is needed." While state and regional networks have done a good bit to help overcome this disadvantage, the involvement in professional associations, the exchange of ideas and experiences at state and national meetings are invaluable.

Management Ability

As for management skills, because college librarians may have more autonomy than librarians in a university, they need to know how to manage. Most college librarians will not have to manage the numbers of subordinates or the amount of materials that many university librarians will. The type of management skills, then, may be quite different: in a college situation, interpersonal skills may be more important than sheer organizational ability. Also, in a college library, management may be more a shared responsibility—again, because one is required to serve in so many capacities. An interesting development at Dickinson College, where true collegiate management has been instituted, could make this even more important.

At Dickinson, where the library has a professional staff of eight, the role of library director—or chairperson, as the position is called there—rotates to a different librarian every four years. The system has been in effect for almost 10 years, and the staff reports individual satisfactions, even enthusiasm, as well as institutional advantages.²² But for other institutions to make such a radical change from traditional administration it is probably too soon for a really convincing evaluation. If it does turn out to work well, and if it is emulated by other colleges, there will be a real demand for staff members who are capable managers as well as, say, fine reference librarians; an inept chairperson for four years could hinder a library's growth and blunt its effectiveness for a much longer period.

Commitment to Education

One of Pat Battin's requirements was "an intellectual commitment to research librarianship." For college librarians, the counterpart is a commitment to the process of undergraduate education and the role of the library in supporting that process. A college librarian who is an expert on, say, government documents really doesn't belong in that library unless he or she is honestly interested in getting students to use those documents. "The college library has the same *raison d'etre* as the college of which it is a part," Harvie Branscomb wrote, "it exists for the sake of teaching or educating undergraduate students."²³ I've seen too many librarians, in colleges as well as in universities, who view the libraries as ends in themselves—the procedures, the organization of the collection as their *raison d'etre*. That's surely unfortunate in a university situation, but it becomes disastrous in a college, because undergraduates need librarians' help and encouragement. Without the staff's commitment to the process of undergraduate education, without an interest in helping young people grow intellectually and culturally, without the desire to help students learn how to learn, to show them how to find, evaluate and organize information for themselves so that they can, after their formal education is over, become more effective and creative members of society—without those aims as part of the staff ethos, a college library can easily become simply a warehouse, a place where information and materials are available to students if they want or need to use them, but not a library that plays an active role in the educational process.

Let's return to the question: should the preparation of college librarians be different from that of other academic librarians? We can see that neither the preparation nor the personal qualifications need to be very different. It is an oversimplification to say that one group is interested in working with scholars and/or scholarly materials while the other is interested in working with undergraduates, but to apply Moffett's usage of a continuum with somewhat different dimensions, one can say that each group *tends* toward one end or the other. Both interests are of course important, but for different agendas; there's no question that the styles of work, the measures of accomplishment, the kinds of satisfactions for each agenda are also different.

A parallel with academics is not inappropriate. There are those academics who are most interested in research and publication, either in doing their own or guiding others, or both. They are the recognized scholars, the leaders in their disciplines, who occupy major university positions. Then there are those academics who think that conveying their disciplines, contributing to the development of young people's appreciation and abilities is more important; for them, the college classroom, the teaching/learning process is the way to professional satisfaction. It is this group which college librarians identify with, this group which college librarians serve by supporting and by enhancing that teaching/learning process. There are other rewards, other satisfactions, other pleasures in being a college librarian, but none so great as making that contribution.

RECRUITMENT

Can library schools aid in recruiting or training for this role? To some extent, yes, but the most effective recruiting needs to be done before then. Library schools, after all, no matter how good a job they do, can't make over the personalities or the talents of their students, and if we want candidates who are really empathetic with the purposes and processes of undergraduate education, the colleges themselves will have to be responsible for recruiting them.

Lawrence Clark Powell wrote years ago that "our profession does not automatically perpetuate itself. A good measure of a library . . . is the number of students or clericals it has recruited for librarianship. . . . Every student who works for us is a potential librarian. . . . The best recruits are those who are inspired by the librarians for whom they work."[24] Powell was addressing his own university library staff, but his words are even more appropriate for college librarians. To most university undergraduates, the library staff is unknown; college librarians, on the other hand, can and often do have a very different relationship with students. The student body at the small residential college is almost a captive audience; that, plus the close working relationship between students and librarians, should make recruiting efforts feasible. Wheaton College in Illinois recently provided an example of what can be done. With the cooperation of the campus career development office, the library staff plus outside speakers held a well-attended seminar for students, to publicize careers in library and information science.[25]

Beyond the efforts of individual libraries or librarians, the library and the higher education associations and consortia ought to work together. Recruiting quality personnel for college libraries is, after all, in the interest of both groups. In his talk, Moffett expressed the hope that "the Great Lakes Colleges Association (and perhaps other college consortia) can be persuaded to offer some internships in college library administration. . . . By so doing we may be able to . . . counter some of that bias which discourages good people from seriously considering careers in smaller institutions."[26] Moffett was more interested in getting librarians to think about careers in college libraries; just as important is getting college students who are interested in higher education to think about college librarianship as a crucial and exciting aspect of higher education.

The Association of American Colleges, or the Council for the Advancement of Small Colleges, or any number of state or regional consortia, working with the Association of College and Research Libraries, or the College Libraries Section, or regional or state college library networks should begin planning such programs soon. The need for quality recruits for college librarianship was never more urgent. In the section "Qualifications of the Librarian" in his classic *The Administration of the College Library,* Guy R. Lyle quoted from Louis R. Wilson's "The Role of the Library in Higher Education." In that talk, Wilson spoke of the qualifications needed for

> the librarian who is to become a successful administrator, a wise counselor in the use of books, and a force in shaping college instructional policies. It insists that the librarian must be a person of imagination and initiative, that he must have a sound understanding of library administration and some subject field, and that he must know how to relate the use of the library to the educational program of the college.

Lyle then went on:

> One might add . . . he must be a person of character, integrity, and professional idealism. . . . These ideals include an unshakable belief in the importance of books, an ambition to make them easily and conveniently available, and a faith in the ability of librarians to share with others their enthusiasm in bringing books to readers.[27]

Wilson's words were written almost a half-century ago; Lyle first added his comments less than a decade after that. With only minor modifications, that combination of qualifications would be quite appropriate today—and tomorrow. We ought to begin to find ways of making sure that the next generation of college librarians can assume the roles that a quality college education deserves.

NOTES

1. "1981-82 Library Data for a Selected Group of Liberal Arts Colleges (900-1450 FTE)," compiled by Lisa Bailey and Dan Bedsole, Austin College, October 1983 (mimeographed).
2. "Indiana Private College Library Survey, 1984-1985," collected by Larry Frye, Wabash College (mimeographed).
3. Allen B. Veaner, "1985 to 1995: The Next Decade in Academic Librarianship, Part II," *College & Research Libraries* 46 (July 1985): 295.
4. Charles Maurer, "Close Encounters of Diverse Kinds: A Management Panorama for the Director of the Smaller College Library," in

College Librarianship, ed. William Miller and D. Stephen Rockwood (Metuchen, N.J.: Scarecrow Press, 1981), p. 98.

5. William A. Moffett, "Reflections of a College Librarian: Looking for Life and Redemption This Side of ARL," *College & Research Libraries* 45:338-349 (September 1984), p. 344.

6. Peter Dollard, "A Paradigm for College Libraries," in *College Librarianship,* ed. William Miller and D. Stephen Rockwood (Metuchen, N.J.: Scarecrow Press, 1981), pp. 42-43.

7. Lester Asheim, *Library School Preparation for Academic and Research Librarianship; A Report Prepared for the Council on Library Resources* (Washington, D.C.: Council on Library Resources, 1983).

8. Patricia Battin, "Developing University and Research Library Professionals: A Director's Perspective," *American Libraries* 14:22-25 (January 1983).

9. Harold Borko, "Trends in Library and Information Science Education," *Journal of the Association for Information Science* 35:185-193 (May 1984).

10. John Budd, "The Education of Academic Librarians," *College & Research Libraries* 45:15-24 (January 1984).

11. Edward G. Holley, "Defining the Academic Librarian," *College & Research Libraries* 46:462-468 (November 1985).

12. Barbara Moran, *Academic Libraries: The Changing Knowledge Centers of Colleges and Universities,* ASHE-ERIC Higher Education Research Report, No. 8, 1984 (Washington, D.C.: Association for the Study of Higher Education, 1984), especially pp. 54-59 on The Preparation of Academic Librarians.

13. W. Boyd Rayward, "Academic Librarianship: The Role of Library Schools," in *Issues in Academic Librarianship; Views and Case Studies for the 1980s and 1990s,* ed. Peter Spyers-Duran and Thomas W. Mann, Jr. (Westport, Conn.: Greenwood Press, 1985), pp. 100-114.

14. Robert D. Stueart, "The Education of Academic Librarians" in *Academic Librarianship: Yesterday, Today, and Tomorrow,* ed. by Robert Stueart (N.Y.: Neal-Schuman Publishers, 1982), pp. 231-245.

15. Veaner, "1985 to 1995."

16. Irene B. Hoadley, Sheila Creth, and Herbert S. White, "Reactions to 'Defining the Academic Librarian,'" *College & Research Libraries* 46:469-477 (November 1985).

17. Battin, p. 23.

18. Veaner, p. 298.

19. Stueart, p. 234.

20. Harvie Branscomb, *Teaching With Books, A Study of College*

Libraries (Chicago: Association of American Colleges [and] American Library Association, 1940).

21. Branscomb, pp. 86-87.

22. Joan M. Bechtel, "Rotation Day Reflections," *College & Research Libraries News* 46:551-555 (November 1985). For a further discussion of the plan's rationale and background, see Dorothy H. Cieslicki, "A New Status Model for Academic Librarians," *Journal of Academic Librarianship* 8:76-81 (May 1982); and Joan Bechtel, "Academic Professional Status: An Alternative for Librarians," *Journal of Academic Librarianship* 11:289-292 (November 1985).

23. Branscomb, p. 81.

24. Lawrence Clark Powell, *A Passion for Books* (N.Y.: World Publishing, 1958), p. 125.

25. Jonathan D. Lauer, "Recruiting for the Profession," *College & Research Libraries News* 45:388-390 (September 1984). I'm indebted to this article for reminding me of Powell's essay and the book it's in.

26. Moffett, p. 345.

27. Guy R. Lyle, *The Administration of the College Library,* 4th ed. (N.Y.: H.W. Wilson, 1974), pp. 136-137.

4

Small Public Libraries

Sara Laughlin

A TRADITION OF AUTONOMY

In the best cases, local governance assures appropriate public library responses to local needs. In many instances, however, strong verbal support for the small public library by trustees and community leaders has not translated into an adequate financial base to pay for modern library service. Compared even with the most conservative minimum standards, many small public libraries fail to meet expectations for open hours, qualified staff or basic facility requirements like a telephone. The development of community-based planning processes to arrive at reasonable local goals and objectives requires insightful local participants, strong leadership by the library director and trustees, and a willingness to work to improve substandard services. Nancy Bolt and Corinne Johnson observe that "Often trustees do not know what kind of service is possible from a properly supported library."[1] Lack of experience with good library service may hamper others as well.

There are several obstacles to fully professional small public libraries. Underqualification of staff is perhaps the most critical. Many small public libraries are unable to pay competitive salaries to attract qualified applicants. New employees often are local residents willing to work part time at an hourly wage with few if any benefits like paid holidays, health insurance or retirement plans. Paid only for open hours (often fewer than 15 hours a week), they must maintain the collection and the building, cover the desk and handle all reference and interlibrary loan requests. Many of these employees have no library education and have never even used a library other than the one in which they are employed. Someone, usually the director, must train them in the most basic skills of circulation management and question negotiation. They rarely are given any training in dealing with patrons, any overview of the purpose of the library or any information about the library's role in the community.

Underqualification may extend even to the director of a small public library. Perhaps the most pressing need is to develop staff to assume leadership positions. Directors, too, are recruited locally and paid minimum wages; they receive few benefits and lack adequate library education. In Indiana, for example, 89 of 239 public libraries did not meet minimum staff certification requirements in 1985, whether by passing tests or completing library courses.[2] Some directors lack even the prerequisite of two years of college; others ignore notices of noncompliance for as long as possible with the support of trustees who are desperate to keep a director. In other cases, directors spend years going to school part time to complete educational requirements that are designed to convey the basic knowledge and skills necessary to lead a library. In the meantime, the library receives less than the full measure of management and direction that might be expected from a full-fledged professional. These individuals are truly not within reach of the lowest rung of the continuing education ladder; they have not yet mastered the basics. In assessing staff development for small public libraries, it is therefore important to remember the unmet need for basic professional education.

Isolation, geographic and professional, limits development of staffs of small public libraries through attendance at regional, state and national continuing education offerings. Large libraries may give staff members the use of the library car, or reimburse them for the use of their own cars. They can be sure that the library will remain open and adequately staffed in their absence. Small public libraries, however, have none of these support mechanisms. Their staffs may be forced to attend such conferences at their own expense on their days off or to close the library in order to attend. Faced with such difficult choices, it is no wonder that small libraries are underrepresented.

What remains to these homebound librarians is local support. Yet many are also professionally isolated. With little formal training and few local resources, human or bibliographic, it is difficult to find adequate information for initiating a new program or evaluating a current one, for improving procedures or for moving in new directions. The status quo is the path of least resistance for all but the most creative and self-sustaining public library directors.

The third major barrier is lack of community support. Local budgets for all sizes of libraries have been pinched in the last decade by rising costs and falling tax supports. Small public libraries have especially felt the crunch, as many were caught offering only basic services in outdated buildings where heating and cooling costs increasingly encroached on materials budgets. There was simply no money to shift from another budget category. Cautious decision makers often did not respond with increased funding. In fact, many library trustees did not even realize the extent of damage to library service.

The source of the communication failure may be traced again to lack of leadership on the part of the directors. Hired to run the library, they never saw themselves—nor were they expected to act—as advisers to the trustees, so while they waited for the trustees to give them more money, the trustees waited to be asked, assuming that everything was as it had always been. If directors did ask, they often did it without adequate background information and without the necessary support from patrons and community.

To sum up, directors and staff of small public libraries need professional education, often at a basic level. They face real barriers of inadequate or incomplete education, geographic and professional isolation, strained financial resources, and lack of support from governing authorities.

POTENTIAL FOR LOCAL SERVICE

In spite of all the limitations faced by the small library, there are many signs that decentralized community services may be coming of age. Lynn Roberts has used the major trends identified by John Naisbitt in *Megatrends* to predict the staff development needs of the Denver Public Library.[3] Many of the trends incorporate characteristics that have often been viewed as deficiencies of the small public library.

While small libraries will have to be very creative in providing access to the enormous quantity of information available through computer technology, the new ability to find and retrieve information offers a renewed rationale for the existence of small outlets. It demands a new high tech image for the local library, an understanding of the new technology and the acquisition of the interview, search, and organizational skills needed to deal with instant information. Most of all, technology demands flexibility and a willingness to give up some of one's traditional autonomy, since computer-based information is no longer within the control of the individual library.

The small public library will have to deal with telecommunications, hardware and software vendors, industry-wide standards, and database protocols and contracts established for a national or international clientele. Technological innovation will also compel small libraries to adjust their short-term planning to incorporate long-range plans for expensive technology. Materials budgets may shift from acquisitions to access, as full-text databases replace encyclopedias, journal reprints replace hard-copy magazines indexed in *Reader's Guide,* and as the image of the library changes from that of a recreational reading center to a full-fledged information center.

Small public libraries may turn their traditional role as community centers into an unexpected asset. Bolt found that small libraries in Massachusetts did not consider themselves community centers. However, respondents did mention many community services and collections. She suggests that the small library could serve as a community center and know the interests of individuals in ways not possible in a larger library.[4] Roberts cautions that staff will need additional training in public relations, outreach and communications skills. Managers will have to develop more interpersonal skills to maintain the delicate balance between technology and personal interaction.[5]

Decentralization

The trend toward political decentralization also favors small public libraries, since more citizens will actively participate in local government and more funding decisions will be made closer to home. Of course, as Roberts points out, library supporters and staff at every level will have to hone their political skills and make a convincing case for library support.[6] Bolt found that the deciding factor in how well libraries in Maryland met citizens' needs was not the size of the library but the quality of its management.[7] Within the library, too, staff will demand more participation in decision making, which will require that the director have training in managing staff input, from skills in participative management to facilitation, group process and effective meetings.

Decentralization will affect the library's relationship with the larger library world as well, as informal local or even regional networks replace formal hierarchies. Small libraries will find themselves participating in cooperative purchasing and cataloging agreements, automation projects, and reciprocal borrowing plans, reference referral services and document delivery systems. Governance may expand beyond the local board of trustees to include participation in or leadership of networks with the attendant responsibility for long-range planning, consensus building and goal setting in a broader information context. From a menu of options for small libraries in Massachusetts, Bolt offers three choices involving cooperation—contracting for service or consolidating two libraries into a larger unit or establishing formal agreements between two libraries for sharing of staff or other resources.[8]

Community analysis skills will be called upon as people move toward more self-help; as population shifts affect all small public libraries by either expanding or diminishing their clientele; and as life choices become more difficult because of a multiplicity of options. All these trends will demand from library staff an ability to envision a changed future and plan for a particular role in it.

Emerging Needs

The societal trends outlined above set the stage for a newly important role for small public libraries. Such a shift in the mission, definition and image of the library presents a significant education and communication challenge. Roberts was not the first to pinpoint automation and management skills as the two areas of greatest need in continuing education and staff development. Studies and needs assessments over the past few years have confirmed that these are the prime concerns of the library community.

In 1984 Nathan Smith, Maurice Marchant and Laura Nielson reported on a study designed to determine how the educational needs of public librarians are changing and to compare these changing needs with those articulated by directors of research libraries in a 1982 study by Marchant and Smith.[9,10] Smith and his colleagues received responses from 157 of the largest public libraries in the U.S. They found important similarities between competencies needed now and expected to be needed in five years by large public libraries and research libraries. Skills seen as most highly desirable for entry-level professionals in the present included the traditional general reference, bibliography and organizational skills as well as human relations and research skills. In five years, human relations, general reference and research will be joined by library automation and online retrieval skills.

The greatest increase in need for competencies fell in two clusters—automation, online retrieval and computer programming, and human relations and managerial skills. A core list of ten much-needed competencies fell into four areas: technology, including library automation and online retrieval skills; improved communication and cognitive skills, including human relations and analytical skills; a deepening intellectual base, including knowledge of library issues and library philosophy; and the traditional skills of organizing information, familiarity with general bibliography and general reference material, and knowledge of collection development theories and practices.

Most public library directors responding to the survey agreed that entry-level library professionals possessed satisfactory reference and bibliography skills, but few possessed computer, supervisory, and business skills such as budgeting, accounting, planning, managing-by-objectives, measuring, research, group decision processes and committee work.

Public and research library directors agreed that almost all entry-level competencies should be acquired during preprofessional library education. They agreed on areas of needed improvement in competencies in technology and managerial areas. Neither group of respondents suggested areas that could be eliminated from library education curricula to make room for education in new competency areas.

A survey of the continuing education needs of professional and nonprofessional library staff, trustees and volunteers in all types and sizes of libraries in Indiana, conducted by the Indiana State Library in 1982, found that, as in other studies, the preferred methods of continuing education were those most convenient and accessible—reading published information and attending workshops or live lectures.[11] Least favored were those most demanding and expensive—internships and college courses. Among the topics respondents would be interested in learning more about, those in management and automation outscored all others. Under management, public relations, dealing with problem patrons, communication, staff development, budget methods, evaluating staff, time management, and supervisory skills were rated most highly. In the automation area, automated circulation, automation training, and planning for automation were the leading topics. In the technical services category, collection development and weeding received significant responses. The similarity between the needs identified by large public and research library directors and those selected by Indiana librarians leaves no doubt that technology and management are the two areas of greatest need for additional education.

To date, no one has surveyed directors of small public libraries to determine which competencies are sought, which are found and which are lacking. Results of a study like Smith's would certainly produce valuable information. The Indiana needs assessment included staff and trustees of small public libraries as 27% of the respondents, which may be a valid indication of the percentage of the total library staff in the state they represent. At the institution level, however, 195 (82%) of Indiana's 239 public libraries serve populations of fewer than 25,000 persons and 148 (62%) serve fewer than 10,000. In 1984, those 148 libraries served 625,693 citizens or 12% of the state's population and expended $6,721,232 or 10% of total library expenditures.

Unfortunately neither the demographic information nor the continuing education list were coded by size of library, so it is impossible to define exactly the particular continuing education needs of small public libraries based on survey results. My experience and annual needs assessments in the Stone Hills Area Library Services Authority (ALSA) area suggest that small libraries share the needs of the rest of the profession, if sometimes at a more basic level.

PHILOSOPHIES OF LIBRARY EDUCATION

The argument still rages between proponents of a broad-based philosophical library school education and those who demand training in the functional skills that produce competent entry-level practitioners.[12]

In 1923 W.W. Charters was hired by ALA to edit a series of textbooks using job analysis, a "scientific" method he had used successfully with other professions. He described librarianship as an assemblage of unrelated processes which could be independently analyzed, recorded and then taught by library school professors to produce an "interchangeable part for the library . . . a mechanism that would run like clockwork."[13] Although the initial volumes of the series were generally well received, the project was discontinued by ALA, probably due to sharp criticism from John Cotton Dana.[14] Dana felt, as others have, that since the job analysis approach assumed that current practice was right, it produced a fragmented, static description of the profession which would impede change. In 1972 Jesse Shera observed:

> There was no hint . . . in the text on cataloging that [Charters] ever considered the fact that the catalog is only one key to the resources of the library, that it is but a segment of the total bibliographic system, or, indeed, that it is in any way related to bibliographic organization as an intellectual endeavor.[15]

The compartmentalized job analysis approach is still in use in the library profession. The 1977 California Library Selection Project employed strict task analysis to derive 36 skills currently used by library staff members.[16] The surveys by Chalfant and Smith listed 19 competencies defined somewhat more broadly. The 1984 King Research study sought to "identify, describe, and validate" current and future professional competencies.[17] Competency areas were organized first of all by professional level, function performed and type of organization—for example, entry-level cataloger in a public library; second, by generic areas across levels, functions and types; and third, by environments, that is, either professional or nonprofessional, career ladders and professional self-evaluation mechanisms. Joan Durrance has suggested that the problem of "arriving at the status quo" surfaces in even the most effective continuing education needs assessments, which produce "yesterday's needs rather than tomorrow's."[18]

The most basic problem with the job analysis or competency-based approach is that it makes a norm of the existing pattern. As Herbert White has pointed out, if professionals currently do too much clerical work, those tasks will be included in the job description. What should be asked, he maintains, is not "What are you doing?" but "What should you be doing?"[19] I might take the question further and ask, "What are you capable of handling that the library should be doing?"

The competency-based approach focuses on definable skills as the task analysis approach analyzed particular segments of a job. Both methods are useful within limits. Both arose from a need for a quantifiable, scientifically based result. Both suffer from overcategorization and a lack of orientation toward the future. It is time to turn from simplistic formulas and needs assessments and to focus the newly developed planning and communication skills of the profession on the problem of education and development of librarians.

A PROPOSAL FOR SHARED RESPONSIBILITY

Others have reasoned that the responsibility for professional development must be shared by the library school, the library and the individual. I propose for small public libraries that the library network or cooperative must become the fourth partner, involved both as advocate for professionalism and small library needs and as a primary source of training and continuing education.

Schools of library education currently face pressure from

declining or stable enrollments and rapidly changing technology. Practitioners (who are sources of both recruitment and placement of graduates) and students (who want marketable skills) pressure schools to train people to fill existing job descriptions. W. Boyd Rayward has noted that practitioners are "irreducibly pragmatic." They are subjected to a barrage of social, political, fiscal and technical decisions. From their viewpoint, knowledge is empirical, ahistorical and for immediate use.[20] Library schools feel the pressure being exerted on higher education in general to return to basics. Budgets tied to enrollment figures and state funding formulas restrict the library schools' ability to recruit and develop high-quality faculty.

Within its one-year structure library education must maintain the delicate balance between theory and practice that will prepare graduates for specific entry-level positions while it empowers them to advance in the profession, grow with technological and institutional changes, meet increased responsibility for staff, budget and buildings, and face critical decisions in the best interest of the community.

Basic Curriculum

Nevertheless, to the library school belongs the responsibility for laying the critical foundation, for creating an atmosphere of reasoned inquiry within which learners and professors can explore theories of communication, organization of knowledge and human information-seeking behavior. Flexner defined a professional as one whose work contains essentially intellectual operations with large amounts of individual responsibility, derives raw material from science and learning, turns raw material to a practical end, has educationally communicable techniques, tends toward self-organization and is increasingly altruistic in motivation.[21] The "intellectual content" of librarianship is the "man-book interface," according to Shera, who included in the model curriculum of library education basic understanding of knowledge acquisition and dissemination, communication theory, and understanding of the principal constraints and weak points in communication, both at the individual and societal level.[22]

Also included in his view of the basic education of librarians is understanding of the library in the social process, including its role as conservator of cultural heritage and transmitter of cultural education. Shera noted, for example, that trends toward longer life expectancy, more college education and more leisure time for adults would compel libraries to define their role in meeting the intellectual needs of adults, in addition to continuing their role in serving children. Shera's conceptual outline for the library in the social process includes community analysis, community development, cooperative community planning through coalition processes, political responses and a host of other contemporary concerns.

The basic curriculum would also include knowledge of how to promote reading—for citizenship and enrichment. It would focus on the library's role in disseminating information for immediate and practical use. It would include theories of bibliographic organization. Shera's model for library education connects the profession of librarianship to the highest intellectual endeavors and democratic values. Professional education should create user-orientation while developing a body of theoretical knowledge against which to measure the appropriate role for a particular library. Staff in small libraries need these skills no less than those in other libraries.

The educational needs of staff of small public libraries fall into three categories—operations, management and leadership. Operations includes easily analyzed tasks such as book selection and weeding, cataloging and processing, or circulation. Management includes budgeting, staffing, evaluating staff and services, problem solving, managing collections and maintaining buildings. Leadership includes building and maintaining community, board and staff relations, developing network and professional relations, planning for technological innovations and other changes, and developing funding and lobbying.

Library education must cover all three areas, but it should concentrate on developing leadership skills. Despite pressure from practitioners, alumni and students, despite limited resources, there is simply no other time or place where the essential theoretical foundations can be laid; there are no other teachers with access to the depth and breadth of literature necessary to support such study; there can be no second chance. Library directors agree that library philosophy and issues are essential for even entry-level professionals. Those who have worked with staff who lack professional education uniformly say they lack a broad view, although they can function well within the established structure. In short, library education must go beyond competencies training to make the linkages between technical and public services, between services for children and adults, between academic, public and school libraries and the emerging information profession. There is no lack of intellectual material to be explored and there is a critical need for professionals with a broad conceptual grasp.

Leadership

In an article about the lack of leadership in the profession, Donald Riggs points out that "Leadership begins where management ends."[23] The purposes of leadership are to infuse the library with significance beyond the requirements of day-to-day operations, to promote and protect values, to envision new horizons and to care for and develop staff members. Leadership is the mechanism for achieving the important role for libraries that Shera envisioned. Library education, then, must not merely teach the intellectual content of the profession, it must empower graduates to provide the kind of leadership that will be necessary if libraries are to respond to the information age.

For small public libraries, facing as they do the enormous challenge of modernization and the barriers of limited budgets, isolation and understaffing, leadership is the fulcrum upon which the future balances. Those whose staffs lack sufficient belief in the importance of the cultural and social role of libraries may shortly find themselves the victims of proud autonomy and shrinking resources. Those able to activate the intellectual values of librarianship into creative and well-planned change may survive to deliver information-rich service to their community.

Operations

Operations training becomes both simpler and more difficult

as the library profession is more and more oriented toward computerized systems. With each system, indeed with each generation within each system, there are new protocols, procedures and standards. Now more than ever, it is impossible to teach a library school student how to operate every online database, every circulation system or every microcomputer. The choices are simply overwhelming, and there can be no certainty that the student will end up working in a library with the same system. In fact, those opting for small public libraries may find no automated system at all. The only alternative for library schools is to teach the theory that underlies the individual systems.

Community-based planning and missions for libraries further obviate the need for practical school training in service-delivery skills. Services may be radically different from one library to the next, depending on the clientele, even though both are derived from valid planning processes. The new professional must be able instead to review the library's mission and planning documents and understand how current operations were selected or to participate in organized planning as the need arises.

To the library falls the task of training the new professional in day-to-day operations. In many small public libraries, there is no one to train a new director but individuals from the board of trustees. The first trial for many new directors comes in identifying the trustee who is knowledgeable and willing to spend enough time to give an orientation to the community and its funding and budgeting process, to board practices and expectations and other essentials. In the first month the new professional may put communications and critical thinking skills to the test in grappling with a new town, a new institution and a new employer with seven personalities. Surviving the orientation period is but the first of a constant barrage of challenges facing the librarian and requiring continuous mastery of new skills. New trustees are appointed regularly by various political bodies, funding possibilities arise and disappear, buildings become obsolete, staff changes, technology changes and the community changes.

Regional library cooperatives play a valuable role in the orientation of new directors by connecting them to colleagues with experience in other libraries, by introducing them to neighboring librarians and by helping them solve problems as they arise.

Regional cooperatives can also facilitate planning, consult on automation projects and conduct board development seminars. They can help ameliorate geographic isolation by providing news about current issues and opportunities. They can disseminate information on technological or managerial innovations. They can act as intermediaries in interlibrary agreements and cooperative planning.

If the director of the small public library has other staff members, in many cases they will have no library education or experience. They will, however, be charged with performing many of the daily operations and may be the only ones in the library for long stretches. Imitation is the main source of training for these staff members. If there are other people with more experience, they will watch them; if there is no one else, they will emulate the director. Chances are, they will see little of the library literature; they will attend few state association meetings, unless at the district level; they will know few staff members from other libraries.

In the best traditional training scenarios, the library director had a list of areas in which to orient the new employee and time to explain or demonstrate procedures. The person was considered trained at the end of the probationary period. This may be inadequate to the demands of the changing world. How will small libraries train support staff in the new complex technological systems? More than ever before, a training procedure must be in place, since it is increasingly unlikely that the new employee will have any knowledge of an automated circulation system or interlibrary loan procedures.

There is an opportunity for regional cooperatives to become more involved in support staff orientation and training. With careful assessment of the most pressing needs of small library staff orientation, self-instruction programs could be designed to cover many areas, in either printed or computer formats. The cooperative would respond to the requirements of small libraries in designing and producing the packages, which would then be used in the library whenever a new person was hired. Working through its cooperative each small public library could have a high-quality orientation package.

Operations training must be done at the library. In small

public libraries, new directors must use all the resources available to become familiar with the community and the library. They must continue to turn to regional cooperatives for up-to-date information and consultation. New technological systems and standardized procedures will make it imperative that support staff be oriented to the library and have well-designed instructions. They must also be trained in communications skills, since they will be meeting the public.

Management

Education for management is the most difficult of the three areas to assign to any group. Responsibility must be shared by the library school, the library, the individual and the regional cooperative. Basic management is currently taught in library schools, often to unwilling and inexperienced students who came to school to become reference librarians or children's librarians or because they liked to read. To many, the concepts of management are restrictive and uninteresting. Yet it is these very students who find themselves as entry-level professionals in small public libraries supervising and evaluating squabbling support staff, submitting budget proposals or writing grants, designing summer reading programs and trying to build a reference collection. In six months, when the long-time director retires, they are promoted, and must deal with problem patrons, book selection, the board, community groups, censorship problems and the leaking roof. The library school must at least lay the foundation on which these new managers can build. There is, for all their unpopularity, a reason for management courses in library school.

Management skills, like leadership skills, must be constantly nurtured. They accumulate with exposure and experience, as well as with education. Management techniques have undergone extensive change in the last decade and every year brings a new approach to some part of planning, budgeting, controlling or evaluating. No professional librarian can rest comfortably for long on management skills acquired in library school.

For small public librarians, facing the enormous challenge of managing technological change and interpersonal relations, acquiring ongoing management training is difficult at best. For them, it must consist of a mix of self-study, attendance at conferences and more sustained exposure during workshop series or courses. Expenses will also have to be shared between the individual, who may have to give up days off or vacation; the library, which should support registration fees and travel expenses; and the regional cooperative, which will make available within reasonable distance workshops or other opportunities that are inexpensive or subsidized.

Continuing Education

The bulk of management training will fall into the area of continuing education. It will follow professional library education and be founded on its basic intellectual tenets. Much remains to be done to define the responsibilities of various components for assessing need, designing programs, paying for and recognizing library continuing education. Several states have completed comprehensive long-range plans for continuing education and the literature holds numerous examples of successful programs around the country.[24] Sandy Stephan urges libraries to begin comprehensive long-range development of staff.[25] What is lacking, it seems to me, is a grassroots movement among small libraries to demand that their needs be met, either regionally or at the state level, or failing that, even a perception that a staggeringly large need exists at all. Herbert S. White confirms that from the library school perspective, at least: "The problem is not with the provision of educational opportunities. There are plenty, and if there were a demand for more there would be more. The problem is that there is hardly any demand for what is offered."[26] There are, of course, individuals facing specific problems who call their regional consultant and ask for help, and from the consultant's viewpoint the questions often sound familiar. All too often the call comes a week after an excellent workshop on the topic which would probably have answered the question.

The next step must be to get a grip on the obstacles faced by small public libraries, on the most pressing needs that they have articulated in formal planning and informal conversations and on the resources available to meet those needs, and then to deliver appropriate training.

Southern Indiana is a good example of how this can be done. In Stone Hills ALSA, 15 of the 17 public libraries serve populations of fewer than 25,000. Underfunded and understaffed, most are housed in outmoded buildings. None has an automated cataloging or circulation system, but all have access to interlibrary loan and reference referral and document delivery. Also in the district is Indiana University, with its highly ranked library school, which has 15 faculty members and a cadre of doctoral students. In the region and in Indiana and surrounding states there are a wealth of consultants, speakers and other human resources. Stone Hills ALSA has conducted assessments on an annual basis to determine staff development needs and within a yearly plan for service has conducted successful workshops and advertised others available at Indiana University and elsewhere. A monthly newsletter reaches 450 library staff members.

Nevertheless, it is unsettling to see the same topics emerge year after year. Have the workshops failed to reach the target audience? Is the need more comprehensive than the one-day program we planned? I fear the answer to both questions is Yes. The barriers against which our potential audience struggles prevent some from coming; for them, it doesn't matter that we held a workshop because their problems remain. Those who come often receive only a superficial overview, since we have not actively involved the library school.

I believe regional cooperatives like Stone Hills ALSA are perfectly suited to sponsor long-term comprehensive staff development programs for small public libraries. Cooperatives are physically close to their members and understand their needs and limits. They are not constrained by as many bureaucratic demands or traditional role expectations as a university, state library or state association might be. They have a mandate from members for continuing education and work on a daily basis with libraries facing real problems and options. They have a grassroots structure of governance that allows ideas and needs to be articulated by small public libraries.

Successful Programs

John Allred warns that "Updating can mean grafting new ideas onto an old paradigm of professional service . . . or it can assist in creating new paradigms of service, allowing 'old knowledge' to take on a fresh significance."[27] The problem of grafting continuing education programs onto old paradigms of graduate education or professional association programs is one of the most serious facing continuing educators trying to reach the small library audience. Elizabeth Stone's survey of state librarians showed that 60% of the states were trying new delivery systems like video, self-study packages, cable or teleconferencing.[28]

The library literature contains reports of several examples of successful programs around the country in which new methods of reaching those in need have been used. All these programs have participative planning processes and new styles of delivery. They have attempted to solve current needs in innovative ways. Most have applied adult education principles of participant involvement.

- Responding to a 1979 change in the library certification law which added the requirement that directors of public libraries serving fewer than 2000 population be certified, Wisconsin used its closed-circuit Educational Telephone Network to make a public library administration course available to 200 remote sites.[29]
- In Maryland, the continuing education specialist from the state library helps public libraries establish long-range staff development plans.[30] Maryland libraries developed and adopted Public Library Associate Bylaws and Guidelines which make 60 hours in-service training or 6 academic credit hours in library science a requirement for certification at the paraprofessional Library Associate level.
- A two-day summer microcomputer camp for librarians, sponsored by the micro users group in North Carolina, attracted participants from all types of libraries.[31] They were introduced to fundamental operations and BASIC program language and then were allowed to select three of four hands-on tracks—database management, spreadsheets, word processing or public access microcomputers.

- The University of Wisconsin has implemented a Certificate of Professional Development in Library Management.[32] In three required and four to five elective courses offered around the state, practitioners focus on an intensive examination of administrative problems.
- The Illinois State Library has increased access to information on continuing education by making an online continuing education calendar and a human and material resources database available to anyone with a modem.[33]
- Michigan developed a series of programs on issues and challenges facing librarians in the next 10 years.[34] The "Issues Forum" was cooperatively planned and funded; the programs held in six different locations attracted an average 115 individuals who participated in discussion sessions following presentations. Topics ranged from "Productivity in Libraries" to "Multiple Directions of Librarianship" and "Censorship."

New Modes of Continuing Education

Lowell Olson's proposal for new modes of continuing education comes closest to creating a new paradigm for staff development.[35] Understanding adult learning behaviors, he proposes that continuing education for librarians be informal, accessible and conveniently scheduled. It must recognize participants' needs and allow them to be involved in planning. Programs must be collaborative and flexible, interdisciplinary and related to and enhancing of job performance. They must capitalize on the immediate environment and be a model for independent lifelong learning. Seen in the context of these requirements for adult learning, the demands of staff of small public libraries for convenient, inexpensive and relevant experiences do not appear to be so unusual. Olson suggests that they are typical adult learners with definite goals, a wealth of experience and very structured schedules that limit participation.

He incorporates all these behaviors into a new educational structure which he calls a "collegium," in which five to seven librarians and a faculty mentor would identify and select a learning experience from a list of possibilities. His example included visits to libraries, reading professional literature related to job concerns, exchanging positions, arranging seminar luncheons with specialists or conducting a research project. Some activities would be carried out individually, some in groups. Olson proposes that the collegium be sponsored jointly by a library school and a library. The regional cooperative might also facilitate the arrangement and scheduling of activities for small public library collegia. The small number of individuals involved would create an informal, collaborative and personalized learning environment. The variety of options available would assure that time spent would be directly rewarded by enhanced job performance, since projects could address practical problems in as much detail as necessary.

Olson's model offers exciting possibilities for staff of small public libraries. In the Stone Hills ALSA area, for example, where several small libraries struggle independently with community analysis and planning while library school faculty teach these units each semester, they could meet in the collegium to share problems and results.

The collegium idea brings into sharp focus the extent to which continuing education has been grafted onto old systems. When educators complain that no one enrolls for their offerings, perhaps it is because they are inconvenient, expensive and only marginally useful to practicing librarians. When small library practitioners complain that they can't come or that they need more practical help, perhaps they are equating current offerings with dozens of two-hour conference programs the suggestions from which they were unable to implement when they got home.

It is true that both library schools and small public libraries face substantial hurdles to a productive interchange of information. It is equally true that both groups have been too narrow in estimating resources and developing creative responses. As Allred pointed out, creating new paradigms for library service is much more difficult than grafting new services onto old organizations of knowledge. The time has come to develop new paradigms for lifelong library learning. Regional cooperatives can play a crucial role.

NOTES

1. Nancy M. Bolt and Corinne Johnson, *Options for Small Public Libraries in Massachusetts* (Chicago: American Library Association, 1985), p. 7.
2. 1985 statistics from the Extension Division, Indiana State Library.
3. Lynn Roberts, "Megatrends: Implications for Staff Development," *Colorado Libraries* 9 (Spring 1983): 8-11.
4. Bolt and Johnson, p. 46.
5. Roberts, p. 9.
6. Roberts, p. 10.
7. Bolt and Johnson, p. 7.
8. Bolt and Johnson, p. 14.
9. Nathan Smith, Maurice Marchant and Laura Nielson, "Education for Public and Academic Librarians: a View from the Top," *Journal of Education for Librarianship* 24 (Spring 1984): 233-45.
10. Maurice Marchant and Nathan Smith, "The Research Library Director's View of Library Education," *College and Research Libraries* 43 (November 1982): 437-44.
11. See unpublished report (Indiana State Library, June 1982), "Library Information Media Continuing Education Needs Survey."
12. See Herbert S. White, "Defining Library Competencies," *American Libraries* 14 (September 1983): 519-25, and responses by Mark Plaiss, *American Libraries,* 14 (October 1983): 618, and Martha Childers, *American Libraries* 15 (January 1984): 17-18.
13. John Richardson, "Theory into Practice: W.W. Charters and the Development of Library Education," in *Reference Services and Library Education: Essays in Honor of Frances Neel Cheney* (Lexington, MA: Lexington Books, 1983), pp. 209-24.
14. Letter by John Cotton Dana, *Bulletin of the American Library Association* 22 (January 1928): 12.
15. Jesse Shera, *Foundations of Education for Librarianship* (New York: Becker & Hayes, 1972), pp. 243-44.
16. Anthony Gerczak, *Library Selection Project: Job Analysis Report: Phase I* (Sacramento, CA: Selection Consulting Center, 1977).
17. José-Marie Griffiths, "Our Competencies Defined: A Progress Report and Sampling," *American Libraries* 15 (January 1984): 43-45.

18. Joan Durrance, "Continuing Education," *Journal of Education for Librarianship* 23 (Spring 1983): 311.
19. White, "Defining," p. 519.
20. W. Boyd Rayward, "Conflict, Interdependency, Mediocrity; Librarians and Library Educators." *Library Journal* 108 (July 1983): 1313-17.
21. Abraham Flexner, "Is Social Work a Profession?" *School and Society* 1 (June 26, 1915): 902, 904, and 906.
22. Shera, p. 49.
23. Donald E. Riggs, "Leadership Is Imperative," *Technicalities* 5 (November 1985): 9-11.
24. Alice Naylor, "And the Search Continues," *Journal of Education for Librarianship* 24 (Winter 1984): 208-11, mentions comprehensive continuing education plans in Indiana, Oregon, Louisiana, Texas, the Mountain Plains states and Wisconsin. Elizabeth Stone, "Continuing Professional Education," in *ALA Yearbook,* 1983, pp. 96-99, surveyed 50 state librarians. Of the 25 who responded, 50% said their state had an operating continuing education state plan.
25. Sandy Stephan, "Continuing Education in Maryland," *Public Libraries* 23 (Spring 1984): 26-27.
26. Herbert S. White, "Continuing Education—Myth and Reality," *Indiana Libraries* 4, No. 4, (1984): 138-45.
27. John Allred and Judith Bowen, "Implications for Professional Education: Librarians as Adult Learners," *Library Trends* 31 (Spring 1983): 669-86.
28. Stone, "Continuing Professional Education" (1983), p. 96.
29. Dottie Hiebnig, "Wisconsin Idea at Work: Cooperative Development of a Public Library Administration Course," *Public Libraries* 22 (Winter 1983): 153-55.
30. Stephan, pp. 26-27.
31. Duncan Smith and Robert Burgin, "Micros in the Carolinas," *Public Libraries* 23 (Summer 1984): 61-62.
32. Elizabeth Stone, "Continuing Professional Education," in *ALA Yearbook,* 1985, pp. 106-108.
33. Ibid.
34. Joan Durrance, "Issues Forum—Creative Staff Development in Times of Economic Stress," *Public Libraries* 22 (Fall 1983): 118-20.
35. Lowell Olson, "New Modes for Continuing Education," *Bookmark* 41 (Summer 1983): 207-11.

5

Corporate Libraries

Elin B. Christianson

The question of what constitutes appropriate educational preparation for a career in special libraries is becoming increasingly important as employment in special libraries grows, forecasts predict continued growth and larger proportions of library school graduates find employment in special libraries. It is a difficult question for library educators who must seek common ground on which to base a coherent program yet recognize and provide for the diversity of requirements in the field. It is an important question for practitioners who seek to maximize the efficiency and effectiveness of their libraries by hiring well-qualified professional personnel. And most of all, it is an important question for students who plan a career in special libraries.

Corporate libraries and information centers—that is, information services in private, for-profit organizations—make up a significant sector of the special library field and more than adequately represent the special library functions and characteristics that shape personnel needs and employment opportunities. This chapter explores the functions and characteristics of corporate libraries, the personnel needs that arise from them and the translation of these needs into appropriate educational preparation.

Both the diversity of corporate libraries and the uniqueness of each library are characteristics in which corporate librarians take pride. It is true that corporate libraries are uniquely situational: any one library's subject scope, services, size and structure are influenced by the library's environment—the parent company—and will differ from any other library's. Yet there are certain functions and characteristics that corporate libraries have in common and by which they are often described and identified as a type of library. While application in any one situation may differ, these functions and characteristics hold true in the aggregate and provide a framework for discussions of corporate libraries. These functions and characteristics include an emphasis on providing information service, a predominately small staff size, the dynamics of the library's place in and relationship to its parent company and a high degree of subject specialization. They exert a strong influence on professional personnel needs and, in turn, on educational preparation in library and information science and subject qualifications.

LIBRARY AND INFORMATION SCIENCE

Corporate libraries exist to serve the information needs of their parent companies and are characterized by their emphasis on information service. The services of any one library depend on the needs of the company and on the resources the library can muster. Some libraries provide only basic acquisitions, control and reference services; others offer an extensive array of sophisticated information management services supported by specialist staffs of abstracters, indexers, literature specialists, data analysts, records managers and other information specialists. While traditionally focused on externally generated information, many corporate libraries are also involved to some degree with internally generated substantive or research information. Corporate library work centers on organizing, creating, and providing access to information. It requires familarity with information resources and knowledge of how to organize and provide access to them, how information is used, how to communicate with information users, how to analyze and evaluate information and how to transmit it to users. All this knowledge should be found in good library and information science education programs.

Size of Staff

Corporate library staffs are quite small compared to those of other types of libraries. While a few corporate libraries employ 20 or more professionals, it is common to define a library with a staff of 8 or more as large and a library with a professional staff of 3 to 7 as medium-sized. Even these are in the minority: most corporate libraries have a staff of only one or two professionals. Although the larger libraries may develop specialized professional positions, professionals in medium-sized and small libraries tend to operate as generalists, performing several or all library functions. A comprehensive knowledge of the various aspects of library work, versatility and flexibility in performance are therefore important.

Job descriptions and advertisements for professional positions in corporate libraries most often require a degree from a program accredited by the American Library Association. Although the specialized library associations have developed personnel guidelines that specify this degree, adherence is voluntary and sometimes not without argument. The argument, as old as special librarianship itself, is over the relative merits of the professional librarian and the subject specialist. It is most often raised by corporate managers and personnel departments who have some control over library hiring. While some positions in corporate libraries do call for subject specialists rather than librarians, corporate libraries are basically in the business of managing information, and library and information science programs provide an effective foundation for this. The question is one of what constitutes that foundation.

Recommended Coursework

Somewhat surprisingly when one considers the diversity of corporate libraries, the various articles and surveys on employer preferences in library and information science curricula reveal fairly substantial agreement on the basic core of knowledge needed for work in corporate libraries. The recent study by Herbert S. White and Marion Paris provides a good summary of these preferences.

In the study, managers of large and medium-sized special libraries were asked to rate a list of 87 specific courses as prerequisites for either entry-level professionals or beginning positions and to rank each course on a scale from 1 ("essential for anyone we would consider hiring") to 7 ("unimportant for hiring of professionals in this library"). Courses ranked essential (2.5 or higher) by a majority of the respondents were then recommended to be made available to every student. Managers of large special libraries recommended six: basic reference, advanced reference, general online searching, system-specific online searching, advanced cataloging and classification, and cataloging of nonbook materials. Managers of medium-sized special libraries recommended 11 courses: basic and advanced reference, general online searching, collection development, literature of science and technology, database selection, special libraries, introduction to information science, organization of materials (Dewey), advanced cataloging and classification, and general technical services. Both the large and medium-sized special libraries' recommended lists were considerably shorter than those of the academic and public libraries, which ranged from 14 recommended courses for large public libraries to 26 for medium-sized academic libraries.[1]

Michael Koenig surveyed 249 professionals on the information staffs of large industrial organizations about courses they had taken. Respondents identified online searching (83%), general (69%) and specialized (76%) reference, programming (56%) and management/administration (55%) as important or very important in their work. About a third of the respondents found abstracting and indexing, bibliography, cataloging and classification important or very important.[2] Koenig's study did not focus specifically on corporate library managers or on entry-level professionals. His sample was drawn from large organizations with relatively large staffs so the results also reflect the specializations found in professional positions in these libraries as opposed to the generalist positions that predominate in special libraries. The relatively low ranking of cataloging and classification, abstracting and indexing, and bibliography is probably a reflection of the nature of Koenig's sample.

Nevertheless, both studies confirm corporate library needs. General reference, advanced or specialized reference, online searching and bibliography provide the foundation for the corporate library's most important product, information service. Basic and advanced cataloging and classification provide the foundation for information control. Because the computer is rapidly becoming a mainstay in the corporate library for in-house databases and other technical functions as well as for reference, course work in information science (programming, databases, systems analysis) is also considered basic.

Management Training

Where, when and how (and sometimes why) management training should be a part of preparation for librarianship, interests corporate librarians as much as it does their colleagues in other types of libraries. Most corporate libraries are small, with only one or two professionals. In such libraries the professional must be a library manager in addition to being a generalist in information work. Time spent on managerial activities may be less than that spent by managers in large corporate libraries, but planning, budgeting and other managerial activities must be fitted in along with information service activities. New professionals are just as likely to be hired for small corporate libraries as experienced professionals are and they are therefore as likely to become managers their first day on the job. For these new professionals particularly, a course in library management is a necessity. Continuing education programs in management are readily available to experienced corporate librarians through their professional associations. Many corporations offer in-house management training programs which are open to the library staff. But these come after the need is recognized, not before, so it would seem that an introduction to management during the graduate library and information science program is needed to provide the basics.

Other Courses

A special library course is valuable in providing a basic understanding of the theory and practice of special librarianship. The content of the special library course is of particular interest to corporate library managers, who are concerned with whether the course emphasizes one kind of special library over another or covers a variety of applications, what topics it covers and whether or not it deals with the library's all-important relationship to its environment.

Other library and information science courses and special

programs are useful for certain kinds of corporate libraries or for specialized positions in large corporate libraries. Abstracting and indexing are useful for specialist positions and for generalist staff in smaller libraries, who must handle these as well as other activities. A concentration in information science prepares students not only for specialist positions in corporate libraries but also for positions in other corporate information units. Archives and records management also offer potential specialization, both in the corporate library and in other corporate information units.

Corporate library needs for information management skills are readily translated into expectations through requirements for library and information science degrees and through relatively concise recommendations for a basic core of courses in reference, organization of information, information science, online searching, library management and special libraries. There are, however, other characteristics of corporate libraries that corporate library managers would like entering professionals to have some exposure to but which relate to course content more than to distinct courses. One such "like to have," already mentioned briefly, is the library's and the library professional's relationship to the corporate environment. Understanding and operating within this environment is another important aspect of corporate librarianship.

CORPORATE DYNAMICS

Corporate libraries are support units in larger organizations that are in business to produce and/or market a product or a service, not to run a library. The parent company does not establish or support its library as a corporate or public good but as a useful tool in pursuing other corporate objectives. In companies where integrated information management is in place, the corporate library may be a unit of a larger corporate-wide information system, complementing and/or supporting information analysis, management information systems, records management and other information units. Most often, however, the corporate library is independent of an information parent and functions as the single organized mechanism for dealing with the information requirements of the company. The library's function as a support unit and its relative isolation from similar units pose both problems and opportunities for information service which are critical to the viability and success of the library.

Corporate librarians function within the company as information professionals, bringing their expertise to bear on the company's information needs; they are also employees of the organization. Some corporate librarians feel that they are employees first and librarians second. This is not to say that professionalism and professional ethics are ignored; rather it emphasizes the fact that corporate librarians have dual roles to play. As employees at a managerial, technical or professional level equivalent to other managers and professionals in the company, they share not only the status but also the responsibilities and obligations of their corporate peers.

When corporate library managers interview candidates for positions, they look for certain skills and personal qualities. Interpersonal and communication skills are vital for corporate librarians, who are in constant communication with individuals at all levels in the company. Personal qualities such as the desire to engage in intensive information service, the ability to handle competing demands and work under pressure, and an entrepreneurial attitude toward information service are also needed for effective service. These are not skills and qualities possessed by everyone.

Where and how library school students are introduced to the dynamics of the corporate library environment and the qualities and skills needed is perhaps a matter of course content rather than course title. The corporate library in its environment and the qualities and skills successful practitioners need should certainly be covered in the special library course. If a library management course introduces the theory and practice of management in a general as well as in a library context, it can also enhance an understanding of the corporate environment. Reference and online searching courses may introduce interpersonal and communication skills through discussion of the reference process, and clarity in oral and written communication are basic skills needed in all courses. Internships and well-structured practice work can provide valuable insights into the corporate library climate as well as an opportunity to apply the principles learned in classes. There are many drawbacks to internships and practicums, not the least of which is finding corporate libraries willing to cooperate in developing a meaningful experience, but the potential advantages for students who plan or want to explore careers in corporate libraries should encourage library educators and practitioners to develop opportunities for field experience.

SUBJECT SPECIALIZATION

Subject specialization is a basic characteristic of corporate libraries and is the one most often perceived and addressed by both library educators and corporate library managers.

Corporate libraries serve companies in many sectors of business and industry. Many are in scientific and technical fields: computing, electronics, chemicals, pharmaceuticals, petroleum, energy, engineering and transportation, to name a few. Other corporate libraries are in the business and commercial sector, in advertising and public relations agencies, real estate firms, newspapers, insurance companies, banks and other financial institutions, and consulting firms in many fields. As new industrial and commercial sectors emerge and expand, so do companies and, sooner or later, libraries within these companies. In the past decade or so, the energy, environmental control, computer and electronics sectors have grown and expanded with a concomitant growth and expansion of corporate libraries.

Because corporate libraries exist to meet the information needs of their parent companies, their collections and services are geared to the subject interests of their parent organizations and the libraries' professional staffs must be proficient in the information resources of the subject areas and in working with users who are specialists in the field. Subject specialization, then, is a need that arises from the specialized nature of corporate libraries. The difficult part of a response to this need is the definition of what kind of subject specialization, how much is necessary and where it should be obtained.

Science and Technology

Corporate libraries in scientific and technical fields are most likely to seek staff with educational preparation in their fields of interest. At first glance the backgrounds sought seem fairly obvious: chemical company libraries seek professionals with specializations in chemistry, pharmaceutical company libraries look for biology, chemistry or the health sciences. Aerospace company libraries seek professionals with backgrounds in engineering, mathematics or one of the physical sciences. These are simple examples. The interdisciplinary nature and variety of scientific and technological work today can create complex demands for subject competencies in interdisciplinary fields as well as in the basic sciences.

For example, Genevieve M. Casey's feasibility study for an educational program to prepare energy information specialists found that no single subject background was perceived as essential by a majority of the energy information center directors surveyed. However, when asked to rate subject areas as either essential or desirable, engineering (either chemical, mechanical, electrical or petroleum) was considered either essential or desirable by 78% of the directors. Chemistry, environmental studies, geology, computer science and physics also ranked high, rated as essential or desirable by over 70% of the directors. Several respondents stated that a broad general knowledge of all the above disciplines was desirable.[3] This last desideratum is particularly interesting because it underlines the interdisciplinary nature of the field and leads to the further observation that while a company's subject interest may be quite specific, the range of topics on which its library is asked to provide information is seldom so narrow. Employees may turn to the library for information in their field of expertise (which in itself may be interdisciplinary); they are also more likely to turn to the library for information outside their own area of expertise. Library professionals with broad backgrounds in the subject and/or related subject areas may be better equipped to deal with the information needs of corporate library users than professionals with narrow specializations.

Business and Commerce

Corporate library managers in business and commercial fields often view subject specializations differently from their scientific and technical colleagues. To be sure, certain specializations are desirable. Business and economics backgrounds are valuable specialties in banks and financial institutions, insurance companies and other business libraries. Other corporate librarians prefer English, sociology, psychology, political science or liberal arts; still others seek various specializations so that the professional staff members complement each other in subject background and are capable of handling information over a wide range of subjects. In addition it is useful to note that the subject backgrounds sought for corporate library professionals are often influenced by or correspond to the subject backgrounds the company itself seeks for other managerial and technical personnel.

How Much Specialization

There is also the question of how much subject specialization and where it should be obtained. Does one need a second master's, an undergraduate degree, a major or minor in the subject, a joint library/subject degree, courses outside the library school, courses inside the library school or will work experience qualify? There are no automatic requirements; each situation dictates its own. Corporate library managers in scientific and technical fields, most likely to find subject specialization essential or desirable, are also most likely to want the subject degree, undergraduate or graduate. In some cases, for example positions that are primarily literature searching or abstracting, the job description might emphasize a subject degree over a library degree, but these are specialist positions and do not dominate the market for staff in corporate libraries.

Corporate libraries in business and other nontechnical fields, on the other hand, are more likely to identify subject specialization as desirable rather than necessary and are more likely to accept a broader range of qualifications—undergraduate degree, major or minor, or appropriate work experience.

For the entering professional and for the corporate library manager, subject specialization is sometimes a necessity and sometimes desirable; it is always an advantage. While there seems to be no one right way to obtain subject specialization for work in corporate libraries, there are opportunities for various subject specialties obtained in various ways and, in turn, various ways in which library schools can enhance prior subject specialization or provide appropriate background. Courses in other departments of the university have traditionally been recommended to students who want to specialize in a particular subject. Specialized courses and programs directed toward specific subject disciplines offered within the library school or jointly with other departments are offered by some schools. The program administered by a library school has the particular advantage of providing a focus on the subject/information/user interface which is at the heart of corporate library information service. Courses and programs for specific types of libraries or information resources—scientific and technical, medical, law, business—are appropriate to some corporate libraries. Few schools, however, can mount an extensive array of these specialized offerings and they should not be substituted for a good, general program in special librarianship.

What corporate library managers want from their entry-level professionals is familiarity with certain subjects, their vocabulary and their literature and information resources. While a library manager must still provide entering professionals with on-the-job training in the library's own subject focus and resources, the professional with subject specialty credentials can begin to be productive more quickly. Corporate library managers want their professional staff to be able to communicate with the library's users—the scientific, technical, professional or managerial staff whom the library serves—and to have their users accept and depend on the library professional staff to understand their information needs and problems and know how to solve them. Nonlibrarians seldom understand what it is that librarians know and do; they do have at least a general understanding of what chemists, engineers or bankers know. The corporate library professional who has an appropriate subject background has an added advantage in gaining acceptance from the library's clientele.

THE NONLIBRARIAN MANAGER

This discussion of educational preparation in library and information science has been based primarily on the expectations and needs of the corporate library manager who is a librarian. It has presumed that the librarian manager controls the qualifications and hiring of new professionals. This is not always true. Nonlibrarian managers are also involved in hiring professional staff and their perceptions of what they need play a significant role in small corporate libraries and in new corporate libraries. As White and Paris point out, "What these nonlibrarians are looking for when they hire an entry-level librarian constitutes an important research question of considerably greater complexity."[4]

When vacancies occur in a one-professional corporate library, the nonlibrarian manager who has the responsibility for the library hires the replacement professional with or without consultation with professional librarians about appropriate qualifications. Nonlibrarian managers also control hiring for professional positions in new libraries, which are created at a yearly rate of between 3% and 5% of all special libraries.

Although little direct research has been done on the question of nonlibrarian manager expectations, research into the formation of new special libraries shows that although managers responsible for establishing new corporate libraries perceive that they need a library, few have a true picture of what its requirements are. Their first step in planning is to hire a librarian, usually an entry-level professional, at the lowest possible salary, or to look for someone with a subject degree in their area in the belief that the new "librarian" will pick up library skills on the job. In short, there are many situations where the employer does not know what qualifications are needed and may have only a vague idea of what a librarian knows and does. In these cases, not at all uncommon among corporate libraries, the new professional, for his or her own sanity as well as for the sake of the library, must bring adequate preparation to the job. Further, this preparation must take place in the library and information science program because on-the-job training in these situations is more aptly called sink or swim.

SUMMARY

At first glance, corporate library managers' needs and expectations for the educational preparation of new professionals entering corporate libraries seem as diverse as the corporate libraries themselves and as individual as the managers who express them. Pessimistic observers conclude that these factors preclude effective educational preparation for corporate librarianship. This is a dark view and one that neither corporate library managers nor library educators can afford to take. Corporate libraries are an important factor in the library employment marketplace and will continue to be so for both library and nontraditional positions.

A closer examination of the needs and expectations expressed by corporate library managers reveals that there is some common ground. Preparation in library and information science and subject specialization are the two major areas of interest to corporate library managers. There is substantial agreement on a basic core of knowledge to provide a foundation for corporate library work. Recognizing that generalist positions dominate the field and that library professionals, new or experienced, in these positions must have the versatility and flexibility to perform a variety of information functions, this core includes courses directed toward both information control and information dissemination.

General reference, advanced or specialized reference in appropriate areas and online searching provide the foundation for information service activities. Basic and advanced cataloging and classification and information science are considered basic for information control functions. Library management and a special libraries course are also important for a basic understanding of how corporate libraries work; whether or not these courses include concepts important in corporate librarianship is of some concern to corporate library managers.

The various forms of practice work (work/study, practicums, internships) are also attractive to corporate librarians, who see them as opportunities for prospective corporate librarians to apply the principles they have learned, to gain some understanding of the nuances of working in a corporate environment and to test themselves in that environment.

There are, of course, specialist positions in the larger corporate libraries and in other corporate information units which call for specialization in appropriate areas of library and information science—cataloging, information management, systems analysis, etc.

Educational preparation in a subject specialization, the second major area of interest to corporate library managers, is less readily defined, not only in terms of the subject itself, but also in how much and where subject specialization should be obtained. Corporate libraries in scientific and technical fields are most likely to seek new professionals with undergraduate degrees in appropriate sciences or, for some positions, master's degrees. Corporate libraries in business and the social sciences are less emphatic in their requirements but do look for appropriate backgrounds. The bottom line is that corporate library managers need professionals who are familiar with the subjects on which the library focuses and the information resources in those subjects and who are able to interact with the library's users.

Subject specialization is a particularly difficult issue for library educators to address because of the variety of subject backgrounds sought and the various acceptable means of qualification. However, the burden of subject preparation does not fall entirely on library education. Students entering graduate library schools bring with them subject majors and minors, undergraduate degrees and sometimes graduate degrees and/or work experience. It is up to the library school to help students match their prior preparation with appropriate goals and to offer educational programs to reach those goals. The library school can help strengthen and enhance or, to some extent, even add subject specialization in several ways, through courses in other departments or within the library school itself through subject-oriented courses or programs.

A more positive view of corporate libraries is that their diversity does not exclude effective educational preparation; rather, it offers diverse opportunities for educational preparation. No one educational track will prepare all students for all positions in all corporate libraries; no one educational track can now prepare all students for all positions in all libraries. Rather, various tracks are necessary for corporate libraries just as they are for other types of libraries.

Corporate library managers' needs and expectations are specific and pragmatic; they center on the knowledge and skills needed for corporate library work. In these practitioners' view, educational preparation for work in corporate libraries consists of a basic core curriculum in library and information science, subject-oriented courses and programs and, for specialized positions, advanced courses in appropriate areas of library and information science. Although subject specialization in particular presents a bewildering array of needs and means of fulfillment, continuing research and dialogue between corporate library managers and library educators should help to determine library education's role in subject specialization more clearly.

NOTES

1. Herbert S. White and Marion Paris, "Employer Preferences and Library Education Curriculum," *The Library Quarterly* 55 (January 1985): 6-10.

2. Michael E.D. Koenig, "Education for Special Librarianship," *Special Libraries* 74 (April 1983): 185-187.

3. Genevieve M. Casey, "Energy Information Specialist Program: A Feasibility Study," *Journal of Education for Librarianship* 24 (Summer 1983): 53-61.

4. White and Paris, pp. 5-6.

6

Medical Libraries

Erika Love

The science and practice of medicine have made such phenomenal strides in the years since World War II that it is not at all surprising that all the related health service fields have similarly burgeoned. Research and education have been compelled to keep up with these rapid developments, and the libraries that serve the medical profession and all the allied fields have experienced a corresponding pressure to expand.

No other special library field can link its rise more directly to advances in the discipline it serves than can medical and health sciences librarianship. A number of professional and educational developments have profoundly affected medical libraries and, even more dramatically, the health sciences library profession itself.[1]

PARALLEL DEVELOPMENTS

In the late 1930s the National Institutes of Health (NIH) began a modest program of assistance to medical research that amounted to less than $1 million in 1946. Ten years later research support had reached $63 million, and it rose to $177 million in 1958. Major categorical disease program support was initiated; every NIH institute awarded grants to stimulate research in its area.[2] As a result, facilities for medical research, education and health care were greatly expanded. Medical schools and hospitals became medical centers; schools of nursing and other health professional programs became part of academic institutions; teaching hospitals broadened their role to support a national trend toward decentralizing professional education in the health care field, moving educational opportunities to smaller communities, Area Health Education Centers (AHEC's) being a prime example. Patient education and consumer health information services made their debut.

New technologies were introduced—photocopying and TWX were only two of many innovations that would transform library operations. Programmable typewriters and computers were tested in developing bibliographic control systems on both local and national levels.[3]

These and other developments during the 1960s—the age of the Great Society—had a decided impact on medical librarianship. A growing overload of medical literature placed an enormous burden on an inadequate number of librarians, who were faced with rising demands for reference and information services. These phenomena were documented in a landmark study conducted by Harold Bloomquist at the request of the National Library of Medicine (NLM). Among other recommendations Bloomquist suggested that "Federal funds should be appropriated to initiate a vigorous program of recruitment, education and training of medical librarians aimed at raising standards of medical librarianship and creating a manpower pool."[4]

Nationwide Guidelines and Federal Funding

Bloomquist's report was followed by two national efforts. The first was the development of *Guidelines for Medical School Libraries*.[5] The second was major legislation that would have a far-reaching effect on the development of health information services and medical librarianship. Publication of the *Guidelines* in January 1965 preceded the Medical Library Assistance Act (MLAA) of 1965 by only a few months. Signed by President Lyndon Johnson in October of that year, it authorized NLM to award grants wherever needed to improve medical libraries,[6] and train librarians and other information specialists.[7] Congress appropriated $4.5 million for NLM grants to library interns and to practicing librarians hoping to improve their communication techniques and pursue advanced training in library science.[8]

With NLM—the only library for a single discipline so designated by an act of Congress—serving as an agent for change and providing both technology and resources, medical librarians suddenly became part of a major national movement in the medical sciences and health care arena. Library construction flourished. The late 1960s and early 1970s witnessed the creation of a new generation of health sciences libraries.[9] Hospital libraries experienced similar growth.[10] Both medical school and hospital libraries played a significant role in the development of NLM's Regional Medical Library (RML) Network.

A National Network

Supported by funding under the MLAA, the program virtually revolutionized the way medical libraries interacted with each other[11] within the RML network hierarchy, which included four levels: thousands of community-based hospital and other local libraries (Basic Units) formed the first level, providing primary information services to the health professions. Some 125 Resource Libraries (RLs), mostly medical school or medical society libraries, made up the second level, helping local libraries provide library materials. The third level encompassed eleven Regional Medical Libraries (RMLs), with facilities capable of reinforcing the Resource Libraries. The fourth level was NLM itself as a "library of last resort," ready to supplement the collections and services of the eleven RMLs. For the first time, the federal government granted aid to medical libraries through a national network. The trial was successful and legislation continued to be renewed through several MLAA extensions.

New Jobs and New Requirements

The development of a national biomedical information resource created new jobs in the medical library field. They demanded a host of new skills and professional qualifications which, in turn, prompted an increased awareness of the need to prepare medical librarians for new challenges. Librarians were needed to function as networkers, outreach librarians, field librarians, trainers and teachers, online searchers, coordinators, builders and grant writers. NLM expressed a growing concern for improving specialized education for medical librarians and for exploration and experimentation leading to the design of new graduate curricula in medical librarianship. The MLAA of 1965 not only fostered academic courses in medical librarianship, it also initiated a series of internship programs which, by the end of the 1960s, had reached a peak where two dozen or more students each year completed internships in health sciences librarianship, thus adding to a growing cadre of well-trained medical librarians.[12] In answer to the need for librarians capable of working with MEDLARS and other automated systems, NLM offered training in Medical Subject Headings (MeSH), indexing, searching and concepts of information storage and retrieval. Indeed, due to the phenomenal growth of U.S. medical centers, medical schools and hospitals—and their associated libraries—the education and continuing education of medical librarians moved to the forefront of discussion.

In September 1967 the School of Librarianship at the University of Washington sponsored an invitational conference that brought together a number of highly qualified persons in the health sciences in general and in medical librarianship in particular. Participants met to consider current needs and requirements and to develop, through working papers and discussion, a graduate degree program in health sciences librarianship.[13]

Online Retrieval

The 1970s brought a new series of events that affected health information management in libraries and posed new challenges to the professional preparation of the health sciences librarian. Most notable was the introduction of the forerunner of MEDLINE the AIM-TWX system in 1970, followed by MEDLINE, the online bibliographic information retrieval system developed out of

MEDLARS by NLM. Introduced at selected sites in late 1971, MEDLINE centers had been established at all United States medical school libraries by 1973. Other online information retrieval systems searchable through Lockheed/SDC followed, with files such as ERIC, PSYC ABS and others. Online cataloging through OCLC was initiated in 1974, and a host of other developments in that decade gave rise to a second conference in April 1979, the Allerton Invitational Conference on Education for Health Sciences Librarianship.[14] Many changes that had occurred in health sciences librarianship in the intervening years were noted:

1. The introduction and widespread use of MEDLINE and other online database services affecting all areas of library operation
2. The inclusion of clinical medical librarians as part of the health care team
3. The identification of the role of the health sciences librarian in patient education
4. The implementation of a new certification code by the Medical Library Association (MLA) requiring successful completion of a competency-based examination
5. The elimination of virtually all post-master's internship programs for health sciences librarianship
6. A job market with an abundant supply of entry-level personnel and an apparent shortage of middle and top management personnel[15]

A content analysis of health sciences library positions available in 1977-78 confirms the last point. Of 414 advertised positions, almost 60% indicated specific experience requirements of up to five years or more professional experience. As many as 193 positions (47%) required either NLM online or OCLC experience, two qualifications that were virtually nonexistent less than seven years before.[16]

Continuing Education

The Allerton Conference also produced a series of recommendations designed to strengthen the continuing education efforts in health sciences librarianship. It suggested that "stress be laid on cooperation, compatibility and coordination instead of on competitiveness," as the regional medical libraries, library schools and other agencies "become more involved in continuing education for health science librarians." Finally, the conference recommended that "library directors communicate with library schools as to what competencies need to be addressed in the library school curriculum and what continuing education activities would be most useful."[17]

One would have hoped that this challenge would have been answered by library directors, and that a lively dialogue would have ensued between library practitioners and library schools concerning curriculum choices for the health sciences librarian. Yet, while the literature abounds with studies of professional education in librarianship, the voice of the practicing health sciences librarian has hardly been heard since this challenge was issued. The *Bulletin of the Medical Library Association,* a bellwether for medical library practitioners, supports this observation. How has the coverage of education for librarianship varied in this quarterly library journal from the 1960s to the present? The 1960s mined a rich lode of comment on this topic by a broadly representative group of practitioners. Dozens of entries appear in the journal's annual indexes under the heading "Education of Librarians"; from 1964 to 1969 alone, there were 118 entries.

This lively interest may have been due in part to the fact that during the 1960s, internships in medical librarianship and degree programs existed together as alternative avenues of entry into medical library practice. Eventually academic courses in medical librarianship prevailed so that, by the early 1970s, most internship programs had ceased to exist, along with their federal support funds. Perhaps this explains why the 1970s and 1980s are almost devoid of articles by practitioners on the subject of education. In 1982, the last year the term "Education for Librarianship" was used at all in the *Bulletin,* two articles appeared under this heading—one describing a course for "untrained library managers," the other on continuing education. Fortunately, the term was abandoned altogether in 1983, and the reader is now referred to "Continuing Education," where two important studies that address the formal preparation of the health sciences librarian are found.[18,19]

In an effort to pursue the Allerton Conference recommendations, a study group on the Medical Library Association's (MLA's) role in the educational process for health sciences librarians was created in the spring of 1980. The final report from this group covered recruitment, the master's level program, field experience, post-master's specialist's certificate and degree programs, doctoral programs, continuing education and certification. It concludes with a series of short- and long-range recommendations.[19] While the report emphasizes MLA's role in the educational process, the recommendations, particularly in the area of recruitment and field experience, deserve careful study by practitioners.

MEETING CURRENT AND FUTURE NEEDS

In the spring of 1985, the Library Education Section of the MLA sponsored a session whose topic was the question "Are library schools meeting the current and future needs of our profession?" In an attempt to ascertain their views on the competencies that should be addressed in the library school curriculum, a number of health sciences library directors were surveyed informally. They were asked to comment on (1) important qualifications in the new library school graduate, (2) the role for the new graduate on his or her first job and (3) opportunities for professional and career development offered by the library to the new library school graduate. The sample included 30 academic health sciences libraries chosen from the *Annual Statistics for Medical School Libraries in the United States and Canada for 1983/84*. To gain a profile of these libraries, the following comparisons to national figures were established: (1) total clientele served and total budget, (2) total staff and total professional staff, (3) distribution of library professional staff and (4) staff development funds.*

---

*The statistical data in Tables 6.1 through 6.6 were presented in a paper delivered by Erika Love at the annual MLA Meeting, "Are Library Schools Meeting the Current and Future Needs of Our Profession." New York, May 28, 1985.

Total clientele served ranged from 473 students and faculty to over 15,000. Total budget went from $350,000 to almost $3 million, with the national mean approaching $1 million. (See Table 6.1.)

Table 6.1: Clientele Served and Total Budget

	Total Clientele		Total Budget	
	Survey	National	Survey	National
High	15,552	15,552	$2,836,291	$2,836,291
Low	473	353	342,821	137,713
Mean		4,200		$ 964,096

Important Qualifications

The value of this informal survey was not so much in well-focused responses to a structured set of questions but rather in the spontaneous observations of experienced library administrators and, in some cases, their staffs. Comments concerning desirable qualifications of the new library school graduate divided naturally into three groups. The first included library and information science skills that would come from the core curriculum courses in library science: bibliography, classification, information management and other relevant skills. The second group included subject expertise, such as a degree in a natural or life science, computer and data management skills, courses in business administration and other specialty courses or subjects that would enhance their background in librarianship. The third category stressed personal attributes and the general attitude of the individual toward the profession. These included good verbal and written communication and interpersonal skills, stamina, self-esteem, enthusiasm, intellectual curiosity and an inquiring mind, thus reflecting a commitment of the total professional person. The rate of frequency with which these were cited is shown in Tables 6.2, 6.3 and 6.4.

Roles for New Graduates

On entry-level job descriptions, the survey elicited comments

Table 6.2: Knowledge and Skills

Core knowledge	67%
Understanding libraries and their mission	63%
Familiarity with medical or library milieu	13%

Table 6.3: Other Knowledge and Skills

Problem solving, analytical skills	47%
Computer literacy, data management	47%
Degree in a natural, life science or subject specialty	30%
Organizational implementation skills	30%
Conceptualization skills	23%

Table 6.4: Personal Attributes, Attitude Toward Profession

Team player, communication skills	77%
Enthusiasm, pride, self-esteem	60%
Intellectual curiosity, dynamism	40%

that revealed four distinct schools of thought, all relevant to professional staff size. Table 6.5 shows the range and proportions of library staffs nationwide and represented in the survey.

The assumption here is that a large library with a staff of 70 has a support base different from that of a library staff of twelve, and that a library with a professional staff of 26 will allow a different orientation toward the new graduate from that of a library with only one or two professionals. Thirty-seven percent of

Table 6.5: Total Staff vs. Total Professional Staff

	Total Staff		Total Professional Staff	
	Survey	National	Survey	National
High	68.6	71.5	26.0	26.0
Low	12.8	3.0	5.1	1.0
Mean		30.2		9.8

respondents expected their new graduates to assume management responsibility, think on the job and be rather self-reliant; only 10% expected them to function completely on their own.

One group (33%) expected new graduates to assume a learning role at least during their first 6 to 12 months. A smaller group (13%) thought one year of library school was insufficient to assimilate a curriculum that would adequately prepare them for their future professional role. They called for internship programs in cooperation with library schools.

According to 37% of the librarians surveyed, newcomers should contribute fresh ideas and a different outlook. A smaller group (23%) wanted them to work independently but also to recognize that they are part of a team. Because most work in larger institutions is accomplished through group effort, they felt that there really is no place for those who consider themselves independent professionals. Librarians with the smallest professional staffs (17%) said that their limited staff size made them unable to hire inexperienced graduates as trainees.

Opportunities for New Graduates

All library directors acknowledged the importance of continuing education, but staff development funds ranged from zero to almost $38,000 a year. (See Table 6.6.)

Table 6.6: Staff Development Funds

	Survey	National
High	$37,783	$37,783
Low	730	0
Mean		$ 6,198

Overall, most respondents favored professional development and continuing education. They felt that libraries offer broad exposure to library operations and multiple responsibilities where new graduates may learn a variety of skills and feel free to develop new programs. Directors of larger libraries considered theirs an "innovative, exciting place to work, where research is being practiced on a daily basis and, most important, where recent graduates are offered a chance to fail without threat or punishment, where they can try something new." Yet even among those in the upper range of staff development budgets, not all were prepared to pay the entire cost for continuing education. They expected professionals to contribute a share of their own time, money and effort toward their development, and added that those who participate only in activities paid for by the library with compensated time off reveal a lack of professionalism.

The percentage of graduate librarians on the staff of each library varied. The mean was 34% with a low of 20% and a high of 50%. Some said promotions were made from within whenever possible, indicating that the recent graduate has an opportunity to advance within the institution.

To summarize, responses clearly indicated that health sciences librarians care about the professional growth and development of new graduates. All respondents unanimously agreed that personal attributes, a professional attitude, good communication skills and the ability to be a team player were of equal if not more importance than acquired core knowledge in the library and information sciences.

Other studies conducted earlier confirm that these observations are shared by educators and practitioners alike.[20] Roper asked directors of both degree and internship programs about their primary objectives, then calculated their responses in rank order. Additional comments disclosed that candidates with science backgrounds received special consideration and that personal appearance and personality got high ratings. "A bright, personable candidate who seems to have a high potential for success in the field receives first priority regardless of other factors."[21] Results of a nationwide survey conducted in August 1981 by the Committee on Standards and Guidelines of the Association of Academic Health Sciences Library Directors (AAHSLD) reveals similar skills requirements.[22]

PROBLEMS AND PROSPECTS

These similarities, particularly in problem solving, analytical skills, computer literacy, data management, and organizational and implementation skills, reflect the fact that the library environment itself has become so complex that the operation of libraries requires a host of skills based on different types and levels of education and training. Can these requirements be met in a single year of library school? A comparable assumption in medicine would be that all hospital patient care personnel need the same knowledge taught in identical programs. While a hospital environment is infinitely more complex than that of an academic health sciences library, the growing need for specialization in the library and information management milieu requires expertise that goes far beyond what can be taught in a one-year program. Not every librarian must become a skilled administrator, online searcher, cataloger, library educator or researcher. A few in every library must become expert in performing certain library functions, a feat that might well be achieved in the practical arena and through continuing education. According to Dean Stueart of Simmons College, "Graduate education is and should remain less concerned with the development of specific work skills and more committed to setting criteria which guide in the acquisition of knowledge which then enables people to learn, unlearn and relearn."[23] Clearly, the base of discussion between library educator and library practitioner must be expanded.

While there should be no disagreement that education, practice and research provide the basic elements of a profession,[24] the importance of professional education in librarianship is a topic now under intense and spirited discussion. The medical library practitioner must become more deeply involved in this exchange. Should professional education deal with the practical matters that dominate daily operations, or should it concentrate on the topics that underlie practice? In discussing the future education of the health sciences library professional, the critical question is whether the profession can adapt to a rapidly changing political, social and technological environment.

Crucial Issues

The crucial issues confronting the health sciences librarian of tomorrow are addressed in a report by a Joint Committee to Develop Guidelines for Academic Health Sciences Libraries. The project, sponsored by the AAHSLD and the MLA, was funded by

NLM and the Council on Library Resources. The report, which appeared in final draft form in January 1986 to be published soon, addresses new roles and responsibilities of the library as a partner of its parent institution, the academic health sciences center, and discusses how the library's information management resources and skills can contribute to the institution's mission in research, education, patient care and community service. In a "Summary of Needed Actions," the report calls on outside agencies and organizations to "modify curricula in schools preparing information professionals to produce graduates who are skilled in the administration of information resources and the application of advanced technology to information management, research and education." It further recommends that they "identify and create funding for continuing education and internship programs for retraining professionals in the application of advanced technology to information management."[25]

These recommendations reflect the fact that the development of a profession undergoes certain cycles. Once again, as in 1963, we hear Bloomquist's voice calling for resources to stimulate the development of new programs for the professional preparation of the health sciences librarian.

Planning for the Future

Such discussions cannot take place in a vacuum. Planning adequately for education in health science librarianship, projecting future demands and needs, should be based on adequate knowledge of the present work force. In a major study on the Educational Needs of Health Sciences Library Manpower, Kronick asks:

- How sophisticated and skilled is the existing population of librarians?
- What are the current rates of growth and attrition?
- What are the usual points of entry into the work force?
- What is its composition in educational and demographic terms?
- What types of education should be provided in terms of present demands and future needs?

He seriously questioned the necessity and desirabililty of employing one kind of professional health sciences librarian in all types of health sciences libraries, in all categories of health-related institutions, at all levels of library functions.[26]

Similar concerns were voiced by participants in the 1979 Allerton invitational conference. Two years later, the study group on MLA's role in the educational process for health science librarians reported that "We need to understand who we are, what we do and how the profession is changing."[27] In fact, the recommendations made by this study group in 1981 reflect those of the Kronick study of 1969.[28]

Field Experience and Internships

The study group also looked at field experience and internship programs as a formal component of educational preparation for health sciences librarianship.[29] The question of supplementing academic education with internships is by no means new. Internships in medical librarianship flowered in the 1960s with federal support—and quickly wilted without it. Today, NLM is the only medical library to offer a year's internship as a postgraduate program. During the first 20 years of the program, 66 persons received training at NLM. Approximately three-fourths of the graduates from these so-called associate degree programs remain in the library field, half of them in medical libraries. More than a third remain at NLM.[30]

Through a series of rotating assignments, seminars and related activities, internship in a library should give the newly graduated but inexperienced librarian a carefully planned exposure to the broad field of medical librarianship and to the specialized environment in which the health sciences library must function. Both time for advance planning and an adequate staff are required to guide and teach the newcomer, a staff well aware of the state of the art and capable of transmitting its essence to the learner. Medicine has succeeded in building into its educational program such a series of supervised experiences—internship, residency, postgraduate fellowships and courses, and innumerable more or less formalized continuing education opportunities. The physician's preparation to become a lifelong learner has been reaffirmed in a series of studies.[31,32,33]

In her presentation at the 1979 Allerton Conference, Louise Darling emphasized this neglected aspect of librarianship:

> Other professional schools have taken responsibility for directing internship and residency-type training programs. Why should this not be the case with librarianship? The schools have the educational expertise, the libraries the practical resources for training programs. The two should operate on the same cycle. Sharing the responsibility might conceivably lower costs to the point where internship experience could become a regular feature of the library school curriculum.[34]

CONCLUSIONS

Medical librarianship has grown and matured under the time-honored triad of medical research, education and patient care to the point where health sciences library practitioners seem more aware of the qualifications of the graduating physician, more concerned about accreditation of medical schools and hospitals, and more committed to imparting information-seeking skills to health care practitioners than they are to the qualifications of graduating librarians and accreditation (if any) of academic programs in medical librarianship and the self-instructional skills of librarians.

Health sciences librarians should raise the very questions which they themselves have asked of those medical educators who depend on health sciences library support for *their* educational programs and curricula that produce the physicians of tomorrow. These same questions should be asked of their colleagues in library science academia.

First, are students being taught the skills necessary to evaluate and make use of the library and information science literature? Since librarians must become expert in assessing and managing information resources, the literature of their own discipline is an excellent starting point.

Second, do library schools promote awareness of the costs of information services? Today's librarian must learn to show tangible results for money spent, and in the case of publicly supported libraries—like most of those in the health sciences arena—the additional challenge of emphasizing the public good aspect of library services must be addressed.

Third, how are students being taught while in library school? Are modern means of self-instruction used to reduce the didactic element of classroom teaching? There is much talk about computer literacy, but are library schools updating the students' learning environment beyond the conventional and limited online searching module?

Finally, how are library students learning to identify, formulate and solve problems? How are they being taught to grasp and use basic concepts and principles, and to critically gather and assess data? More important, are they being prepared to become active, independent and self-directed learners in a rapidly changing information environment?

This last is, perhaps, the most fundamental guarantee, not only for professional survival, but to assure that future librarians will remain at the cutting edge of their profession.

Such questions might well stimulate a dialogue between the health sciences library practitioner and the library school faculty. While the lines of communication currently seem somewhat tenuous, such interchange may be encouraged by (1) a sabbatical exchange program for teaching faculty and practitioners, (2) practitioner advisory boards to library school curriculum committees, (3) visiting professorships for practicing academic medical librarians on sabbatical and (4) field experiences and fellowships for teaching faculty wishing to gather research in a practicing environment. These and other ideas are not new; many are, indeed, alive and well in some quarters. Yet each presents unique challenges to both academicians and practitioners. All of them could be successfully implemented if both parties would acknowledge the responsibilities—and rewards—inherent in such cooperative ventures. Other professions have established successful partnerships to enhance the professional preparation of their members. The call is out to medical librarianship as well.

NOTES

1. Susan Crawford, "Health Science Libraries in the United States," *Bulletin of the Medical Library Association* 71 no. 1 (January 1983): 28.

2. W.D. Miles, *A History of the National Library of Medicine* (Washington, DC: U.S. GPO, 1982) (HIH Publication #82-1901).

3. Irwin H. Pizer, "Looking Backward, 1984-1959: Twenty-five Years of Library Automation—A Personal View," *Bulletin of the Medical Library Association* 72 no. 4 (October 1984): 335-348.

4. Harold Bloomquist, "The Status and Needs of Medical School Libraries in the United States," *Journal of Medical Education* 38 no. 3 (March 1963): 162.

5. "Guidelines for Medical School Libraries Prepared by a Joint Committee of the Association of American Medical Colleges and the Medical Library Association," *Journal of Medical Education* 40 no. 1 (January 1965): 1-72.

6. Public Law 89-291, An Act to Amend the Public Health Service Act to Provide for a Program of Grants to Assist in Meeting the Need for Adequate Medical Library Services and Facilities (usually referred to as the Medical Library Assistance Act of 1965).

7. Miles, p. 400.

8. Ibid., p. 402.

9. C.K. Huang, "Physical Facilities of Medical School Libraries in the United States, 1966-1975: A Statistical Review," *Bulletin of the Medical Library Association* 64 no. 2 (April 1976): 173-178.

10. Crawford, p. 35.

11. D. Bishop, "Planning the New Medical School Library in Relation to Local and Regional Information Resources," *Bulletin of the Medical Library Association* 59 (1971): 292-295.

12. Fred W. Roper, "Special Programs in Medical Library Education, 1957-1971," *Bulletin of the Medical Library Association* 61 no. 4 (October 1973): 387-395.

13. Irving Lieberman, ed., *Proceedings, Invitational Conference on Education for Health Sciences Librarianship, University of Washington, Seattle, 10-12 September 1967* (Seattle: University of Washington School of Librarianship, 1968).

14. Robert A. Burke, ed., *Proceedings, Allerton Invitational Conference on Education for Health Sciences Librarianship, Monticello, Illinois, 2-4 April 1979* (Chicago, Illinois: Medical Library Association, 1979).

15. Ibid., p. i.

16. Dean Schmidt, "Qualifications Sought by Employers of Health Sciences Librarians, 1977-1978," *Bulletin of the Medical Library Association* 68 no. 1 (January 1980): 58-63.

17. Burke, p. 156.

18. Robert M. Hayes, "Manpower Issues: Implications for Training and Retraining Librarians," *Bulletin of the Medical Library Association* 71 no. 4 (October 1983): 427-432.

19. "Report of the Study Group on MLA's Role in the Educational Process for Health Science Librarians," *Bulletin of the Medical Library Association* 71 no. 4 (October 1983): 117-122. Also published in the *Annual Report* of the Medical Library Association (1982), pp. 95-143.

20. Fred W. Roper, "Special Programs in Medical Library Education, 1957-1971: Part 2, Analysis of the Programs," *Bulletin of the Medical Library Association* G1 No. 4 (October 1973): 387-395.

21. Ibid., p. 390.

22. Association of Academic Health Science Library Directors, Library Program Profile Survey, 1981, Preliminary Report. AAHSLD Committee on Standards and Guidelines, 1982.

23. *Library Journal*, October 15, 1981, p. 1990.

24. Erika Love, "Research: The Third Dimension of Librarianship," *Bulletin of the Medical Library Association* 68 no. 1 (January 1980): 1-5.

25. *Challenge to Action: Planning and Evaluation Guidelines for Academic Health Sciences Libraries,* Association of Academic Health Sciences Library Directors/Medical Library Association Joint Task Force to Develop Guidelines for Academic Health Sciences Libraries. Final Draft October 1985, revised January 1986, p. 38.

26. David A. Kronick, Alan M. Rees, and Lesliebeth Rothenberg, "An Investigation of the Educational Needs of the Health Sciences Manpower: I. Definition of the Manpower Problem and Research Design," *Bulletin of the Medical Library Association* 58 no. 1 (January 1970): 7-17.

27. Medical Library Association, *Annual Report,* 1982, p. 116.

28. Op. cit., p. 105.

29. Op. cit., p. 106.

30. Miles, p. 465.

31. B.V. Dryer, "Lifetime Learning for Physicians," *Journal of Medical Education* 37 no. 6, pt. 2 (June 1962).

32. L.T. Coggeshall, *Planning for Medical Progress Through Education* (Evanston, Illinois, Association of American Medical Colleges, 1965).

33. "Physicians for the Twenty-First Century: Report of the Project Panel on the General Professional Education of the Physician and College Preparation for Medicine," *Journal of Medical Education* 59 no. 11, pt. 2 (November 1984).

34. Burke, p. 104.

7

School Libraries and Media Centers

Karen K. Niemeyer

> WANTED: School media specialist, MLS preferred, endorsement acceptable. Responsibilities include supervision and maintenance of staff, services, and collections. Of paramount importance is enthusiasm for working with students, teachers, administrators, and community. Must be able and willing to develop and execute objectives; team teach media-related skills within the content area; lead others to consistent use of media center and information skills; demonstrate communication skills; utilize technology; create a dynamic, vigorous media program. Must possess sense of humor, patience, perseverance, and integrity. Confident, eligible candidates should apply to Personnel Director, Carmel Clay Schools, P.O. Box 2099, Carmel, IN 46032.

The foregoing job announcement describes the person—of any age—that the profession needs and that Information Science departments of our universities must help educate and certify as school media specialists.

The traits or qualities are those that school library media specialists need today and will continue to need into the next century. This list of qualities is based on my reading of published and nonpublished literature and my observation of those media specialists I most respect, followed by a determination of what qualities in their work and personalities elicited that respect. The 24 qualities resulting from such consideration are

- enthusiasm
- library know-how

- self-confidence
- teaching skills
- leadership
- management skills
- stamina
- a catalytic nature
- professional concerns
- dedication
- program advocacy
- clarity of vision
- political savvy
- perseverence
- patience
- listening and speaking skills
- curiosity
- writing skills
- an inclination toward public relations
- honesty and tact
- a sense of humor
- a desire to continue learning
- professional association commitment
- flexibility

The first eight are listed in order of importance, but the balance are in no particular order. Indeed, it would be difficult to assign an order, for the importance of each will vary with the working situation and with the experience of the individual, both areas to be considered later in this chapter.

My credentials for compiling this list include a bachelor's degree in Education; a master's in Library Science; twenty years as a media specialist, including eleven years as a supervisor of twelve media specialists in nine schools; three years of teaching an administration course to graduate library students in an ALA accredited library education program; and leadership roles in state and national media associations for the last four years. These experiences have provided innumerable opportunities for me to observe and converse with practicing media specialists.

Research in the library profession has documented how important the librarian is to a successful library program. Experience has likewise taught us that books, filmstrips, space, and excellent facilities will not necessarily result in an outstanding program: the librarian or media specialist is the key.[1] The term *media specialist* will be used for the balance of this discussion to describe that person who directs a building-level media program in a public or private school encompassing any combination of grade levels from kindergarten through grade twelve. This discussion will focus on the qualities desired in a media specialist *from a media supervisor's point of view as an employer and advocate of quality media programs,* not from the point of view of a principal or personnel director. Media supervisors across the United States are trying to educate their school administrators and Boards of Education as to what to expect of school media specialists. Many school administrators do not yet understand how much teaching expertise and curricular support an outstanding media specialist can provide; they are content to accept the level of service offered by the media specialist in their building.

A school media program, staff and student development, the school curriculum, and relationships with the community are in a continual state of process. Respect earned by any media professional varies with that person's ability to affect positive change. The following characteristics determine the media specialist's success as a change agent.

ENTHUSIASM

When asked what qualities he expected of a media specialist, one Indiana media supervisor said, "Those of a cheerleader!" Those attributes include enthusiasm, a smile, energy, and assertiveness. The individual style may vary, with one person demonstrating a pleasant manner and quiet support of the goals of a dynamic program, while another may exhibit almost boisterous zeal and vigorous activity to achieve a similar goal. I look forward to a shift in emphasis in university preparation of school media specialists; those planning to enter the field must move from the traditional style of static aloofness to one of dynamic involvement in the educational process of our schools.

Without enthusiasm the stereotype of the librarian as a bossy, cranky woman with her hair in a bun, sensible shoes, reading glasses on a chain, sweater tied over the shoulders, hushing finger to lips and a higher regard for her books than for the people who use them persists. That was the result of an informal survey of U.S. school superintendents and employees and of community members reported by a Salem, Oregon, associate school superintendent in 1982.[2] Without enthusiasm, the perception that there is little need to employ media specialists will persist. Clerks can handle circulation procedures, teachers can teach the Dewey Decimal System, and office aides can keep track of audiovisual equipment distribution. What makes the difference? The presence of an enthusiastic, informed media professional can create a cohesive, dynamic program that is less likely to be achieved in the absence of such a person.

LIBRARY KNOW-HOW

It is essential that potential media specialists have a thorough background in most of the traditional library and audiovisual courses. Until such time as robots select accession-numbered books from closed stacks and lasers read them from compact digital disks on a regular basis, the Dewey Decimal and Library of Congress classification systems will be used; media preservation and repair techniques will have to be taught to clerks and volunteers; reference services will be needed; collections will have to be developed and balanced (or unbalanced) as need dictates; and facilities will have to be designed for optimum research and learning.

However, there are areas traditionally neglected by schools of library and information science that are equally essential. While it may not be feasible to institute many new courses, existing courses should be examined carefully and areas of emphasis modified. The best media specialist has a combination of "people skills" and professional knowledge; people skills have typically been regarded as things a university cannot teach. The university creates an end product with professional knowledge, but on-the-job experience guided by a media supervisor or building principal modifies the end product to create a successful media specialist who works well with a variety of publics to promote a viable, visible media program. Continuing education opportunities will assist current practitioners, but universities must accept their role in preparing practitioners of the future.

University professors argue that library school students need a background of theory to apply to the various situations they will encounter on the job, and I agree. However, I also believe that specific examples and experiences drawn from "Real World 101" are absolutely essential, both to preserve the students' interest and to prepare them at least adequately for entry into the world of school media work.

Since there is no room for more courses in a student's schedule, those already in the curriculum must be modified to allow for additional areas of emphasis. Is it essential to spend time on the history of libraries, of librarianship, of paper and of books? In today's schools we are deciding that the history of the computer can be taught in five minutes, rather than in two weeks, as formerly thought. The area of emphasis is on using the computer as a productive tool. We do not have to teach the history of the pencil in order to teach writing: we teach how to shape letters and how to write creatively. There are areas of the library school curriculum that should be left to the curious student to study independently, just as the student who wants more information on the development of the computer may pursue it individually. Such a revision would allow the library school to include units on self-confidence, teaching skills, and leadership and management skills.

SELF-CONFIDENCE

Although adequate preparation in the traditional library curriculum has been the major strength of university programs, it is the student teaching, practicum or field experience, coupled with successful job performance, that generally provides a media specialist with a feeling of self-confidence. A healthy ego and a strong, confident voice could be promoted prior to that time, however, to help determine which individuals could make the greatest contribution to the profession. Image development, guidelines for dress, and stress management techniques are no longer nonessentials but should instead be part of the library school curriculum. Only those students who demonstrate knowledge of these areas as well should achieve a recommendation for a media certificate. This extreme is essential if we are to effect a rapid positive change in the media programs of our nation's schools, for to be most effective, one must be perceived as a person with authority. For example, a person viewing two men standing and talking, one in a short-sleeved and the other in a long-sleeved shirt, will assume that the one with long sleeves is the decision maker; the other does manual labor. Accurate? Maybe. Fair? No. Realistic? Yes.

A state media conference planner and elementary media specialist was sneering at the offering of a workshop on "Dress and the School Media Specialist" until another media professional described her experiences with professional image and dress; a university audiovisual instructor added that he detected a noticeable difference in treatment by colleagues whenever he wore casual clothing instead of a business suit. A new acquaintance makes an assessment of a person during the first 60 seconds, making assumptions about income level, social activity, community status, level of education, etc., based on impressions gleaned from appearance. Again, such an assessment is not presumed to be fair, merely realistic. These are understandings that may be taught to library school students in order for them to be more effective within the school climate earlier in their careers. Imaging, visualization, "fake it till you make it" and "success breeds success," are techniques and slogans that need not wait to be learned in continuing education courses; the spiral of success must begin early in the education and career of a media specialist and may be frequently reinforced during the university years.

TEACHING SKILLS

School media specialists realize that it has usually been necessary to obtain a subject-area teaching degree before they could be hired in a school. Yet the debate continues: "Am I a teacher first and a librarian second, or a librarian first and a teacher second?" Since 1980 many articles have been written about the fruitlessness of formally teaching "library skills" in a vacuum and about the importance of the "role of the teacher-librarian as a teaching partner, something quite different from a teaching adjunct."[3] Roy Lundin defines the teacher-librarian as one who coordinates and facilitates the organization and use of educational resources. That role contains two primary parts: resource management and cooperative planning/teaching.[4] He confirms Ken Haycock's assessment that "the single most important role of the teacher-librarian is cooperative program planning and teaching with classroom teachers. The major shift for the teacher-librarian from determining what the student is to do, to cooperatively determining what the student is to learn, has resulted in the teacher becoming the primary focus."[5]

Although studies show that principals do not fully understand this team-teaching role of the media specialist, teachers are even less receptive.[6] However, a two-year project in eight elementary, junior high and high schools in Carmel, Indiana, has demonstrated that once teachers and media specialists have planned, taught and evaluated together a unit of instruction that is within the content area yet features media skills, neither the media specialist nor the teacher wishes to return to the old way of teaching media skills in isolation. Both report that the integrated style is more work and more fun.

Needed today are publication of more examples of such integrated teaching and more university units of study, even courses, in cooperative planning. Ken Haycock suggests these could include consideration of curricular entry points, strategies for involvement, skills to work with professionals one dislikes, scope and sequence of research and study skills K-12, process for developing school-based policies and strategies for implementing innovation.[7]

LEADERSHIP

Although the bulk of the media specialist's time should be spent as a member of the educational team, considering instructional and curricular issues, other areas should be receiving emphasis as potential candidates are enrolled in library science classes and as administrators evaluate the media specialists in their employ.

Leadership skills include developing rapport with students to foster productive use of media facilities and collections, rather than an overriding concern for administering discipline and maintaining order. However, self-preparation to master new technology in order to teach teachers how to use it is a second form of leadership. Guiding a policy through Board of Education approval is a third form. Knowing when to follow instead of lead is also part of leadership.

Developing the ability to take appropriate risks is a skill that is often foreign to the nature of educators. Yet knowing when and how much to risk is a result of practice, consideration of alternatives and the desire to progress toward accomplishment of the goals of the media program.

MANAGEMENT SKILLS

Although some media specialists resent the term *management* because they equate it with *manipulation,* such skills are sorely needed by today's professional.[8]

"There is little doubt that the flood of information . . . is completely unmanageable by any person."[9] Media specialists have been trained to organize information but find it impossible to cope, even with the aid of automated retrieval systems. However, they are best suited to helping students and staff select relevant details from the mass of information in order to make intelligent decisions. They are also the logical persons to assist teachers with their organization of the information products used in teaching.

Many media specialists need to institute a "work simplification program" that includes analysis of the work of each staff member or volunteer, development of a work distribution chart, consideration of the staff's interests and abilities, examining the location of tools, and eventually making changes based on that analysis and on discussion with staff members. In so doing, the media specialist must remember that only about 37% of library work requires professionally trained librarians and that they should concentrate on those parts that require their skills.[10]

Lessons may be learned from business and industry. The authors of *In Search of Excellence* call the above reminder,

"Sticking to your knitting."[11] If each media specialist carefully examines what he or she does in a working day, enough clerical, nonprofessional tasks could be eliminated or transferred to allow adequate time for accomplishing professional tasks. Likewise, many clerks are performing tasks that do not relate appropriately to the focus of the media program.

"People skills" have been emphasized in *The One-Minute Manager* and many other popular books intended for readers in the business world, but educators should find them useful as well. Media specialists must accept the challenge of learning and applying the skills of catching students (and staff and principals) "doing something right" and offering praise,[12] of developing productivity through people and creating in *all* students and staff the awareness that their best efforts are essential and that they will share in the success of the school and the media center. Peters and Waterman quote a General Motors manager as saying there is but one key to a people orientation—trust:

> Some will abuse it. "Three to eight percent," he says, with a smile at the precision of his estimate. Nonbelievers will give you "an infinite number of reasons why workers can't be trusted. Most organizations are governed by rules that assume the *average* worker is an incompetent ne'er-do-well, just itching to screw up." He gives a symbolic illustration: "Ever go to parks? Most are peppered with signs that say, STAY OFF THE GRASS, NO PARKING HERE, NO THIS, NO THAT. A few say, CAMPERS WELCOME, or PICNIC TABLES FOR YOUR CONVENIENCE. One tells you that you SHOULDN'T. The other says that you SHOULD, urges you to join in, take advantage of the facilities." Such a difference in assumptions is monumental in its impact on people, he argues persuasively.[13]

Such a change in assumptions would create a major difference in most schools and school media centers.

Another area of management for most media specialists is clutter. We are trained to collect, preserve, classify and organize clutter. There are, of course, lessons on weeding, but they are usually given less emphasis, and many of us work six inches off the top of desks covered by papers that we have not assigned to proper places. Three recent titles have gained considerable popularity among persons plagued by clutter and mess: *Clutter's Last Stand, How to Put More Time in Your Life* and *The Organized Executive*. The first helps you identify junk and clutter and realize what clutter is doing to you; it then gives practical direction on dejunking. "Getting the clutter out of your life can and will rid you of more discouragement, tiredness, and boredom than anything else you can do."[14] The second explains how to cope with both home and work in a practical, realistic way, accepting the fact that most of us cannot close the door and tell a secretary to hold the telephone calls, a recommendation often made in other time management books.[15] The last, whose subtitle is *New Ways to Manage Time, Paper and People*, gives tips on how to set up files, how to establish a check system to avoid missing deadlines, etc.[16]

Managing people should not be considered by the school media specialist as a negative task, one to be avoided by a people-oriented media program. Knowing how and when to delegate is a skill often lacking, but once it is mastered, it will allow students, clerks and volunteers to feel positive about their contributions to the media program, while allowing the media specialist more time for planning and decision making.

Another book may be helpful for the school staff, especially after backsliding has taken place and old habits have returned—paper, clutter, lack of time, etc. *I Want to Change but I Don't Know How!* was written by two psychiatrists who "want to share what [they've] seen of the process of change and show some ways to master it."[17]

STAMINA

Two media specialists, in separate conversations, expressed the opinion that the best media specialists were also good actors. They defined an actor as one who has the ability to carry on in a positive way, in spite of aching feet, weariness, sniffles and other human frailties. Building-level media specialists are on their feet 6 to 10 hours per day; yet must always appear happy to greet students, willing to work with them and interested in their projects. A person in poor mental or physical health will not be able to provide the best in media service to students and staff. Stamina is the key—moral and physical endurance—combined with a pleasant manner. This is not to imply that those with physical handicaps should not be employed as media specialists, for there are enthusiastic, knowledgeable wheelchair-bound professionals, for example, who direct exciting media programs. Their disabilities have not destroyed their energy nor their enthusiasm for working with people.

CATALYTIC NATURE

The most successful media specialists are those who embrace their role as a catalyst, not bemoaning the fact that they seldom see tasks through to completion and receive total credit for them, but rejoicing in their role of idea generator, spark plug, brainstorming specialist and troubleshooter. In 1980 the twelve Carmel Clay media specialists hung a 3-foot "C" above their desks as a continual reminder that their role was that of a catalyst, an agent that precipitates a process or event, often without being involved in or changed by it. Since that time, I have noted the term used in the literature and am pleased that the role of catalyst is an acceptable one. It is a role that is not instinctive to all persons who assume the responsibilities of media specialist; it is a stance that requires understanding, development and practice.

PROFESSIONAL CONCERNS

A skill related to that of serving as a catalyst is the ability to look beyond oneself and adopt an attitude of service, of being able to ignore slights (whether intentional or unintentional), and to work patiently with those who do not yet understand the nature of a media program. The media specialist must be willing to admit that there is *always* a better way to do a job and the best way is *never* accomplished.[18] Willingness to consider alternatives, to grant to students and staff the opportunity to try it their way, is a sign of maturity and self-confidence. Contributing time to a legislative effort or to writing for the profession are manifestations of the ability to look beyond one's own immediate needs and to provide instead for the concerns of others or the library profession.

DEDICATION AND LOYALTY

Qualities to be developed in a teacher or media specialist are loyalty to the school, the administration, the program, the staff and the students, coupled with a dedication to improving the media profession. Support for the goals of the school district's media program is required, as is support for the goals of the building-level program.

Although it is natural for any teacher to spend a major portion of the first year in a newly adopted school system making references to past experience—"When I was in _____ School, we did it this way"—such references should diminish as the teacher develops an identity with and dedication to the present school and its programs.

PROGRAM ADVOCACY

"Put simply, if the teacher-librarian doesn't sell the program, nobody will, and it *is* a given fact that teachers have no idea of the role of the teacher-librarian at the beginning of their careers."[19] A very great need of today's media programs is for program advocates—media specialists who do not complain: "The math department never uses the library," or "I only see Mrs. Smith when she crosses through the media center on her way to the mailboxes or lounge." Instead, the effective media specialist is able to articulate his or her role as a member of the teaching team and state the focus of the media program and methods for progressing toward the goals.

VISION

A useful tool is a sense of vision or clarity of vision—the ability to dream big dreams, consider the future, outline where the program should be in a few years and then define steps to bring that vision to reality. Reading materials such as *Futurist* magazine and information from Naisbitt and others, and observation of trends in current professional media literature will help foster clarity of vision.

CREATIVITY

The abilities to release the mind from tradition, to consider alternatives and to make transfers of learning from one application to another are essential skills of the best media specialists. Inspiration and instinct may also be components of creativity, but extensions of the skill of looking at an opportunity from many perspectives is the element that is needed.

POLITICAL SAVVY

Media specialists have long resisted involvement in the legislative process, but that is only one form of political savvy that is helpful for today's media programs. Awareness of the power plays within the school system, knowing which teachers are supportive of the media program and being aware of the importance of image to the effectiveness of a media specialist are important skills. Some administrators may have concern about loyalty to the school system after the media specialist has served as chair of the school system's salary negotiating team. This may not be fair, but it is realistic. It is also an example of political savvy that is often ignored.

OTHER SKILLS

Also important for media specialists are

- Perseverance and persistence—the ability to continue an effort, in spite of failure or disappointments, always reevaluating the effort to insure that the objective is still valid
- Patience—with the recalcitrant student or teacher or with a project that is moving slowly and patience to wait for the opportune moment to offer a suggestion, provide assistance or implement a program
- Listening and speaking skills—including the willingness to hear what the speaker is really saying, rather than adding one's own assumptions of intent; realization that one learns more by listening than by talking; being an active listener,

interested and alert, not passive; being willing to master speaking skills in order to reasonably promote the media program
- Curiosity—recognizing that lifelong learning is promoted in students by teachers and media specialists who demonstrate their own curiosity for new techniques, skills and areas of knowledge
- Writing skills—working to develop varying styles as appropriate for writing policies, procedural statements, manuals, public relations materials and other materials
- Inclination toward public relations and a willingness to study the techniques of promotion; to borrow the best in order to promote the media program; to form committees that involve students and community members, even though it might be simpler to make the decision in isolation
- Honesty and tact—being willing to talk with a teacher to resolve problems, being willing to admit to one's biases, able to criticize and praise as needed, yet able to avoid injuring unnecessarily
- Sense of humor—the ability to laugh at oneself, to accept errors as opportunities for growth, to smile with a student or teacher at the vagaries of school life
- Desire to continue learning—a willingness to read professional literature, to take advantage of continuing education opportunities, approach each conference or workshop with the feeling that there is always something new to learn (technology included!)
- Professional association commitment—the recognition that one can both receive from and contribute to the efforts of one's colleagues in the profession, coupled with a willingness to carry one's share of leadership responsibility and to offer suggestions
- Flexibility—the ability to accept and even respond positively to change, to study trends and consider those with merit; the ability to evaluate and eliminate an objective once it no longer seems appropriate; the ability to revise goals when necessary, recognizing that the process of helping teachers rely on media services—of creating in students the knowledge that media resources can influence their efforts

both in school and throughout their lives—is continuous. By accepting this premise, the media specialist will find more enjoyment in the daily challenges and opportunities and will be able to expend energy planning for and guiding the process of change rather than resisting it.

CONCLUSION

These are my expectations for media specialists who would provide the best program to the students of today and tomorrow. These are the needs of the media centers and libraries in our schools.

Fortunately, each media professional already has some of these qualities, but none of us yet possesses them all. Each has an area requiring balancing or strengthening.

In addition, the various school environments require different amounts of any one quality. A media program with strong faculty support will require less program advocacy than one that is perceived as a study hall or opportunity for teachers' free periods. Yet some advocacy will still be required. A media specialist with an MLS degree and experience may have less need for obtaining additional courses and knowledge of the profession than the person with an endorsement and the feeling that "I don't know enough about collection development."

Where are the traditional skills of book repair, bibliography development, cataloging and storytelling? They are within each of the 24 categories discussed above. However, for the school media profession to become vital and visible; to have maximum positive effect on teachers, students and the school curriculum; to meet the expectations of school libraries and media centers striving for the best possible programs, only the most enthusiastic, knowledgeable and confident media catalysts will do!

Robert Maidment said, "There are three ways to get to the top of a big tree: (1) climb it, (2) sit on an acorn, (3) make friends with a big bird."[20] The school library media profession needs the dynamic, informed media specialist who is capable of using all three methods and has library/media knowledge coupled with self-confidence to be able to determine which approach to use. Career counseling of a radical, almost brutal, totally honest sort is required of the universities who are preparing students for the school media field. These institutions must provide to the university students themselves and to the school media profession an integrity that results in the generation of enthusiastic, informed media specialists who are people-oriented, curriculum-supportive, leadership-wise and management-trained.

NOTES

1. Shirley Aaron, *School Library Media Manual, 1984* (Littleton, CO: Libraries Unlimited, 1985), pp. 3 and 9.
2. Homer Kirns, "Media Specialists: An Endangered Species," Address at Association for Educational Communications and Technology Conference, Anaheim, CA, January 1985.
3. Ken Haycock, "Editorial—Hard Times...Hard Choices," *Emergency Librarian* 9 (May-June 1982): 5.
4. Roy Lundin, "The Teacher-Librarian and Information Skills—An Across the Curriculum Approach," *Emergency Librarian* 11 (September-October 1983): 8-9.
5. Haycock, p. 5.
6. Judy M. Pitts, "A Creative Survey of Research Concerning Role Expectations of Library Media Specialists," *School Library Media Quarterly* 10 (Winter 1983): 166-167.
7. Haycock, p. 5.
8. Alice Evans Handy, "Successful Management Techniques—School Library Style," *The Book Report* 4 (November-December 1985): 12-13.
9. Lundin, p. 8.
10. Mildred Donahue, untitled and unpublished paper, Carmel Clay Schools, Carmel, IN, n.d.
11. Thomas J. Peters and Robert H. Waterman, Jr., *In Search of Excellence* (New York: Warner, 1982), p. i.
12. Kenneth Blanchard and Spencer Johnson, *The One-Minute Manager* (New York: Morrow, 1982), p. 40.
13. Peters and Waterman, p. 236.
14. Don Aslett, *Clutter's Last Stand* (Cincinnati: Writer's Digest Books, 1984), p. 6.
15. Dru Scott, *How to Put More Time in Your Life* (New York: New American Library, 1980).

16. Stephanie Winston, *The Organized Executive* (New York: Warner, 1983).

17. Tom Rusk and Randy Read, *I Want to Change but I Don't Know How!* (Los Angeles: Price/Stern/Sloan, 1980), p. 8.

18. Donahue, p. 1.

19. Haycock, p. 5.

20. Roger von Oech, *A Whack on the Side of the Head: How to Unlock Your Mind for Innovation* (New York: Warner, 1983), p. 49.

8

Federal Government Libraries and Information Centers

Patricia W. Berger

In recent years, assessments of the educational needs of librarians and technical information specialists in the federal government have been fairly frequent and frequently wrong. To be sure, the government's December 1968 Qualification Standards, which are used to establish professional librarian positions in the federal government (GS-1410 Series, Grades 7 through 15), state that federal librarians must possess a "full professional knowledge of the theory, principles, and techniques of librarianship."[1] Further, the standards cover such typical library/information center functions as selecting and acquiring materials; cataloging, classifying and indexing; bibliographic, reference and literature searching services; library management and systems planning activities; "strengthening library service"; and developing "information retrieval systems."[2] On education, the government's Qualification Standards for librarians are quite precise: to qualify at the GS-9 level, which is the entry level for professional positions in the federal government, applicants must hold an undergraduate degree and must have completed either all requirements for a master's degree in library science or two full academic years of graduate study in library science. Technical Information

---

A contribution of the National Bureau of Standards. Not subject to copyright.

Specialists (GS-1412 Series, Grades 5 through 15) need an undergraduate degree and two years of graduate education in their specialty to qualify at the GS-9 level.

POSITION-CLASSIFICATION STANDARDS

Another document that sets out government expectations of its librarians is the February 1966 Position-Classification Standards for GS-1410 jobs. These standards stipulate that "Federal libraries may operate as (A) general libraries, (B) research libraries, (C) special (or technical) libraries or (D) academic libraries."[3] Distinctions between the duties of professional librarians and those of library technicians are set out in the Position-Classification Standards for Library technician jobs (GS-1411). Librarians "must possess a knowledge of library principles, theories, and techniques and of literature resources sufficient to permit free movement to [all] functional areas or to other library organizations"[4] while technicians "typically are proficient in one or more functional areas in the particular organization in which they are employed."[5] Technical information specialists must have sufficient competence in their fields to enable them to abstract, index and analyze source materials efficiently and effectively.

Sounds neat and orderly, right? Wrong! In 1978, just 10 years after the Qualification Standards for librarians first appeared, Winifred Sewell was asked by the Federal Library Committee to undertake a review of staffing problems in government libraries because "directors of federal libraries . . . [are] hampered in finding and retaining professional personnel [due to the outdated] Civil Service Commission standards."[6] (No such complaint was voiced by the technical information specialist community.) Sewell's review identified several problems, two of which were traceable to unrealistic evaluations of what education federal librarians need. First, in any one year, most federal agency personnel specialists see less than six personnel actions for librarians; therefore, they tend to classify *very* conservatively the education, knowledge and skills librarian positions require. This problem is further exacerbated by the age of the standards. They were developed prior to the emergence of our national and international library networks and before large-scale applications of automation in federal libraries had begun. For these reasons, the standards do not describe, much less credit, the expanded knowledge and skills that federal librarians have acquired in order to function effectively in today's rapidly changing technological environment. To ameliorate these difficulties and to accommodate future change, Sewell recommended that the Civil Service Commission substitute "general guidelines" for the 1966 and 1968 standards and that "a panel of information professionals" be used to "monitor classification/qualification actions and [to] administer the guidelines."[7]

Sewell found that depth of knowledge and breadth of knowledge are treated unevenly in the standards because the documents do not stipulate that federal librarians may well need both in order to work effectively. Sewell noted that while "the depth of knowledge of the specialist [as] indicated by the Ph.D. degree is clearly recognized, . . . breadth of knowledge is not credited, even though a generalist who has two B.S.'s or two M.S.'s is often more valuable than the specialist."[8] Therefore, Sewell recommended that new emphasis be placed on the "need for a combination of subject [knowledge] *and* functional education and experience." Sewell observed that "rather than ask for an information degree or a subject degree, employers will ask for both so that what is now needed is a means of identifying the individual's . . . [competencies] in detail."[9] To do this, she suggested that "programs in the various [library] schools be surveyed; that curricula be updated frequently to satisfy changes resulting from new technological or intellectual developments; that information on curricular changes "be communicated to those working with federal librarian standards and guidelines"[10]; and that sophisticated hierarchies of subject matters, functions, skills and institutional settings be developed to "increase the precision of match between the job and the applicant."[11]

CONTINUING EDUCATION

Sewell's review of the GS-1410 Qualification and Classification Standards alluded to but did not specify a major flaw in both documents: the standards do not set out requirements or assign credit for continuing education (CE) activities. Instead, federal library and information center work is described in terms that imply that extended education is not required to maintain practitioner competency and proficiency. This is a singularly narrow view of an occupation that is usually represented wherever there is a long-term United States presence; one that is expected to provide the professionals to run and to manage whatever types of libraries and information centers the federal government may require, wherever and whenever they are needed.

In 1974, Dr. Elizabeth W. Stone and her colleagues at the Catholic University of America's Graduate Department of Library Science issued their final report to the National Commission on Libraries and Information Science (NCLIS) on continuing library and information science education. The report and the project it describes were undertaken as "a response to the commission's request for 'a nationwide program of continuing education for personnel in the library and information science field.'"[12] However, the CE needs of federal librarians appear to be underrepresented in the report. This is unfortunate since the federal government is the largest employer of library workers in the United States. Indeed, a 1972 survey of federal libraries identified 2313 libraries in government organizations, 64% of which were in libraries in the Department of Defense.[13] Nevertheless, only five of the 108 librarians interviewed for the NCLIS Project were identified as federal librarians and all five worked in civilian agencies. In addition, while the project surveyed a total of 271 libraries and library organizations, federal library survey representation was limited to the three national libraries; namely, the Library of Congress (LC), the National Library of Medicine (NLM), and the National Agricultural Library (NAL). None of these three libraries resembles other libraries in the federal government and their CE needs are quite different from, for example, the needs of Department of Defense librarians or those of USIA librarians serving in countries unfriendly to the United States. However, earlier, in 1970-71 Kortendick and Stone surveyed the CE needs of the federal library community.[14,15] Some of their earlier work was incorporated into Stone's NCLIS report. In addition, Dean Stone told the author that "many" federal librarians who were not identified in the NCLIS report received CE questionnaires during the course of the study. In any case, the report's recommendations did not result in comprehensive changes to CE programs for librarians chiefly because NCLIS took no action to implement them.

In 1982, Alphonse Trezza, Director of the Intergovernmental Library Cooperation Project, submitted a report to LC and NCLIS. Entitled "Toward a Federal Library and Information Services Network: A Proposal," his study was primarily designed to examine and assess library resource sharing within and without the federal community.[16] Trezza undertook a comprehensive survey of federal library needs and resources in three sections of the country. He also held meetings with many of the librarians in these three regions. In all, Trezza surveyed 473 federal libraries in the Midwest, South, Southwest, Far West and Hawaii. In addition, he visited 30 federal libraries in the Washington, DC, area. He learned that while federal librarians considered the current Office of Personnel Management (OPM) Qualification and Classification Standards outdated, they considered the OPM's proposed 1981 revisions totally inadequate. He also found a "need and desire for training," especially "training opportunities in the areas of library automation, management, planning, research, and evaluation."[17] To date, Trezza's observations about these CE needs have generated little discussion or action.

NEW QUALIFICATION AND CLASSIFICATION STANDARDS

On December 8, 1981, just four months before the Trezza study was published, the OPM distributed first drafts of its proposed new qualification and classification standards for librarians (GS-1409 and 1410), library technicians (GS-1411) and technical information specialists (GS-1412). In all, seven documents were released for public review and comment a few days before Christmas. OPM declared that the seven documents represented the distillation of two years of study, analyses, interviews and writing by two seasoned senior occupational specialists.[18] (Within two years after the release of these drafts, both specialists had retired from federal service, as had their boss; and their boss's boss had been reassigned—rather abruptly—to another part of OPM.)

In 1979, when they began their work on the new standards, the OPM specialists were given copies of the Sewell Report. In addition, they spent time discussing job qualifications and expectations with federal librarians, library directors, library technicians and technical information specialists. (Later in the standards development process, OPM would claim to have interviewed several library educators as well, although who was interviewed, when, and what was discussed, was never disclosed.) After several months of public dialogue, the OPM specialists hibernated. In December 1981 they reappeared with the seven proposed standards, whereupon their analyses and conclusions met outrage and strong opposition. More than 500 letters were sent to OPM and to members of Congress describing the drafts as unrealistic and debasing and expressing indignation that OPM presumed to be the national arbiter for what constitutes appropriate education for librarians. Why this unanimous, national boo? Because the proposals disallowed the degree of Master of Library Science (MLS) as the basic educational requirement for librarianship, relegated all federal librarians who were not managers to a new, nonprofessional series and abolished the technical information specialist series, scattering its population either in "subject" series, such as chemistry or mathematics, or in the library technician series.

A PROFESSION IN NAME ONLY

In addition to devaluing the MLS, OPM proposed that certain kinds of nonprofessional, on-the-job experience be considered adequate to qualify for professional federal library work and therefore substitutable for formal education in library science. In effect, OPM's proposed standards for the federal library workforce minimized the need for the MLS and redefined librarianship as a profession in name only.

There was something schizoid about OPM's persistent rationalizations regarding its findings and about its unremitting unwillingness to revise the standards even after it became clear they had missed the mark. The information community was not alone in its objections to the drafts; many, if not most, agencies of the federal government took exception to OPM's findings and spelled out their differences in discussions and detailed, written critiques. The result of all this ferment was an impasse between OPM and that community of persons and organizations with a stake in the educational foundations of librarianship—an impasse that began in December 1981 and continues today.

COMMERCIAL ACTIVITIES OR LIBRARIES?

A second federal document that diminishes the professionalism of federal librarianship and in so doing diminishes also the educational expectations for federal librarians is Circular A-76 of the Office of Management and Budget (OMB). The 4th revision of A-76 was issued on August 4, 1983, in order to set "procedures for determining whether commercial activities should be performed under contract with commercial sources or in-house using Government facilities and personnel."[19] Library operations are listed as one of 109 "Commercial Activities" which agencies should study for contracting-out to the "private," i.e., nonfederal, sector. What makes this document particularly pernicious is its stress on products produced and their associated costs, and its lack of emphasis on the intellectual skills, special knowledge and quality service that have distinguished our profession's contributions in the past. In addition, the thrust of A-76 is to reduce the salaries of federal librarians, an action that will widen the present dollar gap between librarians and all other professions in the federal workforce. Taken together, this combination of the induced erosion of the educational foundation for librarianship and the increased disparity between librarians' pay and the pay of other professionals could well result in a future reclassification of federal librarians as nonprofessional workers.

The Federal Library and Information Center Committee (FLICC) includes an active education subcommittee that tries to respond to some of the expressed educational and training needs of federal librarians. In the fall of 1985, for example, FLICC cosponsored with the Department of Agriculture's Graduate School a number of Federal Librarian Update Seminars. In addition, in 1984 and 1985, FLICC presented and repeated three seminars on implementing OMB's Circular A-76. Thus far, however, these seminars have been available chiefly to persons in the Washington, DC, metropolitan area.

The problem of CE support for "field" federal librarians is a difficult one which their agencies must address almost single-handedly. Some agencies do just that. For example, within the Department of Defense, the Army, Navy and Air Force have developed training and educational programs that provide, at a minimum, annual workshops and seminars to satisfy some of the specialized educational and training needs of military librarians. Similarly, the Federal Interagency Field Librarians (FIFL) meetings, which are held in the fall of each year, were developed and are convened by a consortium of civilian agencies in order to extend CE opportunities to federal librarians throughout the United States.

THE MEDLARS TRAINING PROGRAM

Perhaps the most comprehensive and structured continuing education program offered by a federal agency is the MEDLARS training program of the National Library of Medicine (NLM). NLM's program developed as a result of the Medical Library Assistance Act (MLAA) of 1965, which established the library's leadership role in developing a national health sciences library and information system network. Today, NLM's training is available to librarians and health sciences professionals in all parts of the country. In 1982, Matheson and Cooper issued a report that examined "the implications of changing information technologies for faculty, students, and practitioners" and suggested "specific strategies for strengthening the existing information systems which undergird the health services enterprise."[20] The authors developed three sets of recommendations directed at three separate, major sectors in the health sciences community. To the professional associations and societies sector Matheson and Cooper recommended

> that professional health library and information science associations and organizations, in conjunction with academic health sciences center libraries, with the support of the National

Library of Medicine and other agencies, enter into formal agreements with at least four major accredited schools of library science, information science, and/or management science (a) to develop appropriate curricula and a variety of methodologies and approaches to train health information specialists with the knowledge and skills necessary to develop, manage, and improve technologically advanced academic health sciences center libraries and academic information resources management networks, (b) to develop and offer opportunities to retrain and retain talented mid-level career librarians to function as academic information network entrepreneurs and developers, and (c) to recruit and train a cadre of health information specialists who can bridge the disciplines of the health sciences and information sciences and serve as teaching and research faculties in developing academic health sciences and medical information sciences education programs.[21]

To the public and private agencies sector, the authors recommended

that private agencies, foundations, and corporations, as well as federal and state agencies, give top priority to funding projects that introduce information and knowledge management skills throughout the health professions education continuum as a key component in stimulating and supporting lifelong learning. Special incentive programs should be developed and offered to encourage rapid integration of information technologies in the learning and practice of the health professions."[22]

It is clear from subsequent discussions of the report that members of the health sciences community consider it a seminal document, one that will serve as a blueprint for strengthening of health sciences information resources and networks for years to come.

FUTURE NEEDS

On November 22, 1985, the Federal Library and Information Center Committee (FLICC), the District of Columbia Library Association, the Special Libraries Association's (SLA) Washington, DC, chapter, and a DC committee called the Committee on

Information Hang-ups convened a 3-hour meeting at LC to discuss "Future Needs for Library and Information Education." The deans of three accredited library schools participated in the discussion as did the Chair of a Media/Library Department in a Washington, DC, university. One theme permeated three of the four presentations: namely, that the rapid, pervasive technological changes of today preempt orderly, stable curriculum development; therefore, now more than ever, library schools must teach students how to adapt to change quickly and often and how to remain technologically competent and technologically sensitive.

That these are not easy tasks was underscored by one speaker who expressed her frustration by asking, "What do you do [about curriculum development] when there is no [technological] state of the art?" The heads of two other speakers nodded in agreement. Several partial remedies were mentioned, such as integrating computer technology into a wider range of library school courses, helping library science students acquire "technological comfortability" and training both librarians and library users to be "information literate."

In his 1980 report on the education of librarians, Dr. Ralph W. Conant observed that:

> Professional education has three basic functions. It determines who enters the profession and what qualifications and educational standards they must meet to qualify for professional practice; it provides formal instruction for those who seek to qualify for professional practice; and it supplies the profession with qualified people, provides continuing education, defines the objectives of the profession and anticipates its future needs.[23]

He also said that "nearly every profession depends upon its system of education to be the primary entry point for new professionals." Therefore, the faculties of professional schools are "the natural gatekeepers of the profession" who are responsible for providing students "with an education that can serve as a basis of competence as well as a basis for acquiring further knowledge and skills." He noted that "what sets a profession apart is its readiness to guarantee the competence and motivation of its members." However, establishing library curricula to assure continuing professional competence has been impeded by a lack of functional relationships between the educators and the practitioners. . . . Library school faculty seldom invite nearby librarians to participate in curriculum planning. . . . Conversely, library educators are seldom invited by library administrators to participate in planning and policy discussions . . . nor are educators regularly consulted on present and future job opportunities.[24]

As a result, "criticisms of the curriculums of graduate library schools are mainly focused on the need to bring course content up to date and to anticipate needs for the future."[25]

Conant concluded that while "practically every profession expects its educational system to select and train its future leaders . . . the evidence of this study . . . is that library education is so estranged from the profession that normal channels for the development of future leaders are missing."[26] He recommended establishing "a permanent national forum for library education . . . to develop a planning process and plan for professional library education."[27] And he urged that "every practical effort . . . be made between library educators and working librarians to close the gap between them."[28]

Viewed in the light of Conant's findings, the lacunae characteristic of federal librarianship in recent years are not surprising, nor are they atypical of conditions in other areas of the profession. But one wonders whether the recent, egregious excesses of OPM and OMB might have been avoided had this communications vacuum not existed between library educators and practitioners. While such reasoning tends to oversimplify complex problems, it does point to a possible remedy. Communications between these two groups must begin now, and it must continue in earnest and often in order to resolve not only library educational issues but also to search for solutions to additional problems that could become future obstacles to our profession. We must learn to bridge the "mutually damaging gap" that Sewell identified in 1978 and that Conant described in 1980; otherwise, we are headed for greater disaster in the future. Fortunately, the health sciences information community appears to have begun already to address the problem vigorously and at the national level. It is up to the rest of us to follow their lead.

NOTES

1. U.S. Civil Service Commission, "Qualification Standards, Librarian Series, GS-1410" (Washington, DC, December 1968) (TS121).
2. Ibid.
3. U.S. Civil Service Commission, "Position-Classification Standards, Librarian Series, GS-1410" (Washington, DC, February 1966) (TS60).
4. U.S. Civil Service Commission, "Position-Classification Standards, Library Technician Series, GS-1411" (Washington, DC, June 1966) (TS62).
5. Ibid.
6. Winifred Sewell, "Study of Federal Library/Information Service Staffing as Affected by Classification and Qualification Standards," prepared for the Federal Library Committee (Washington, DC, 1978), p. 1.
7. Ibid., p. 32.
8. Ibid., p. 2.
9. Ibid., pp. 29, 30.
10. Ibid., p. 35.
11. Ibid., p. 30.
12. Catholic University of America Graduate Department of Library Science, *Continuing Library and Information Science Education: Final Report to the National Commission on Libraries and Information Science* (Washington, DC: U.S. Government Printing Office, 1974), p. 1-1.
13. *Survey of Federal Libraries, Fiscal Year 1972:* A report prepared by Edwin E. Olson for the National Center for Education Statistics and the Federal Library Committee (Washington, DC: U.S. Government Printing Office, 1975).
14. James J. Kortendick and Elizabeth W. Stone, "Education Needs of Federal Librarians," *Drexel Library Quarterly* 6 (1970): 264-278.
15. Martha Jane K. Zachert, *The Government Library: Simulation for the Study of Administration of a Special Library—The Federal Library Model,* 3 parts (Washington, DC: The Catholic University of America, Graduate Department of Library Science, 1971).
16. U.S. Intergovernmental Library Cooperation Project, "Toward a Federal Library and Information Services Network: A Proposal," submitted to the National Commission on Library and Information Science and the Library of Congress (Washington, DC: U.S. Library of Congress, 1982).

17. Ibid, p. 53.

18. U.S. Office of Personnel Management, "Tentative Standards for Bibliographic-Information Analysis Series, GS-1409 (Classification and Qualification); Library-Information Service Management Series, GS-1410 (Classification and Qualification); Library-Information Service Assistant Series, GS-1411 (Classification and Qualification); Grade-Level Evaluation Guide for Professional Positions Providing Information Services," 7 parts (Washington, DC, December 8, 1981).

19. U.S. Office of Management and Budget, "Performance of Commercial Activities," Circular No. A-76 (revised) (Washington, DC, August 4, 1983), p. 1.

20. Nina W. Matheson and John A.D. Cooper, "Academic Information in the Academic Health Sciences Center: Roles for the Library in Information Management," *Journal of Medical Education* 57 (October 1982): part 2, p. 1.

21. Ibid., p. 79.

22. Ibid., p. 81.

23. Ralph W. Conant, *The Conant Report* (Cambridge, MA: The Massachusetts Institute of Technology, 1980), p. 13.

24. Ibid., pp. 121-122.

25. Ibid., p. 122.

26. Ibid., p. 124.

27. Ibid., p. 193.

28. Ibid., p. 196.

9

The Information Industry

Dr. Herbert R. Brinberg

Unlike libraries, whose role is either acculturation, including the preservation of our cultural heritage, or information service to scientific, technical, business or other specialized fields,[1] the information industry consists of businesses whose objective is to generate profits from the creation or handling of information.

WHAT IS THE INFORMATION INDUSTRY?

There are differences of opinion as to which businesses are to be included in the industry. In his pioneering work, *The Information Economy: Definition and Measurements,* Mark U. Porat included a wide range of information-using and -producing companies—from those in knowledge production, such as publishers, through insurance companies, to producers of electronic gears. Porat's objective was to measure the importance of information and information handling in the U.S. economy. He concluded that information-related activities accounted for over 50% of our gross national product.[2]

The Harvard Program on Information Resources Policy also takes a broad view of the composition of the information business, categorizing it not as a single homogeneous industry, but rather a group of industries to whom information is an important ingredient in their economic activity. These diverse businesses—from publishing to banking, from communications to the postal service—and their information products and services were presented pictorially on an information business map that positioned them in accordance with the characteristics of their information-handling activities. A recent Harvard information business map is shown in Figure 9.1.

More than eighty products and services are noted on the map. The axes of the map are (1) services and products and (2) content and conduit. Displaying business activities along the products/services axis serves to highlight the vertical integration of the information business. The conduit/content axis highlights the differences between companies traditionally thought of as information producers, such as publishers, and those that provide the means to record and transmit information.

The map shows that the constituent industries involved with information are diverse. Some constituents exist to acquire information, others to package, store, process, transmit or distribute it. Some companies handle information as a service, while others produce and market products to allow companies or individuals to collect, process or distribute their own information. Many companies are involved in a wide mix of these functions.[3]

As meaningful as they may be for analyses of the implications of information for social or economic policy, broad definitions such as Porat's and Harvard's are not as relevant here. Although these businesses employ librarians or information specialists just as they employ engineers or accountants, their primary activity is not to market or sell information products or services.

For the purposes of this chapter, I define the information industry as those organizations whose principal business activity is to create, assemble, organize, manage or distribute *content*—the "stuff" of information—through any medium appropriate to the user, but especially through new technologies or innovative information-handling methods.

Of course, information companies publish books, journals and other ink-print products. But not all publishers fit within this definition of information companies. Some publish to entertain, some to teach, others to philosophize and many to enrich our lives with literature, history and art. On the other hand, the information companies dealt with here create and distribute materials to help solve problems or to improve decision making. Whether

The Information Industry   157

Figure 9.1: Information Business Map

Copyright 1986, Program on Information Resources Policy, Harvard University.

SERVICES ←

								PROFESSIONAL SVCS
GOVT MAIL	MAILGRAM			BROADCAST NETWORKS	DATABASES AND			
PARCEL SVCS	E-COM	TELEPHONE	VAN's	BROADCAST STATIONS	VIDEOTEX			FINANCIAL SVCS
COURIER SVCS	EMS	TELEGRAPH		CABLE NETWORKS	NEWS SVCS			ADVERTISING SVCS
OTHER DELIVERY		OCC's	CABLE OPERATORS	TELETEXT				
SVCS		IRC's						
		MULTIPOINT DISTRIBUTION SVCS						
		DIGITAL TERMINATION SVCS		TIME SHARING SERVICE BUREAUS				ON-LINE DIRECTORIES
		SATELLITE SVCS	BILLING AND					
	PRINTING COS	FM SUBCARRIERS	METERING SVCS		SOFTWARE SVCS			
	LIBRARIES	MOBILE SVCS			SYNDICATORS AND			
		PAGING SVCS	MULTIPLEXING SVCS		PROGRAM PACKAGERS			
			INDUSTRY NETWORKS					LOOSE-LEAF SVCS
RETAILERS								
NEWSSTANDS			DEFENSE TELECOM SYSTEMS					
			SECURITY SVCS					
				COMPUTERS				
				PABX's		SOFTWARE PACKAGES	DIRECTORIES	
							NEWSPAPERS	
			RADIOS	TELEPHONE SWITCHING EQUIP			NEWSLETTERS	
			TV SETS				MAGAZINES	
PRINTING AND			TELEPHONES MODEMS	CONCENTRATORS				
GRAPHICS EQUIP			TERMINALS	MULTIPLEXERS			SHOPPERS	
COPIERS			PRINTERS					
			FACSIMILE				AUDIO RECORDS	
CASH REGISTERS			ATM's				AND TAPES	
INSTRUMENTS			POS EQUIP					
TYPEWRITERS			BROADCAST AND				FILMS AND	
DICTATION EQUIP			TRANSMISSION EQUIP				VIDEO PROGRAMS	
FILE CABINETS			CALCULATORS					
BLANK TAPE			WORD PROCESSORS					
AND FILM			PHONOS, VIDEO DISC PLAYERS				BOOKS	
PAPER		MICROFILM MICROFICHE	VIDEO TAPE RECORDERS	MASS STORAGE				
		BUSINESS FORMS		GREETING CARDS				

PRODUCTS →

← CONDUIT   CONTENT →

ATM—Automated Teller Machine; E-COM—Electronic Computer Originated Mail; EMS—Electronic Message Service; IRC—International Record Carrier
OCC—Other Common Carrier; PABX—Private Automatic Branch Exchange; POS—Point-of-State; VAN—Value Added Network

Source: "Mapping the Information Business," by John F. McLaughlin with Anne E. Birinyi, Program on Information Resources Policy, Harvard University, Cambridge, MA, 1980.

economic, financial, scientific, technical, medical, legal or managerial, the information products and services they produce are used by businesses, governments, professional firms and not-for-profit institutions to improve their performance and more effectively realize their particular missions. These are the information companies that have a growing need for the professional talents and skills that should be the product of library schools or schools of information sciences or studies.

Information and Information Technologies

The driving forces behind the emergence of the information industry have been the computer and the communications and optics technologies developed during the past 30 years, combined with significant developments in intellectual technologies, such as software and new classification schemes, which alter the ways in which ideas and data are organized and the ways in which people and machines are arranged and integrated. These forces have been rapid and recent: the first commercial computer was installed in 1951, FORTRAN was introduced in 1955, xerography in 1957, computer typesetting in 1965 and the personal computer in 1981.

At first, development of products and services using these new technologies was more likely to be undertaken by not-for-profit institutions or the federal government. Chemical Abstracts, MEDLARS, even DIALOG (funded by NASA), are leading examples. The underlying motivation to adopt these emerging technologies was public service, education and the spread of knowledge in the tradition of librarianship. Indeed, many were funded as a direct result of government efforts to spread scientific and technical knowledge in response to the challenge extended by the Russian launching of Sputnik.

Digitizing ink-print products enabled new tools to be developed to extend and improve traditional library skills like cataloging, indexing, abstracting and thesaurus development, and to enhance the ability of librarians and intermediaries in collecting and providing relevant data, documents and literature.

As the technology for information handling evolved, entrepreneurs saw an opportunity to capitalize on these technologies by conceiving and commercializing new information products and services. Many publishers, at best seeing a new delivery system in the making or at worst feeling that the market for their traditional products was threatened, entered the market with electronic versions of their books or journals. New delivery systems and new services were introduced. These rapidly led to user interaction, faster retrieval, on-demand publishing and, ultimately, the desk-top library. Whether in the not-for-profit sector or, increasingly, in the commercial sector, these information products and services were research-oriented—they were conceived by librarians for use by librarians or intermediaries.

The growth of computers required new skills, such as knowledge of database construction, computer operations, software capabilities and telecommunications. More recently, the emergence of the personal computer and the evolution of a new machine-oriented intellect—including expert or knowledge-based systems—has resulted in an even more dramatic change in the nature of information handling.

The personal computer is causing a shift in the balance of forces in information transfer from the provider/publisher to the customer/user. Until recently, the information provider was the "gatekeeper" of knowledge, deciding what to disseminate and how. The user was essentially a passive/reactive searcher of what was made available. With the personal computer, the supply/push of the past is fast becoming the demand/pull of the future—so-called end-user computing. This has far-reaching implications:

- The end user is learning to access electronic libraries directly and is demanding that the information product be relevant and simple to utilize and, therefore, not requiring an intermediary. *Result:* The creators of information must be end-user sensitive, with both content and the means of accessing it.
- End users are becoming computer literate with internal information, specific to their companies or jobs. In the past, such material was obtained from record centers or data processing centers. End users now are bringing together, on their desk tops, both internal and external information. *Result:* The creators of information must think about ap-

plications as well as sources that lend themselves to interpreting internal and external content.
- End users are interested in putting information to work and are seeking methods by which the information will lead to improved decisions and better performance. *Result:* Creators of information must think about decision support systems and models, not merely data and documents.

The advent of end-user computing and the dominance of action-oriented information is causing rapid change in the scope and complexity of the information profession. Moreoever, because content and technology are increasingly interwoven, the separation of the roles of the participants in the information creation process—author, editor, publisher, systems analyst, information scientist, distributor—is blurring.

Recognizing this trend, a number of library schools have modified their curricula to include a variety of courses geared to the new technologies. Several schools have revamped their mission to become schools of information sciences or information studies. Nevertheless, in many instances, although the emphasis has shifted away from the librarians' role of preserving the records of society's achievements and of providing the intellectual means to access them, the focus continues to be on traditional library activities.

In reaction to this trend, automating the library and improving information retrieval merely moves the process from card catalogs and bookshelves to a terminal—except that we count databases rather than number of volumes. Moreover, the culture of the library schools and their philosophy of information has changed quite slowly despite the rapid changes in the perceived value and use of information.

Other schools and disciplines have been filling the education gaps. Computer sciences programs, often growing out of engineering curricula with a stress on mathematics and logic, address the issues of computer and information processing systems, the architecture of hardware and software systems and the application of computers to the solution of problems in science, engineering, process control and business.

Business schools have also recognized the emergence of information as a resource and have established programs to train students in the management of information and in the application of information technology and systems to decision making. The culture of the business schools has been compatible with the culture of information industry companies. Information providers and facilitators are willing to invest in development of information products and services because they perceive a market need and, therefore, the prospect for profits. The mission of business schools has been primarily to train individuals to serve in profit-oriented organizations. Library schools have often eschewed the profit motive.

In short, curriculum development in management information systems (MIS), decision support systems (DSS), modeling and simulation and, more recently, information resources management (IRM) increasingly are preempting what should be the natural and evolutionary role of library/information schools to educate those who must cope with the vast accumulation of knowledge itself.

Does this mean that information companies cannot or should not look to library/information schools for future talent? Not at all! Nor does it mean that all library schools should abandon their role of training people to protect and diffuse our cultural heritage. But with technology moving us toward a whole new world of information products and services that will be offered for sale by commercial companies and will be created and marketed by professionals and managers with a business as well as a service orientation, a new culture is required. New curricula, as well as a business-oriented track, plus a desire to serve this particular constituency are necessary.

WHAT DOES THE INDUSTRY NEED?

The information industry's requirements for trained people, not unlike those of other industries, are diverse but essentially fall into three classes: information technicians, information professionals and information-literate managers. Each group requires specific training and brings different talents to an enterprise. While the level of expertise will differ, the appropriate mix of these skills is essential for success.

Information Technicians

These knowledge workers represent the basic foundation of the workforce in information industry companies. They contribute traditional library-oriented skills to the development and production of information products and services, such as indexing, cataloging, coding, and searching and retrieving; and they contribute newer skills, such as programming, online editing and database construction.

The Information Professional

With the growing complexity of both the technology and the environment, the information industry has an increasing requirement for information professionals who are not only proficient in specific areas of expertise, but also broad-based, well-educated individuals in touch with the needs of society and in tune with our cultural setting. These individuals must also be attuned to the business world and knowledgeable of the business tools necessary to operate in the profit-oriented environment of the information industry.

Managing the Enterprise

The third essential requirement is management—especially middle management—to run a profit-oriented information enterprise. These managers require a sound foundation in business practices, a comprehension of the content base of information products and a fundamental knowledge of information technology and its applications. They also require the skills needed to build a business, from product planning and development to motivating and directing people. The manager must possess the flexibility necessary to respond effectively to the fast pace of change in both technology and markets.

Previously, these skills were addressed in several ways: some were provided in schools of library and information sciences, some were provided in schools of business and management, and some were offered in programs in computer sciences. However, the time has come for an integrated program that can serve the needs of the information industry and provide the leadership for the information age.

Such an integrated program must be offered at the graduate level. Undergraduate library and information programs can and should train individuals in librarianship and in the skills needed to become an information technician. The graduate program should address the broader needs, moving students from a task orientation to the innovative and strategic outlook required of the professionals and managers for the information industry.

Importance of a Liberal Education

Undergraduate training in the liberal arts and sciences is the essential foundation and background on which to build appropriate professional and managerial skills for the information industry. Increasingly, in the judgment of knowledgeable managers in the information business community, the employee who is the product of a comprehensive liberal education gains both vision and perspective about the culture and society in which the information industry operates. Such individuals demonstrate a greater receptivity to new ideas and think more conceptually, while groping for creative and meaningful ways to employ the new technology in product/market development.

TOWARD A NEW CURRICULUM

The education of information professionals and managers for the information industry should offer training in a specialized field while at the same time providing a broad perspective on the nature of information, its creation and its use. The range of subjects can be encompassed in four knowledge areas: the underlying concepts of information; business principles and practices; information technology and content management; and information policy. Each of these major areas is examined separately below.

Concepts and Foundations

An information professional must have a comprehensive understanding of information itself. This requires familiarity with the underlying theories of the information sciences, an understanding of human information processing, and familiarity with the results of modern research and the theory of human cognition. There must be a knowledge of the information-seeking behavior of information users and an understanding of the influences and factors associated with humans needing, using and acting upon information.

The language and syntax of communication is evolving as the form and substance of the symbols we use are changing. To deal with this, the information professional should understand the basic concepts of oral, written and visual communication.

This foundation in theory, concepts and psychology is a requirement for those professionals who enter the information industry. It is essential to developing new means of organizing, transferring and using information.

Business Principles and Practices

Adequate training in the principles and practices of business is probably the area that has been least addressed in the traditional library/information graduate programs. I am referring here not to a substitute for a business administration program but rather to (1) creating an awareness of the role of business in society and how it operates; (2) developing an understanding of the economics of information, its supply and demand, how it is valued and how it is priced; (3) acquiring a basic knowledge of the tools of business and, to the extent appropriate, of management; and (4) understanding how information flows in a business environment and how it is used in the decision-making process.

Information industry firms too often have been frustrated by the narrowly trained information professional. They have been faced with two choices: train the information professional in business and management—in-house or at a continuing education program—or recruit business school graduates with some knowledge of information technology and develop their skills in information handling. Neither of these approaches is wholly satisfactory, but the pendulum appears to be swinging toward the latter.

This is unfortunate. The essence of information products is the content, not the technology. Library/information schools are content-oriented; they should build on this predisposition in an environment that not only trains but encourages its students to opt for a career in business.

Four objectives of a "module" on business principles and practices can be suggested. Each addresses the subject from a different perspective. The first describes and analyzes the business environment in which the information professional must function—the information company is, after all, in business to make a profit. The curriculum must address the ethics of business, its modus operandi and its relationship to other institutions. This will alleviate the often inaccurate perceptions of the world of business that deter students from such a career.

The second objective is to understand the value of the information itself. Increasingly, information is viewed as a valuable resource, but only recently has serious work been undertaken on how to value the contribution of the information to problem solving, to decision making or to productivity improvement. The only objective value of information in economic terms today is the price of "traded" information in the marketplace. More knowledge of the true economic contribution to the user will aid in assessing needs, developing new information products and services, and establishing more realistic prices for them.

Third, if information professionals are to grow within a business enterprise, they must be familiar with business nomenclature and tools. Profit and loss, return on investment, planning and budgeting, and market share must be as familiar to them as bits, bytes and bauds. Professionals aspiring to management must also understand management principles and marketing concepts and strategies as they apply to the unique commodity called information.

Finally, to develop and market information products and services effectively, one must understand how information is used by the customers in their business setting. To be useful for market monitoring, product planning, production scheduling or financial control, information must improve performance. The information junkyard is filled with products and services that didn't meet that test.

Information Technologies

It is a truism that familiarity with information technologies and significant competence in one or more of them is, or should be, at the heart of library/information schools' curricula. The graduate program requires expanded courses to provide comprehensive indoctrination in this burgeoning technology.

Information technologies, as used here, are both machine technologies and intellectual technologies. Machine technologies include computers, telecommunications and optical systems. Intellectual technologies deal with the way information is organized, manipulated and utilized.[4] A list of the most significant technologies indicates something of the expanding range with which information professionals must cope:

- Mainframe computers and operating systems
- Microcomputer-based information systems
- Image and graphics storage, retrieval and transmission systems
- Telecommunications systems
- Information networks
- Office automation
- Systems analysis and design
- Database design, evaluation and management
- Programming
- Online systems and electronic publishing
- Artificial intelligence
- Decision support systems
- Computer modeling and simulation

Obviously, it would be impossible to master all these technologies. Nevertheless, it is essential that the information professional be adequately familiar and comfortable with them, while at the same time developing a specific expertise in one or more.

Increasingly, information is multidimensional—text, numerics and graphics are being integrated while local and external databases are being merged. The delivery systems by which information providers offer their products are multiplying: first print, then microform and online, now laser disks. The information company must be ever flexible to meet the market needs to tie the content with the appropriate delivery system. The information professional must be flexible and must assist in this process.

Information Policy

I have stated a number of times that information companies are in business to make a profit. However, they are also citizens. As such they must deal with the political, social and legal issues regarding information as a worldwide force.

Some of these issues hit home more directly than others. For example, legislative and case law on intellectual property rights is of direct concern to the information provider. Censorship and privacy are perhaps issues of less immediate concern, but they must be understood. National and international information policy, especially transborder data flow, are also important—although more directly to some companies than to others.

A well-trained information professional must be aware of the impact of information and information technology on society. The information age is more than a cliché. It is a reality.

SUMMARY

The objective of this chapter has been to identify the professional and managerial requirements of the information industry and its expectations concerning the broad-based education of individuals to meet these needs. The curricula proposed encompass four major areas and can be outlined as follows:

    Concepts and Foundations
        Information theory
        Human cognition
        Communication

Business Principles and Practices
   Business ethics
   Economics of information
   Business tools
   Information flows
Information Technologies
   Machine technologies
   Intellectual technologies
Information Policy
   Political aspects
   Legal aspects
   Social aspects

The information industry needs broad-based, well-trained information professionals and managers. Information professionals need the appropriate education to perform in a manner that contributes to the company's growth and advances their own career. For the library/information schools to attract and maintain the patronage of the information industry, they must adapt their curricula to provide the programs that develop individuals with the competence, interest, creativity and enthusiasm to build and sell the information products and services of the future.

This conclusion recognizes that library/information schools have constituencies other than the information industry. However, while the course suggested here tilts rather sharply away from librarianship toward a broader competency, it will also be congenial to the new and emerging careers in information resources management for governments and not-for-profit institutions, as well as the information industry itself.

NOTES

1. J. C. Donohue, "Information Resources Management: Passing Fad or New Paradigm?" *Information Management Review* 1, no. 2 (Fall 1985), p. 68.

2. M. U. Porat and M. R. Rubin, *The Information Economy: Definition Measurement,* 9 vols. (Washington, DC: Government Printing Office, 1977), pp. 22-29.

3. B. M. Compaine, ed., *Understanding New Media: Trends and Issues in Electronic Distribution of Information* (Cambridge, MA: Ballinger Publishing Company, 1984), pp. 20-22, 65.

4. H. R. Brinberg, "The Contribution of Information to Economic Growth and Development," in *Organization and Economics of Information and Documentation,* ed. by Bibeke Amundsen, *Proceedings of the 40th Federation Internationale de Documentation (FID) Congress* Copenhagen, Denmark. 18-21 August 1980, p. 24.

II
Educational Preparation Programs

10

Graduate Education for the Library Profession

Herbert S. White

EVOLUTION OF LIBRARY EDUCATION PROGRAMS

There is neither space nor need for a full account of the history of library education in the United States and Canada. It must suffice to point out that the parallel pattern of development for librarianship in both countries is similar to that for the medical and legal professions. In both these fields aspiring candidates would work as odd-job assistants under senior advisors until they gained competence; the guild system concept of an apprenticeship followed by a period of time as a journeyman before reaching the stage of master was quite similar to what was found in the professions, although the nomenclature differed. As both law and medicine established separate university-based educational programs, followed in both cases by practitioner-dominated postgraduate learning processes for which the library profession has not found an equivalent, so librarianship moved gradually from training programs operated in large public libraries to educational programs located in universities. The change was slow and gradual, however. The programs developed by Melvil Dewey at Columbia University and later at Albany were unabashedly training programs, and the mid-1920s still found a mixture of public library–based and academic institution–based vocational training programs.

Shift Toward Graduate Education

C. C. Wiliamson's landmark report for the Carnegie Corporation in 1923 signaled a dramatic shift. Professional training, Williamson argued, "calls for a broad general education represented at its minimum by a thorough college course of four years plus at least one year of graduate study in a properly organized graduate school."[1] It is interesting to note that despite his breakthrough call for graduate education, Williamson continued to use in both the title and text of his report the word *training*. Confusion about the meanings of these terms persists to this day, and they are often used interchangeably, or run together as if they were one thing called *educationandtraining*. In Europe, the phrase *library education* has still to gain major acceptance, and the units of the International Federation of Library Associations (IFLA) still refer to their missions in this framework of training programs.

Nevertheless, the Williamson report sparked an upsurge in library education at the postbaccalaureate level. Originally offered as second bachelor's degrees, master's degrees began to appear after World War II, when the upsurge in educational opportunities prompted in part by the returning veterans and the GI Bill of Rights caused phenomenal growth and increased vigor and confidence in the higher educational establishment in general and in library education in particular. By the end of the 1940s the second bachelor's degree had virtually disappeared, and library education was generally viewed as a graduate professional experience culminating in the achievement of a master's degree, most commonly the Master of Library Science (MLS).

Role of Undergraduate Programs

This is not to suggest that undergraduate programs for the preparation of librarians disappeared. They did not, and they continue to this day. As Daniel has pointed out, undergraduate programs are even developing at schools that have concentrated up to now on graduate library education.[2] Most of these are housed in Schools and Departments of Education, in which many graduate programs also originated. For the latter, there is a clear pattern that suggests that only as library science programs gained total autonomy were they able to achieve whatever level of identity and prominence they have achieved. This point is noted because graduate programs in library education are once again facing suggestions of merger and incorporation, this time not with departments of education but with the disciplines of communication, computer science and journalism. The risks are probably the same.

There are no really accurate statistics that suggest how many of these undergraduate librarians there are because their degrees are frequently not library but education degrees. Nor do we know where they get jobs. Without doubt a major source of employment is the school system, in which equivalencies for library education through further course work in education are generally accepted and where the requirement is more likely to be certification than the achievement of an educational degree. In addition, small public libraries are often willing to accept undergraduate librarians (or for that matter librarians without any formal education) as a matter of convenience or perceived economic necessity.

This point needs to be stressed because the validity of a master's degree depends entirely on the profession's own willingness to perceive and enforce the need for it. Nonlibrarians faced with the need to staff libraries have not been prepared to accept without question the necessity of graduate educational qualification, and recent efforts by the federal Office of Personnel Management (OPM) to downgrade educational qualifications by a reliance on "competencies" that are nothing more than the memorization of facts and the acquisition of skills through repetition always remind us that we face a potential of returning to pre-Williamson levels. The search for equivalencies in the name of economy or affirmative action to bypass both the time-consuming and expensive graduate degree is for this profession potentially far more dangerous than for others and requires a continuing attitude of vigilance and even belligerence, precisely because what we have is not automatically granted to us.

Despite these concerns and caveats and despite the continuing existence of undergraduate courses and preparation programs, the premise of a graduate degree at the master's level for initial professional work in the library field had received general acceptance by the early 1950s. Through the development of certification criteria, job descriptions in academic and large public libraries, and later increasingly in special libraries and smaller public libraries, called for a graduate degree either as an initial qualification or as a credential to be achieved within a certain period of time.

ACCREDITATION

The process of accreditation, as a balance between educational and practitioner expectation, is also a very common procedure for what are called the terminal master's degree programs. Administered nationally by the Council on Postsecondary Accreditation (COPA), accreditation for the library profession has been assigned to the American Library Association (ALA). ALA first took responsibility for accreditation in 1924 through its Board of Education for Librarianship. In 1956 this was replaced by the Committee on Accreditation (COA), which serves to the present time. *Standards for Accreditation* were initially formulated and approved in 1951, and new standards were instituted in 1972. With only minor modifications, these standards have been in effect since that time. The standards and the accreditation process are designed to safeguard the quality of library education through a process of annual reports and site visits normally at seven-year intervals. The standards are not prescriptive: they are designed to ensure both a minimum consistency in accreditable programs and to ensure that the programs fulfill their own promises and expectations.

Weaknesses of Accredited Programs

The present process of accreditation has been criticized by a number of individuals, including this author.[3,4,5] The bulk of the criticism has asserted that the standards are not demanding enough, and that they set minimums without in any way acknowledging higher-level quality or even excellence. At the present time accreditation is a binary process. Programs are accredited or they are not, and there is no differentiation between acceptable and superior or outstanding programs. Schools that reach for a higher standard do so as internal decisions even in the face of increased cost, and without recognition or even acknowledgment.

A second level of criticism has been leveled by other professional library associations, who resent ALA's unique control over the accreditation process and argue that their own views and needs are not sufficiently represented. A study undertaken by ALA but with the invited participation of many other professional groups is examining the implications of a changed and broadened accreditation process. The potential benefits and risks of change will be examined later in this chapter. For the present, it will suffice to note both that this review is still in an early stage of development with implementation mechanisms only sketchily mentioned, and that the significant costs of participation in the accreditation process, presently borne in full by the American Library Association, may deter other societies from a fuller participation.

It is the argument of many of the critics that COA has not done enough, but it is difficult to substantiate either claims or counterclaims. The number of programs disaccredited or placed on conditional accreditation is small. About 10% of accredited programs have been so severely criticized, and the number of programs closed by the parent institution without COA pressure exceeds those penalized through the accreditation process. However, all schools receive recommendations for improvement from COA, and it can be argued that it is through these recommendations that improvements have been made, or conversely even further declines avoided.

Accreditation is and will probably always be a totally voluntary process. That is, programs of graduate library education are not required to seek accreditation, and some do not. In addition, programs that are denied accreditation or from which accreditation has been removed are not required to close, or even to change. The effectiveness of the accreditation process lies exclusively in its acceptance by the profession as a guide to initial hiring. In that light, it is formidable indeed. Analysis of job advertisements clearly indicates that virtually all academic libraries, most of the larger public libraries, most state and certification agencies, and an increasing number of special libraries make not only the MLS degree but the MLS from an accredited program a primary requirement of initial hiring.

Unaccredited Programs

Whatever the drawbacks and weaknesses of the present accreditation process, it would appear that the absence of any sort of accreditation and control mechanism poses a far bleaker scenario. As noted elsewhere by this writer, library education programs are under severe economic pressure within their own universities, and the application of Gresham's Law of Economics would suggest that library education programs will get smaller and weaker because smaller and weaker programs are also cheaper programs, unless a force such as accreditation is counterposed against such decline.

At the same time, unaccredited graduate-level programs do exist. Virtually all of them are small, and most are housed in institutions without national recognition and distinction. Their enrollments tend to be small, and for most it consists of a mixture of some graduate and a considerably larger number of undergraduate students, who often take the same courses toward one or the other degree. There is nothing in the professional literature to describe these programs. It is known that some aspire to accreditation, although that is a very rocky path. As a later section of this chapter will describe in greater detail, no presently accredited programs are less than 14 years old, and COA has not accredited any new programs in some time. In seeking accreditation, these programs face a formidable chicken-and-egg scenario. They must achieve accreditation in order to attract students, but they must attract students to be allowed by their parent institutions to develop the faculty size and resources to warrant serious consideration for accreditation.

Other programs appear content to continue to offer a mixture of undergraduate and graduate degrees to what is primarily a local constituency. The potential source of undergraduate students has already been mentioned, but graduate degree candidates in unaccredited programs may be seeking to fulfill very narrow and limited career goals, the limitations of which they may not fully understand. They may already be employed in an organization that accepts an unaccredited degree, or they may find that a specific local situation will accept such an educational framework, perhaps because of an unwillingness or perceived inability to compete in salary for graduates of an accredited program. If students consciously make such an educational decision in full understanding of its implications, and if the recruiting program spells out the limitations, that may be rationale enough. However, it frequently happens that relocated librarians with nonaccredited MLS degrees find themselves disqualified from many job opportunities. This would suggest that the significance of accreditation is not fully understood by and explained to students.

The present process of accreditation provides much of whatever quality control we have at present. Little more can be said about unaccredited graduate programs. This writer sees no real place for them and would prefer that they either make the effort to gain the strength to seek accreditation or refrain from offering such degrees entirely. There is little likelihood that any will pay attention to that preference.

GROWTH OF ACCREDITED GRADUATE-LEVEL PROGRAMS

The number of accredited graduate-level library education programs grew rapidly in the 1960s and 1970s, as universities expanded in response to growing enrollments, federal funding initiatives and the perception erroneously and gratuitously promulgated by the U.S. Department of Education that there was a desperate shortage of librarians. It should be noted that only ten years later there were dire predictions of a desperate oversupply in librarians which were just as inaccurate. In 1986 we again hear complaints about shortages, both in general and in very narrow specializations, and it appears that the perception is based on the accumulation of individual reactions from those who are trying to either fill vacancies or find jobs. Unfortunately, university administrators, guidance counselors and students have reacted significantly to both of these erroneous or at least simplistic signals.

It is quite possible, however, that additional graduate library education programs would have been started in U.S. and Canadian universities in the 1960s quite aside from any reality of need, because these were euphoric times in higher education, and virtually every university wanted at least one of everything. Only five of the presently accredited library education programs in the United States were formed before 1900, and it took 30 years to form 13 more. By contrast, 14 programs now accredited by the ALA were started in the 1960s, and four additional ones between 1970 and 1972. The year 1972 is widely recognized as a turning point in higher education, marking the start of the less than generous educational policies in existence now and for the foreseeable future. No presently accredited programs came into being after 1972, but in the twelve years after 1960 one third of the presently accredited U.S. programs had their birth. For Canada the situation is even more dramatic. There are currently seven accredited graduate programs. Of these, two existed before 1930. There was no change for the next 30 years, after which the other five were established.

For reasons already described, these fledgling programs sought accreditation, and accreditation was quickly forthcoming. There is no evidence that this should not have occurred, at least insofar as these institutions might be compared to already accredited programs. There were indeed students in abundance; federal funds for loans and scholarships were plentiful; and there was, in particular, support for minority candidates. By the mid-1970s COA had reached its high-water mark of 69 accredited programs. The term high-water mark can be used with some confidence. In early 1986 that number is 61, and it will probably decline further.

It would serve no particular purpose to discuss specific reasons for the closing of specific programs, except to point out that COA was not instrumental in most of these cases. It is true that there are instances of COA disaccreditation which led to a university decision to close, but there is also an example of a disaccredited program that worked to regain accreditation and succeeded. Accreditation and its loss are, after all, not arcane processes. If a program is denied accreditation it is told quite clearly why this occurred. It need do little more than follow the injunctions and explanations, and that yellow brick road will lead right back to Oz. Of course, implementing those recommendations inevitably requires organizational support from the parent institution, and most directly organizational funds.

DISTRIBUTION OF GRADUATE PROGRAMS

There is no pattern to the existence or absence of library education programs, a point made with considerable vehemence by Eshelman.[6] However, given the fact that the COA does not encourage or start library education programs—it only evaluates them—there is no reason to expect any logical sort of distribution. How many library education programs at the graduate level there should be has been a matter of continuing controversy. On the one hand, there is compelling evidence that there are already far too many, given the number of students, the size of faculties, continuing decreasing trends in both categories and the fact that library education programs are almost inevitably the smallest such programs, at least in major universities. At the same time, there is the possibility that much library school attendance is based on local availability and convenience, and there are no significant migration patterns that track students from areas no longer served by a library education program to other schools hundreds or thousands of miles away.

While we want good programs and perhaps larger programs, we also want nearby programs, within commuting distance or convenient for evening attendance after a day on the job. This push for fragmentation is much of the argument in the plea for survival of admittedly weak graduate programs. They argue that they serve only a local constituency, and therefore "they do no harm." The conflict between the desires for quality and critical mass on the one hand, and for local convenience on the other, is a serious one which this profession has not even begun to address. What happens to potential students for whom there no longer is a convenient library education program? Do they attend other schools? Do they choose other professions? Do they elect nonaccredited or undergraduate degrees, or find library work without any degree? There are probably at least some examples of every one of these situations. What complicates the problem further is the fact that in the United States higher education is not a federal, but a state or local initiative. Private universities have no geographic constraints but generally charge high tuition. In public universities, for which the tuition is far lower, that benefit is restricted to citizens of the taxing unit, except for a few exchange relationships.

What happens to prospective librarians when there is no library education program in the state, or when the state is large and the nearest program is 400 miles away? There are no clear answers, but some of the proposed solutions border on the ridiculous. It was at one time seriously suggested that the state of Indiana, in which no locality is more than 200 miles from Indianapolis, required four or five library education programs. That, of course, is the ultimate in prioritizing convenience. There is some middle ground, and library school programs that are both entrepreneurial and service oriented have looked at extension courses and the use of television. Quite properly, COA is concerned about the implications of such changes on the quality of the educational program being provided.

To repeat, there is no geographic pattern to the establishment of library education programs, and the recent closings of programs at Minnesota and Denver have left even larger holes. Unlike many other educational disciplines, library educational elitism is not centered in the Ivy League, or even necessarily on the East Coast. Only one Ivy League institution, Columbia University, has a graduate program in library education. At the same time, another major private university, the University of Chicago, has had a prominent role in library education for many years. There simply are no clearly discernible patterns. Some library education programs are located in major state universities (North Carolina, Rutgers, Texas, Maryland, Michigan, Illinois, Indiana, Wisconsin, UCLA and Berkeley, among others). Some are located in state institutions that originated with a much narrower mission (Clarion, San Jose, Emporia). Still others are in more specialized and smaller private universities for which the library education program, despite its small size, may be a highly visible and major educational program (Simmons, Pratt, Drexel). Two of the programs are located in historically black institutions, and their student bodies and faculties still reflect that orientation. About half of what is an unfortunately very small number of black faculty members at accredited programs teach at Atlanta and North Carolina Central.

There are eight accredited library programs in the state of New York, five in the New York City area, with an additional two within an hour's drive. By contrast, there are only three for the entire state of California, considerably larger in both size and population, and none in the neighboring states of Nevada and Oregon. The closing of library education programs at Minnesota and Denver has left a 1500-mile stretch from Kansas to California with only one small library school in between and with nothing in the northern tier of states between Madison, Wisconsin, and Seattle, Washington. There are three library education programs in North Carolina but none in Virginia, only one each in the heavily populated states of Ohio and Michigan, but two in the city of Denton, Texas. There is no pattern to this geographic distribution, and as further schools may close the situation may become worse. Each university makes its own decisions based on its own perceived priorities, and there is little likelihood of new accreditable programs. It hasn't happened in fifteen years, and conditions have not become more favorable.

SCHOOL CLOSINGS

Why do some library schools close, and why do others survive and even grow? It is an important question, because growing attention to these campus-wide political concerns by library educators may well contradict some of the expectations and hopes of library practitioners.

Library education programs close for reasons that are both apparent and complex. The obvious reasons are those shared with the larger university system. Universities suffer from a decline in students brought about largely by declining pools of college-age students; they suffer from the reduction and potential elimination of federal support funds for research and higher education, from economic malaise that affects the support of colleges and universities in some states and localities, and to some extent from the disenchantment with higher education as the solution proposed in the 1960s for all of society's troubles.

Other issues are more complex and more unique. For example, library schools in major multiversities must compete for recognition and attention, but they can find ample opportunities for cooperative and dual degree programs. Library schools in smaller institutions may be more appreciated and more noticed, but the university may lack overall resources or even interest in supporting research priorities or major equipment purchases. None of these reasons fully explains why some mediocre and even poor library education programs survive without difficulty, and why some nationally recognized programs, such as the one at Case Western Reserve (established in 1904, with a distinguished cadre of alumni and boasting the famed Jesse Shera) are closed. Political awareness and sensitivity are being recognized as important attributes for academic administrators, as they begin to be seen as crucial for successful librarians.

Risks and Dangers for Graduate Educational Programs

What are the risks for graduate library education programs? Fundamentally, they can be categorized into four groups, and failure in any one of the four can kill a program. The four groups are discussed below.

Low or Declining Enrollment

Financial constraints are usually cited as the reason for closing library schools because it is the easiest answer to understand and accept. It is far from the only reason. Nevertheless, it is important, and particularly important in certain institutions. It is crucial in those universities for which student enrollment plays a large role in the university budget. This applies in particular to private universities and especially to those with smaller endowments. When student fees fund the university, enrollment becomes crucial. In universities in which the student contribution to the overall budget is small, enrollment becomes less significant, and the university may even urge or require the school to limit its acceptance of new students on the premise that more students cost more money. This is true for some U.S. state universities such as those in California, and for Canadian library schools. The willingness of such schools to lengthen their programs to two years will draw further comment later. It will suffice at this point to note that the "risk " of losing students as a result does not bother them. It may even be considered an advantage.

High Cost of Operation

Graduate education programs are expensive. In most academic disciplines the high cost of graduate education is balanced against the lower cost of large freshman seminar courses, particularly when these are taught by graduate students. For departments of English and economics that balance works quite nicely. Undergraduate students support graduate education, and graduate students are low-paid teachers for the undergraduates. Library education, without an undergraduate base, looks expensive and is expensive on a dollars-per-credit-hour basis, and it shares that distinction with only a few academic programs, such as law.

A Lack of Professional Distinction

Library education programs are sparse in the kind of major research and publication that characterizes other disciplines, and library faculty members are not as likely to bring in major grant support, because no federal agency supports basic, let alone applied, library research. This concern becomes particularly significant in major universities with "star" faculties, in which competition for funds can be brutal. This concern for greater academic distinction underlies the suggestion by Rayward that perhaps library educators are already too responsive to practitioner training preferences for their own good in the academic institution.[7] We must add to that the fact that faculty in other disciplines have never understood what academic rigor exists in our profession. As this author has noted elsewhere, there is nothing in their experience with academic libraries that suggests that librarians do more than acquire lots of materials.

A Lack of Political Clout

When university presidents begin to suspect that their law

schools are losing quality or that enrollment is declining, they usually look for a new dean. They do not close the school, in part because they perceive the law school as a part of the university's mission and long-term goals and in greater part because the school's powerful alumni wouldn't allow it to be closed. Library schools do not have powerful alumni, and they share that distinction with programs in nursing and home economics—all, incidentally, perceived as "women's professions." To some besieged university administrators, closing an academic program becomes a symbolic gesture. When it comes to closing library education programs it can be little more than that, because the process does not save enough money to make a difference.

In summary, then, graduate library education programs are in a continuing state of danger, a danger they share in part with their academic colleagues in other disciplines, but one that is in part uniquely their own. Given the foreseeable prospects for higher education, it takes no crystal ball to predict that more library education programs will close. Although there are those who would argue that this might be just as well because there are still too many library schools, this process of random closing follows no pattern and does not necessarily select either overpopulated areas or weak schools. It certainly has not in the past. Nor is it at all certain that, if the COA applied more stringent standards and as a result other programs became disaccredited and perhaps closed, remaining schools would be strengthened and would benefit. For a variety of reasons including tuition cost, part-time attendance, and hiring patterns, participation in library education remains largely a local or regional process. This is not likely to change until public and special as well as academic libraries expand their recruitment activities nationally. This would entail reimbursement of interview expenses for losing as well as successful candidates and of moving expenses for those selected. Library school deans do not see such a pattern developing. At Indiana University we are probably more of a nationally or internationally involved library school than most state institutions, but even here we recognize that the majority of our students will come from our state and that except for academic librarians, most will find jobs within a 500-mile radius of their homes or of the campus.

Diverse and Contradictory Pressures

Graduate library education programs therefore must respond to a long list of pressures and concerns, and they must try to keep in balance at all times. Overreaction to any one could be fatal.

Pressures from within the University

As already mentioned, in some settings this provides overwhelming pressure to achieve credit hours. Library school reaction to these concerns can include a number of strategies, including undergraduate courses, special degrees and seminars, and dual degree programs. Where the strategy becomes a relaxation of admissions standards, the results are obviously not positive for the profession. Additional pressures come in the need to produce research, to achieve academic credentials, and to lend a research orientation to graduate course content. To the extent to which employers prefer the teaching of "more practical" material, there is an inherent conflict. That conflict is at least as old as 1936, when Robert Maynard Hutchins railed against what he perceived to be the trend toward vocationalism in higher education. It is as recent as 1985, when the Committee on Institutional Cooperation, the group of universities comprising the Big Ten plus the University of Chicago, issued a publication to all accreditation teams reminding them that while comments and suggestions were welcome, prescriptiveness was not and reaffirming that it was universities and not professional associations that made curricular decisions. A library education program that ignores that value system within its own institution does so at grave peril to its health and survival.

Pressures from the Practitioner Community

Rarely a month goes by without an article, editorial, letter or conference program that addresses the question, "What is wrong with library education?" Some of these comments are kinder than others, but all of them approach the problem in far too prescriptive a manner and with conclusions already reached. This is not to suggest that there aren't indeed problems with library education, as there are with public, academic and special library administration. However, educational concerns can't be fixed from the outside; they can be addressed in low-keyed and open discussion. There is little that practitioners can really do about library education programs except to refuse to hire their graduates, and that can work only as an individual action aimed at specific schools and not at entire programs.

Some of the concerns, as already noted, are contradictory. Practitioners want fewer programs or at least better and larger programs, but they also want more geographically convenient programs. Surveys have produced long lists of courses and competencies to be included, but these are sometimes contradictory and make no attempt to fit within a one-year curriculum.[8,9] There is a cry for better students, but the claim that current students are inferior has no substantiation. In addition, it must be clear that library schools have very limited opportunities for recruitment. It is far more likely that they will reject or accept from a pool of candidates, and as already noted, pressures for acceptance are substantial. That pool in turn is self-selected: it consists primarily of individuals who want to follow in the footsteps of the librarians they already know and for whom they already work. The quality of the applicant pool is ultimately the responsibility of the role models.

Problems in Recognition for Higher Quality

In library education, as in other fields, higher quality usually carries a higher price tag. Smaller classes, better equipment, more and highly experienced faculty all have a cost. Where is the return on that investment? As already noted, accreditation has no qualitative levels: it is a binary process. Except for academic libraries, many searches are conducted on the basis of local economy and convenience, and individuals without specific competencies are frequently hired even though more qualified individuals might be available, albeit at a greater distance and at a greater hiring and relocation cost. Graduates of prestigious law, engineering and business schools are heirs to an instant value system that also conveys higher salaries. There is a strange egalitarian reluctance in our profession to attempt to identify quality, let alone reward it. Perhaps that reluctance should not seem strange. The only value systems we do employ, those for academic and public libraries, measure size of collection and circulation statistics. They measure things, not the accomplishments of individuals. What then is the incentive for building a better library education program? At present it must be self-gratification, because that is all there is.

Problems in the Kinds of Students We Attract

Lest earlier paragraphs give the impression that there is no problem with the student population, there most assuredly is. The problem is not so much one of inadequate academic preparation. Many library school students do very well in their classroom work. The problem is rather that the students we attract are not the kinds of people many employers now say they would like to hire. Much of the recent emphasis has been on interpersonal communication skills, on management aptitudes and on entrepreneurial risk taking. Many guidance counselors and prospective students still perceive librarianship as a haven for individuals who have an interest in ideas and some aversion to people, who "like to read" and who are introverted and passive.

Why do these perceptions persist, except as confirmed through observation? Are we really one profession trying, through the backdoor of the educational process, to become another? The shortages in certain backgrounds and aptitudes continue. These include the physical and hard social sciences, computer science and an aptitude for management, which includes a willingness to make decisions and take risks. To these shortages we are in the process of adding yet another, unlikely as this one seems. There is an incipient shortage of students who want to work as children's librarians, and that shortage can only be traced to the years in which we moaned that it was an overcrowded field with no available jobs—untrue as that statement was even then. Some library school students are magnificent raw material for the profession, and most teachers can recognize them at once. Others require a great deal of reorientation of value systems, and for this we have only a year.

LIBRARY SCHOOL STRATEGIES

To respond to this formidable array of concerns, graduate library education programs have developed a diverse set of strategies. Obviously, no school has done all of these things, but most schools have tried more than one. None of these approaches has been instantly and obviously successful. All have drawbacks.

Enlarging the Master's Program

Calling the present program a one-year program is really mislabeling it. The classic MLS program consists most frequently of 36 credit hours divided into 12 courses, sometimes as few as 10, sometimes as many as 15. However, 12 is clearly the norm, as demonstrated by statistics furnished by the Association of Library and Information Science Education (ALISE). That can be completed in one year but is not likely to be. The so-called two-year programs are more likely to be 54 or 60 credit hours. Much publicity was given to the decision by Canadian library schools to move to this so-called two-year program and by the action of a few United States programs in following. That trend, if there was a trend, has now stopped. The enlarged program appealed primarily to those universities for which, because of low tuition, enrollment declines are not a problem. For many of the schools the enlargement of the program involved nothing more than the opportunity to enroll in more elective courses. Although this is not bad, it does not really constitute a philosophical program change.

Library schools are not really free to tamper with their degree requirements if they are concerned about enrollment. As long as other programs are prepared to confer an accredited degree for a smaller number of credit hours, and as long as the profession shows no indication of either preferring or paying higher salaries to graduates of longer MLS programs, little change is likely.[10] Some tinkering that changes the substance while maintaining the appearance is of course possible, and this would include the establishment of prerequisite undergraduate courses, to be completed either prior to or immediately after enrollment. For students who have not recently completed an undergraduate degree in the same institution, that change becomes a de facto increase in course requirements.

Changing the Package

Inhibited as they are from altering the purchase price, schools have looked at making the package more attractive. Strategies have included offering an open-ended market-oriented curriculum, in which desired courses are developed in response to user demand and frequently delivered in off-campus locations. Finding new enrollees is obviously important, because if a new course is offered to the same MLS students within the same degree requirements, that extra cost will gain the school no additional revenues in return. The resemblance between these issues and the marketing concerns of major corporations is not accidental. Adding courses to be taught by the same small faculty at off-campus locations perhaps lacking in resources obviously and quite rightly concerns the Committee on Accreditation.

Another approach, in quite the opposite direction, has involved dropping specialization tracks within the MLS degree. Most commonly these have been those concerned with public librarianship, service to children and the preparation of school librarians. There are two reasons for this action. One is that these disciplines are not perceived as earning a great deal of recognition and credit for the school within its parent institution. The second is the observation that these courses have had declining enrollments, and no longer pay their way. In one sense, the actions are understandable. The fields mentioned are precisely those in which graduates of unaccredited programs and those with library bachelor's degrees have made their greatest inroads. This supports the suggestion that unless controls are established, undergraduate and unaccredited programs can drive out accredited graduate efforts because quality is expensive. Private institutions, particularly those located in close proximity to public institutions offering accredited library programs, can perhaps defend such a decision. It is far more difficult for a state university, particularly when that school is the only one offering an accredited degree to its citizens. Furthermore, and as COA has noted, librarians tend to prepare more for a career than for a specific job; at least the mobility from one kind of library to another is considerable. The elimination of certain disciplines from library education programs would be a serious cause for concern if the practice were to spread. At the same time, the reversal of the trend is squarely in the hands of practitioners. It requires only that they insist on hiring graduates of accredited programs and paying competitive salaries.

Other Marketing Approaches

Other techniques come under the heading of product diversification, and all carry both benefits and risks to the offering institution.

Undergraduate Degree Programs

It has already been noted that these programs continue to exist, particularly as parts of schools of education and in preparation for work in school and small public libraries. In particular in such settings undergraduate programs are considerably cheaper for the university than graduate programs. A more surprising recent development has been the implementation of undergraduate degree programs in library schools that also continue to offer the accredited master's degree. An economic justification for such an action has already been mentioned. The mixture of undergraduate and graduate courses allows for some benefits in the use of graduate students as instructors. In some institutions such undergraduate degree programs in information rather than library science have gained instant popularity, and it is reported that their graduates are very successful in finding jobs. It is less obvious, however, what market these students are being prepared to fill. It is clear that these undergraduate degrees are not intended to be feed-in programs toward graduate education in library science. Such an approach would of course be possible and has even been suggested, but it would deprive us of undergraduate preparation in liberal arts, which employers seem to find at least as attractive. In any case, these undergraduate students prepared in this new environment are not looking for graduate library degrees. They see the bachelor's degree as a terminal job qualification. Are these positions in the "new" information society inappropriate for graduate librarians and do they therefore strengthen response in an area we are not prepared to enter, or are these individuals simply cheaper alternatives for positions that would be more appropriately filled by the graduates of our library education programs? We have no answer to this question, but that does not seem to deter innovators from starting such programs.

Dual Master's Degree Programs

The option of enrolling a student simultaneously in two graduate degree programs is realistically limited to major universities, and such packages can include partners that range from history to music to journalism to public administration to chemistry. The advantage to the library school lies less in securing additional enrollment (because these programs have few students) than in the gaining of interdisciplinary prestige and visibility on the campus. The advantage to the student is economic, since free electives can usually be cross-claimed and the two degrees can be obtained more cheaply. The advantage to employers is particularly great when they seek subject as well as library expertise at the graduate level. There is one final possible advantage. The use of expertise in neighboring disciplines through dual master's programs relieves some of the pressure for teaching library school courses in management, computer science or specific subject bibliography, without the loss of credit hours. At the same time dual master's programs are not likely to gain in major popularity until their value is reflected in starting salaries.

Post-Master's Degree Programs

These degrees, which fall somewhere between the MLS and the Ph.D., are really attempts at continuing education in a more formal setting. They usually provide a great deal of individual latitude in program planning and allow the student the credit that another diploma or certificate brings. The idea has merit in principle, but the economic underpinnings are lacking and will continue to be until receipt of such a post-master's degree is worth something in terms of salary increase or promotion. At present, employers have no formal educational expectations for their professional subordinates beyond the accredited MLS, and some of course don't even require that.

Continuing Education

The significant role of graduate library education programs as providers of continuing education in a whole variety of both informal and formal mechanisms is obvious and is addressed in greater detail by other authors of this book. Despite their small faculties, library schools are anxious to participate in this process, and many have fairly significant programs of annual seminars and workshops. Others have little if anything. The issue is really addressed at two levels. Faculty members, in fulfilling their own service responsibilities for promotion and tenure, do much of the teaching of continuing education courses even when these are offered outside the university. The library school, for its part, must generally develop a program of cost recovery for whatever it proposes to offer. It is not likely that these efforts will expand until and unless a funding mechanism is developed. Funding can come from a government agency, from a library or from the individual students, and the reasons these mechanisms don't work very well at present were explored by this author in a lengthier article.[11] It is not realistic to expect that the financial support will be contributed by the library school or its parent university.

Doctoral Programs

Library school Ph.D. programs were developed parallel to the rapid growth of master's programs, in response to a perceived need and to a massive infusion of federal support funds under President

Johnson's "Great Society" programs. More than twenty doctoral programs in accredited library schools now exist, although some of these produce fewer than one graduate per year. The difficulty is not that these newly minted Ph.D. graduates cannot get jobs. In general they can, primarily as library school teachers, but also as academic library administrators. The difficulty is in the fact that doctoral students in general don't contribute tuition, they require financial support. Doctoral programs can be a financial drain on what are already small schools.

At the same time, library school administrators recognize quite correctly the importance of doctoral programs to the perceived quality of their master's programs and to prestige within their institutions. High-quality faculty members are drawn into research institutions in which their own interests can find better expression, and it is no coincidence that all of the highly rated library master's programs in a whole range of perception studies are in institutions that also offer the doctorate. There are too many library Ph.D. programs for the number of students that enroll in them, and competition for high-quality students is both expensive and unhealthy. At the same time, it must be clear to the reader by this time that the academic model is not one that always operates rationally.

SUMMARY

There are major concerns facing graduate library education programs, and solutions can be implemented only through cooperation and understanding among the constituencies involved. Library educators are not in the same universe or part of the same value system as library practitioners, even though virtually all educators have at one time been practitioners (and sometimes very distinguished practitioners), and although both groups interact in professional societies, in which educators often play a very active and visible role.

Graduate Library Programs Are Overextended

As already noted, library education programs are small, with small student enrollments and small faculty size. According to statistics provided in annual reports of ALISE, the average faculty size has declined steadily over the last several years and has now dropped below 10. Schools with faculties of 14 or 15 are now considered large, absurd as such a term might seem in comparison to the number of instructors of freshman English classes. Some faculties are as small as eight, seven or even six. And yet, the survey cited earlier uncovered an array of 83 courses taught in at least a considerable number of graduate library education programs.[12] While some schools have a formal core and others do not, there appears to be some instinctive sense of what such a core contains. Generally, it includes a course in basic reference, one in collection development, one in cataloging, one in management and one in information science.

It is these last two that pose some difficulty. Should we teach management conceptually, dealing with the development of theory on the assumption that practitioners must have some basic understanding of why people behave as they do? Should we teach skills, such as budgeting and proposal writing? Should we deal exclusively or primarily with problem solving through case studies, recognizing that students bring very little perspective to these exercises? Inevitably, we are drawn to the conclusion that while some management preparation can be undertaken during the degree program, much or most of it should be a part of continuing education.

In attempting to teach an introduction to information science, we run into a different problem. Our students include those who have a genuine fear of and aversion to computers (as some students also feel toward management), while other students have been programming their own personal computers for years. Finding a common denominator is not easy, and perhaps here is the most appropriate use of undergraduate prerequisites.

It is the elective courses, however, that cause the most difficulty. Hardly a week goes by in the life of a dean or director without a letter from some division or round table within the American Library Association or some specialized association, demanding to know what courses we are offering to expose our students to such diverse areas as research libraries, community college libraries (both as distinguished from a more generic course in academic libraries), serials management, an advanced course in government publications, service to minority groups, service to the handicapped and advanced training in subject disciplines. The list is endless, as specialists seek other specialists. Library schools attempt to respond to these demands to a far greater extent than they are realistically able, because their orientation is to a market as defined by employers, and by prospective students who are increasingly aware of what employers look for in résumés. All of this creates a gigantic shell game of shuffling courses to meet a real or perceived demand, all of which takes place within the already defined enclosure of a twelve-course degree program. Without doubt the greatest pressure has been on the addition of computer courses within the library school curriculum, and courses dealing with online searching or microcomputers may not be required but they might as well be, because students feel the need to take them to complete their résumés. This is not necessarily bad, except that it also removes these students from other courses which might be just as important, if not as currently trendy.

The great need is for discussions between educators and practitioners of what can and should be accomplished within a twelve-course one-year program, what can be taught on the job, what can be left to assured continuing education (assuming that we can assure it) and what is presumably unnecessary. All of this will have to happen within a curriculum that can include specializations but must also retain, as COA has wisely insisted, a common core. Observation tells us that students prepared as academic librarians, for example, feel no hesitation about taking jobs as special or public librarians if the opportunity presents itself.

There Is No Emphasis on or Reward for Quality

As noted earlier in this chapter, the pursuit of quality is expensive. At present accreditation differentiates only between accredited and unaccredited programs and makes no other distinctions. Some employers, as noted from survey data, will happily accept all the qualifications they can get but are not willing to pay more for them. Other employers look at salary targets as the primary criterion and will ultimately take what they can get at the offered wage. In what is rapidly again becoming a market of candidate shortage, qualitative distinctions become meaningless. A way must be found to recognize and reward quality beyond the minimum—through the accreditation process or through the employment process, but probably through both.

There Needs to Be a Clearer Understanding of Credentialing

This chapter does not suggest that there is no room for librarians with undergraduate library degrees or for librarians whose graduate degrees are from unaccredited programs. It does argue that there must be a clear understanding of what difference the various levels of education make in terms of job qualification. The accredited MLS is only as good as our own professional acceptance of and insistence on it, and for that matter that is also true of any other kinds of degrees. The recent Merwine case* has exposed a remarkable unwillingness on the part of the American Library Association to protect its own accredited degrees, and the shock waves throughout the profession from that realization may have awakened us to the seeds of self-destruction in our own processes. However, corporate personnel departments and small public library boards still waffle on their insistence on stated requirements when that insistence costs money or leaves positions unfilled. The laudable attempt to provide greater opportunities for minority candidates has concentrated on the much easier and cheaper approach of promoting such individuals directly rather than providing them with the scholarship assistance necessary to obtain the appropriate education.

There are of course equivalencies for the MLS, but those equivalencies are difficult to master on a job, if the knowledge level expected concentrates on issues rather than on specific skills. Skills to perform a specific job can usually be learned on the job, but knowledge acquisition tends to be thwarted by such an isolated and narrow focus. Knowledge can presumably be acquired

---

* In this case an applicant who did not possess a library degree argued that her exclusion from a post that specified applicants holding an accredited degree constituted sex discrimination. Although the jury found for the plaintiff, that finding was overturned by the judge.

through independent study in preparation for an appearance before a peer review board. That process of credentialing still exists in some other disciplines, but it now follows and does not replace what has become an absolute requirement for formal education. Ultimately, we will probably decide that this is the only practical approach in librarianship as well, if we have the self-confidence and self-regard to make it stick.

NOTES

1. Charles C. Williamson, *Training for Library Service: A Report Prepared for the Carnegie Corporation of New York* (New York and Boston: D. B. Updike, 1923), p. 136.
2. Evelyn H. Daniel, "Accreditation," *Library Journal* (April 1, 1985): 49-53.
3. William R. Eshelman, "The Erosion of Library Education," *Library Journal* 108 (July 1983): 1309-1312.
4. W. Boyd Rayward, "Conflict, Interdependence, Mediocrity, Librarians and Library Educators," *Library Journal* 108 (July 1983): 1313-1317.
5. Herbert S. White, "Critical Mass for Library Education," *American Libraries* 10 (Sept. 1979): 468-470, 479-481.
6. Eshelman, p. 1311.
7. Rayward, pp. 1313-1317.
8. Maurice P. Marchant and Nathan M. Smith, "The Research Library Director's View of Library Education," *College and Research Libraries* 43 (Nov. 1982): 437-444.
9. Michael E. Koenig, "Education for Special Librarianship," *Special Libraries* 74 (April 1983): 182-196.
10. Herbert S. White and Marion Paris, "Employer Preferences and the Library Education Curriculum," *Library Quarterly* 55 (Jan. 1985): 1-33.
11. Herbert S. White, "Continuing Education: Myth and Reality," *Indiana Libraries* 4 (1984): 138-145
12. Koenig, pp. 182-196.

11

The Role of the Undergraduate Library Education Program

Ronald Bryson

The rationale for the establishment of the now-traditional standard of the MLS degree as the most appropriate credential for entry into the library field is straightforward and logical. The attainment of a solid base of knowledge, represented by the bachelor's degree in a subject area, followed by the MLS degree, which provides the philosophy, theory, principles and skills of professional librarianship, is a worthy ideal.

There are, however, certain reality factors which have a great impact upon the actual staffing patterns of libraries, three of which seem to be significant: (1) the stage of development of the library; (2) the level of support for library services from the parent institution; and (3) the division of labor, or the staffing structure, within the library.

The social realities of librarianship require that we look carefully at these three factors as important considerations in library staffing because they are also of significance to library education.

STAGES OF LIBRARY DEVELOPMENT

Each stage of library development makes its own demands in terms of the degree of emphasis to be placed upon the traditional library functions, and upon the combination of traditional and evolving roles of librarians.

The Mature Library

A mature library organization can be described as one in which the services provided have established a standard which is accepted and relied upon by the clientele; which exhibits a well-developed bureaucratic structure; which has a well-differentiated staffing structure; which makes use of advanced technology; and which operates in an atmosphere of stability.

The administration of a parent organization (community, school, college, business, etc.) which supports a mature library will probably be at the mature stage of its own development, and will have come to expect a high level of service and the expenses that go along with it. While using good judgment in adjusting to economic and other conditions of the day, such a parent organization will continue to support the ongoing library operation because the library has become a necessity.

Our ideal of the MLS degree as the most appropriate entry-level requirement for librarianship most closely matches reality within the framework of the mature library. The level of support and the development of the bureaucratic structure is such that job specialization is required, is planned for and can be afforded. This is the situation for which the MLS was designed. Due to the fact that the staffing structure is so highly differentiated in the mature library, the bachelor's degree in library science is also useful when it has included a strong second major in a subject or applied area which is related to the library's needs.

Early Development Stage

In the early development stage, the emphasis is on collecting in one place the materials already on hand, securing a suitable facility and organizing the materials for use. This is a sequence of events time honored in librarianship. As Roy Stokes has written "Technical processes—cataloging and classification in particular—have long been considered basic arts in librarianship. . . . This was natural enough in the light of the stage of development of many libraries at the time."[1]

The fact is that organizations today are still starting new

libraries, and many are revitalizing them. Perhaps some organizations will always be occupied in doing so. As this happens, the need for emphasizing the technical aspects will continue.

The use of new technologies will alter our procedures, however, and will allow us to accomplish the updating or the starting of libraries more easily, with less expense and within a shorter period of time.

In this stage of development there is usually a minimum amount of funding available, and often the initial caretaker of a newly forming library is a secretary or clerk who has no library background, but who is nevertheless given the responsibility for the library operation. There are, even today, many libraries in this country which are operating with staff which has little or no training in library science. The extent to which this practice prevails in rural public libraries is described by Vavrek:

> A national survey supported by the H.W. Wilson Foundation indicated that, on an average, 0.9 MLS trained librarians are available in public libraries within populations of 25,000 or fewer people. For populations of 2500 or fewer, the average is 0.2 MLS librarians per library. . . . Volunteers . . . make up 26% and 37% respectively . . . in the two populations. In Pennsylvania . . . volunteers . . . make up 82% of their workers.[2]

For libraries in the early development stage service is usually limited to circulation and location of materials. Reference assistance builds as the staff learns what is in the collection, and as patrons ask for such help, which they may tend not to do, since they will see how busy the staff is. The orientation of the staff is to the internal affairs of the library. Importance is placed upon the tasks and processes required to collect, house and catalog the materials, and to the building of files required to locate, retrieve and circulate them. Since during this stage, the organization and preparation of materials for circulation is still a high priority, the basic Dewey core will suffice, and the more general education the cataloger has, the better. An MLS is not likely to be employed, and in fact, is not really needed in most of these situations. To hire a person with a bachelor's degree would be an achievement in many cases.

The Growth Stage

In the growth stage the services of the library are in great demand and the library secures its place within the organizational or community structure. It is a time in which increased levels of income and necessity lead to the development of new ideas and a review of all aspects of the library operation. Emphasis is placed upon the upgrading of staff, collections, technology and services. The pace of activity increases, the organization loosens up, spirits rise, and events, things and people hum within.

During this stage there is a need for new approaches in all aspects of operation, such as more specific analysis of information needs, the design of more specific services, and the design and implementation of new systems and procedures which use new technologies to deliver the services.

There may also be a need for more subject specialization by library staff members. The best source of this is the hiring of staff with the MLS degree, which increased funds now make feasible. In small libraries, which were started by persons holding bachelor's degrees or even less formal education, the competition of newcomers with higher degrees should produce the motivation for a return to school for the next level of education and training. However, the staff member with a bachelor's degree still has a role to play, even if the motivation to continue formal education does not develop. As these changes occur, the staffing structure begins to require differentiation, and specialization will set in.

The Stage of Decline

When the parent organization fails to prosper and goes into a decline, so does the library which it supports. This may be due to external circumstances which overtake the parent organization so that it can no longer sustain its former position in its field, or it may be due to mistaken judgments or loss of leadership within the organization. In any case, the library will experience all of the negative results that accompany such events. Budgets will be cut, as will hours, areas of service, and orders for materials and subscriptions. In short, any measures that might help to ensure survival of the *entire* organization will be taken.

The toll on the individual is high; the library staff loses its vitality, the pace slows and spirits drop. Competitors who offer the same or similar services draw away members of the clientele. Reorganizations are begun as vain attempts to spark new growth and vitality.

If periods of decline are extended over a long time, some degree of retrenchment can be expected. This could mean the downgrading of positions or outright cuts in staff positions. The goal becomes one of maintaining the status quo while searching for ways to strengthen the library's position until more favorable conditions prevail.

The Stage of Revitalization

If the library has not gone into a permanent decline, a period of revitalization may take place.

Revitalization is based upon new ideas, knowledge of the means of implementing them, and their successful presentation to the leadership of the parent organization. A period of renewed interest in the library will begin as the need for library services is recognized, or as the seriousness of the degree of the library's decline is acknowledged. Development of an earnest and enthusiastic effort to remedy the decline will take shape. Often this occurs when new leadership, espousing new ideas and supporting new technologies, comes into the organization.

Libraries undergoing a second growth spurt, or revitalization, require an active mix of people and backgrounds, and a mix of degree combinations. These all help to generate the ideas and stimulation that combine to create new programs of service.

ACCEPTABLE DEGREE LEVELS

One of the most significant areas of support from the parent organization lies in the established and accepted degree structure within that organization. This will have an effect on the level of hiring of the library staff, and will affect the rank and influence of the library director.

In a complex, mature industrial organization that hires PhD's in research and development, DBAs (Doctor of Business Administration) as specialists in various areas of business, and MBAs in all levels of management, there will usually be no problem in hiring at the MLS level or higher, depending on the level within the organization at which the library is to operate.

In an organization that does not already employ a range of graduate level individuals, the MLS can be seen as an unrealistic standard, and may even be felt as threatening.

Attempts made in the past few years at the federal level to downgrade librarians' positions may stem from a combination of these factors. Librarians have been placed at the lowest salary level of all professions included in the federal hiring structure.[3]

In the academic world, the higher degrees such as the Specialist or PhD are accepted and often expected for positions of leadership or specialization in universities and some colleges. The MLS is the accepted hiring level for the majority of the library professional staff members.

The public schools prefer the range of bachelor's and master's degrees for teachers, principals and other building-level employees, and the certificates earned often require additional credits which do not show up as degrees. An individual who earns the EdS is viewed as a potential administrative candidate if he or she expresses the desire to become involved at that level. Usually, the EdD or PhD is held by top administrators or staff specialists. Because of this pattern, the public schools have retained the bachelor's degree as the first level of professional status for school media librarians, not in opposition to the MLS degree, but in adherence to an established pattern of degree relationships.

MODELS OF LIBRARIANSHIP

A Functional Model of Librarianship

When dealing with library staffing, we think of roles and functions. Each staff member has a role to play and a function to perform, and the role is based on the function. In a great many cases, the same individual plays several roles and serves several, or all, of the library functions.

Roles are dynamic, and provide for the flow of information as people communicate with one another. Functions are relatively static, and provide the framework of purpose within which the roles operate; they give meaning to the roles. Through our roles, we not only fulfill our funcitons, we transfer our thoughts, feelings and energy, thus creating action in ourselves and in others.

During the years of 1967 through 1971 at the Raymond Walters College, University of Cincinnati, my staff and I developed a comprehensive library program, built on the concept of the "active" librarian as suggested by Dupuy.[4] At the same time, I developed my dissertation, "A Theory of Librarianship," one part of which was a conceptual model of the field.[5] The functions identified below derive from that conceptual model.

The Librarian's Functions

The basic process to be carried out in any library is that of dealing with the *primary information* involved; that is, the subject content that has been requested or that the librarian has determined is needed. This process begins with the librarian doing an analysis of the specific individual or group's activities which involve the use of information—the *analysis of information needs*. This information is then fed into

- an *analysis of the media* on the market
- the process of *design and production* of media in-house
- the *analysis of the subject content* for cataloging and classification purposes

Information services are then tailored to meet the needs as specifically as possible. The librarian will *design the systems and procedures* which make all of this operational, and in the role of subject, reference or information specialist, will also *deliver the service*.

Technical and Clerical Functions

To support the librarian, staff members carry out the technical functions which aid in the processing of the primary information. Tasks include file and record maintenance, operation of equipment, manual processing and production of media, searching for and recording of data, and the usual secretarial and clerical tasks.

Administrative Functions

At this level, the *policy-making, organizing, staffing, planning, controlling, communicating and coordinating* activities are carried out with respect to each specific organizational function.

Professional Activities

There are also professional activities that are not part of any specific library service function, but which support the library staff members in their functions. These include library associations and library education.

A Role Model of Librarianship

Hanks and Schmidt have presented an alternate professional model for librarians, which they developed on the basis of General Systems Theory.[6]

General Systems Theory describes any situation in which there is a flow of energy or information back and forth between an enclosed system and the environment surrounding it. In General Systems Theory, an open system that allows for continued exchange and flow of energy or information between itself and the environment tends to develop because of the maintenance of order that is encouraged by constant feedback. A closed system, however, tends to deteriorate as it moves toward greater disorder due to the lack of such an exchange of energy.

Hanks and Schmidt have called their model of librarianship the Open Systems Model because it describes the process by which librarians take energy from the environment in various forms, including money, materials, equipment, space and information, and transform it into products and services. A sample product could be a bibliography, a sample service, bibliographic instruction. The products and services are then injected back into the environment. Feedback is gained by the utility of the outcome. Appropriate modifications are made to improve the product or service, and the cycle is repeated.

Hanks and Schmidt do an excellent job of integrating General Systems Theory with the liaison role of librarians with their clientele, emphasizing that "a profession . . . must interact with its environment."[7] They go on to explain that the client-oriented librarian would "represent the . . . points of view . . . of the community to the library as a whole . . . they would also . . . [represent] the activities and the limitations of the library to the . . . population they serve."[8] They further state that "such a role would require thorough knowledge of both the needs of the clientele groups and the resources in the library and the community."[9]

From this model, they derive several implications for library education, to which we will return.

IMPLICATIONS OF REALITY AND THEORY

Based upon our conceptual models of librarianship (the functional model and the role model), the following is a discussion of those specific reality factors that affect the level at which librarians are hired and the implications for library education which grow out of those factors.

Bryson's Conceptual Model

Using the functional conceptual model as a framework, we can list within each stage of library development the functions in the order of their development and emphasis. As the emphasis changes from that of early development to that of maturity, it is necessary to maintain each of the functions already developed, and to further their development as changes take place in that specialty. The need for the function does not diminish, although the focus changes. In fact, the level of expertise required becomes higher as the technology and processes involved become more sophisticated.

The following are the roles which are defined within the functional model:

1. The *Custodian* organizes the collection and provides circulation of the materials.
2. The *Responsive Librarian* remains focused within the library and responds to requests for services, which are now developed beyond circulation.[10]
3. The *Active Librarian*[11] initiates contact with the key people in the clientele group, analyzes their information needs, and develops services and products to meet those needs, then carries on constant liaison with the group members. This category is equivalent to the open-systems librarian concept of Hanks and Schmidt.
4. The *Innovator* develops new products, services and systems.
5. The *Leader* provides a sense of direction, the motivation to move the group in that direction, and the coordination required to keep things moving.

Appropriate Degrees

What is the most appropriate degree for entry into a library in each of these stages of development? The wide range of situations, each having many variables, would seem to indicate that there could be several reasonable ways to enter the field.

The combination of stage of development, functions to be performed and roles to be played allow us to judge the level of degree and the type of degree that will provide the most utility for the library.

In the early development stage, with its emphasis on the organization of materials and their circulation, the role of custodian is primary. The custodial role is followed by that of the responsive librarian. The bachelor's degree is adequate in this stage, although most bachelor's graduates will be anxious to get into the next stage and become more involved with the clientele.

In the growth stage, and also that of revitalization, while emphasis is placed on the development of collections and services, maintenance of the established functions is necessary. Here, there is a need for the custodian and the responsive librarian functions to continue, while specialists may be needed in subject areas, for both collection development and reference, audiovisual or media, computer systems and administration. The roles of active librarian, innovator and leader develop, as does the degree range required of the staff. The BS is still useful, and the MLS can provide subject and library expertise. There may be a need for sixth-year expertise in areas such as computer systems, administration or subject bibliography.

In the stage of the mature library, all of the functions and roles described in the growth stage continue. Emphasis shifts to the area of administration, as the roles of leadership and coordination become more significant because of the complexity of the library operation. The MLS or higher degree will be required in administration, and higher degrees will become more common in each area of functional specialization, although the full range of support staff, utilizing clerical, technical, bachelor's librarians and MLS librarians will be required.

An Alternate View

Hanks and Schmidt take another view of library education, one that is more highly specialized. However, with respect to the utility of the bachelor's degree, both models are in agreement as to its utility.

Hanks and Schmidt describe the open systems library, and say that, "At the same time that the open systems library would be requiring new client-centered roles for librarians, it would be phasing out the traditional media-centered roles as professional activities."[12] This, of course, is in disagreement with Bryson's model, which indicates that, even as new roles are developed, the old ones continue to be required.

Hanks and Schmidt also say that librarians so oriented would need "substantially more education in the behavioral sciences . . . a focus on information rather than media . . . [requiring] more education in communities, information science, computer science, and even math . . . librarians serving different types of clients would require different types of knowledge."[13]

Everyone writing today agrees on the need for more education, and oddly enough, seem to agree on the areas needed. The major concern seems to be about the level at which the various components should go into the total mix. Hanks and Schmidt recommend "the removal of the master's degree requirement for the practitioners of the functional roles. . . . A bachelor's degree . . . with a designated number of undergraduate library courses would be enough to qualify a person for basic cataloging and reference work as well as for other fundamental positions in the library."[14] They see the client-centered roles as the "province of those with higher credentials."[15]

The question of specializing to the extent suggested here, or whether some might wish to move the training for such client-centered work to the specialist degree level is one to be explored.

This work adds conceptual legitimacy to a role that is certainly familiar to the many active librarians who carry on a heavy load of liaison work with the various groups and the many key people who make up their clientele. The role definition is certainly welcome.

THE BACHELOR'S DEGREE

The role of the undergraduate library degree program is to produce a graduate who is capable of fulfilling the functional expectations and the role expectations of the *active librarian,* at the time of life and at the degree level of the individual student's choice.

Choice is important because experience has shown that this freedom is more significant in a student's school and career plans than having a wide range of electives in the program. The bachelor's degree provides, for the student who wants or needs it, an option that can be a major factor in determining whether or not that person becomes a librarian, just as it may determine whether or not an employer hires a trained person.

Unique Features

Now that the bachelor's degree has demonstrated its longevity and is perhaps enjoying the beginning of its own revitalization period, let us turn to the question of what unique features it might possess.

First, the bachelor's degree can contain an expanded core, more easily than the MLS, which is obligated to have at least five 600-level, advanced courses, most of which are usually electives. Since the field is expanding, the core probably should follow suit. One alternative is to do it at the bachelor's level, using the 500-level courses.

This brings out another feature, which is that the undergraduate degree can be easily integrated with the MLS program in that both can use the same core courses. These also do not have to be cross-listed, since in most colleges and universitites, qualified upperclass students may take 500-level courses.

Taken together, these two features provide a flexibility for the student, who can put together a program of (1) undergraduate library science, with a second major in a subject area, or a second applied area such as business or education, and (2) at the master's level can return to library science and, because of the number of courses already completed, can supplement the advanced courses in library science with study in other areas. Or, the returning student may choose a master's in a subject or applied area. Both approaches can be useful for the individual and for the employer.

Another strong feature is the required practicum, which provides integration of study and work experience, with a significant gain in skills, self-confidence and enthusiasm as a result of working with patrons in a protective and supportive environment. This experience invariably leads to the achievement of a high level of functioning within a short period of time after the student enters a library position.

The bachelor's program emphasizes an active style of service to patrons, which is an excellent foundation for successful practice in librarianship. The concepts and principles involved in interviewing a patron or teaching a library skills unit are based on reality. They are not just concepts; they are actions, and the actor "lives" librarianship.

Finally, the bachelor's degree in library science has one feature that is *not* unique, and which underlies the strength of these other features to a great extent. That is, that there is really very little difference in the BS and MLS graduate's library education.

The undergraduate student usually takes courses that are cross-listed at the 400/500 levels, sits in the same classroom with the graduate students, reads the same material and takes part in the same discussions. The one difference lies in the advanced, 600-level courses which the undergraduate student does not take. In place of these courses, however, the students do take other very useful courses which add as much to their background for library practice as would the 600-level courses. What this means is that bachelor's-level *librarians* are produced who are fully qualified for librarians' positions.

The Administrators Speak

Karen A. Schmidt's survey of undergraduate library science programs found that the administrators of these programs "believe undergraduate programs prepare their graduates for professional positions . . . [but are] divided . . . on the issue of how well equipped their graduates are to adequately assume positions which require the master's degree."[16]

This seeming contradiction may be due to the practice of thinking in what might be termed a "junior/senior" mode with regard to filling a library position. Many organizations are comfortable with accepting a person with a bachelor's degree to fill a librarian's position, with the expectation that the individual must continue to work toward the master's degree while gaining experience. It is understood by both parties that the individual's performance will improve as a result of both the experience and the degree. In order to encourage the attainment of the master's degree, there is often a ceiling on the salary level for the librarian with only a bachelor's degree. These administrators, then, are thinking of supplementing the MLS, not supplanting it, and are willing to feed it through the bachelor's degree.

These administrators also indicated that they "do not believe the ALA should accredit undergraduate programs, nor do they accept that undergraduate and master's degree programs should be fully articulated."[17]

The reaction to further accreditation is understandable in view of the fact that these programs are already responsible to both regional and state accrediting bodies. Since the administrators know they are doing a good job, they feel no need for further evaluation, nor do they want further restrictions or complexities involved in the carrying out of their programs. In addition, the ALA bias toward large programs would automatically eliminate most of them from participation.

With regard to articulation, the issues of flexibility and autonomy in programming are coming to the fore. Full articulation sounds rigid, and a combination of flexibility in choosing level of entry for the student, and autonomy in developing methods of integration of programs for the school are important considerations for these administrators. This reaction is also understandable in that they are responding to an idea rather than to a specific plan or set of proposed guidelines.

The Environment

Evelyn Daniel cites the fact that "there are more undergraduate programs in schools of education . . . than there are accredited graduate library schools."[18] And the publication of the SCOLE (American Library Association, Standing Committee on Library Education) list of schools offering undergraduate library science preparation demonstrated the popularity of bachelor's level study, even after over 30 years of having the MLS as the standard.[19] Daniel continues: "The MLS is not alone. We cannot continue to accept the fiction that the MLS is the first professional degree, or . . . the only professional degree."[20]

Also, Herbert White, reporting on recent developments in library education, cited the renewal of interest in the undergraduate degree as initial preparation for librarianship: "The last few years have seen a sharp increase in the development of undergraduate degree programs at major library schools, not necessarily in librarianship but . . . [in] information technology or information practice."[21] White goes on to say that the reports from the institutions producing these graduates indicate that they are being successfully employed, "frequently in the private sector,"[22] and the concern is " . . . that this could represent a dilution and cheapening of the professional job market."[23]

When this information is reinforced by the moves made by the U.S. Office of Personnel Management (OPM) in deprofessionalizing library positions,[24] proposing to require only a bachelor's degree which includes six library science courses for entry level positions, and when OPM plans at the same time to farm out library operation to the private sector, we see the harm that can come to the profession.

CONCLUSIONS

The Future of the Bachelor's Degree

Based on the longevity of the bachelor's degree programs in library science, their popularity among employers and students, and the constantly changing stages of development of libraries, it appears that there is an enduring place for these degree programs.

The two theoretical views presented here, while differing in some detail, both support the utility of the bachelor's degree in a differentiated staffing structure; the functional model supports its use in all libraries regardless of the staffing structure.

The capability of bachelor's graduates to administer successfully the many small libraries of all types for which they are responsible speaks well for the degree programs in which they were trained. This continued success also speaks for the point that these graduates are, in the fullest sense, *librarians.*

A review of some of the unique features of these programs, such as their flexibility, capability of containing an expanded core, ease of integration in a variety of ways with the MLS degree, their promotion of an active style of service, and their successful and continued use of the practicum experience to build skills, confidence, enthusiasm and a high level of functioning in a short period of time, all speak well for the bachelor's degree programs.

However, in spite of its contribution to the field, and its many good features, the bachelor's degree in library science is still the center of some controversy. This is due to the fact that there are several other professional issues which revolve around it, and which should also be discussed here.

Entry into the Profession

I have dealt so far with the bachelor's degree as it relates to entry into the *field* of librarianship—*not* to the profession. These are two separate questions, and can only be resolved satisfactorily if they are separated.

Entry into any profession becomes more meaningful if it involves a period of successful work experience, and some evidence that this experience has resulted in the achievement of a certain level of maturity in judgment on the part of the individual when he or she carries out professional functions and roles. And this judgment factor goes beyond the level of skills that can be gained from a practicum, because it entails a degree of independence in practice which can only be gained on the job. A professional is a seasoned, knowledgeable person whose judgment has matured through experience.

Accreditation of Undergraduate Programs

A majority of the undergraduate programs are in colleges of education, and have been accredited for many years by the appropriate state and regional agencies. We have seen that the administrators of these programs do not want to undergo further accreditation. Yet there is the urge to reach out and try to encompass these programs and to bring them under the umbrella of ALA accreditation.[25]

Since these programs are mature and well established in their own right, operating as they do within their own structure, it would be wise to go slowly while looking for common needs before further accreditation is considered.

Downgrading of Librarian's Positions

Moves made at the federal level in the recent past have created a crisis for library educators and there is now a need to act reasonably, carefully and effectively. If bachelor's degree programs are accredited, such action will be taken at the federal level as a signal of acceptance of their downgrading of library positions. This will be very difficult to counter later.

On the positive side, it has been obvious for some time that there is a need to establish further criteria for our profession. Now is the right time for us to move forward and do so.

Recommendations

With these points in mind, I would like to recommend a series of steps which could strengthen our position in the long run. The goals on which these steps are based are (1) to establish the legitimacy of a full range of education and training for positions in librarianship; (2) to establish criteria for the profession; and (3) to unify the membership of the library profession. Specific steps which might help to achieve these goals are as follows:

- Let us reestablish the bachelor's degree, in all of its variations, within our range of *accepted* programs, for all types of libraries. Our reason is that it is a useful degree for both individuals and employers.
- Let us make no move to have the COA accredit bachelor's degree programs because (a) this would establish our position as one of acceptance of downgrading at the federal level, and (b) the administrators of the bachelor's degree programs do not want it, and at this time we have a need for unification, not further divisiveness.
- Let us promote membership and involvement in ALISE for all faculty and administrators of all library science programs, regardless of level or lack of ALA accreditation. This will provide a forum for future discussions and development of common interests.
- Let us establish criteria for professional status, not by accrediting a lower degree level, but by reaffirming the validity of the standard we have already established, and building upon it.

My recommended criteria for the attainment of professional status in librarianship are based upon the principle that degree levels alone do not suffice, but that the attainment of a master's degree and a minimum of 36 semester hours of library science do provide a solid, minimal basis for becoming a professional librarian.

- We could accept any reputable master's degree, as long as the individual has included 36 hours of library science, plus practicum, including both graduate and undergraduate work.
- The experience requirement should consist of at least one year of successful full-time employment, which might translate into three semesters for school media librarians.
- Other professions such as engineering, with which we have more in common than with medicine or law, provide appropriate arrangements by which the individual applies for and receives a professional certificate. Professional librarians should do the same.

SUMMARY

While the case for reestablishment of the bachelor's degree in library science seems well founded, the confusion brought about by other professional issues—professional status; accreditation of programs; our standing with our major employer, the federal government—can easily mislead us.

If we deal with library education and training programs from the perspective of the staffing function, we can see much more clearly the levels of training that are appropriate and useful.

If we establish our own criteria for professional status, based upon what we know is the most useful standard, and if we take positive action to align our process of conferring professional status with that of another accepted professional group, with which we have something in common, we will gain credibility over the long run.

As we continue to look more realistically at the world of library education, we may want to make changes in the philosophy of exclusion which has dominated our accreditation process thus far.

And, with regard to our major employer, we must not let our fears of the present destroy our hope and our vision of the future.

Many individual librarians may not like the idea of reestablishing the bachelor's degree, or of accrediting bachelor's programs, or of changing the approach to professional status—or of changing anything at all—but we have no choice. Events are changing around us. We have the opportunity to act in ways that can improve our profession.

What would be the results of taking the steps outlined above? Will bachelor's graduates drive the master's out of business? Not if we reaffirm the master's by declaring it as the base for our new professional certificate. Wouldn't the acceptance of master's degrees other than the MLS dilute its value? No, individuals will continue to choose the degree that suits the field they're going into, and our acceptance of other degrees as a basis for the professional certificate simply means that our membership will become a more realistic proportion of the total population of practicing librarians. Many of these librarians are already in the field, working every day, and are totally unrecognized by the profession of librarianship.

School media librarians, for example, would be allowed to achieve professional status with a master's degree in either library science or in education, plus the appropriate library certification requirements, when these include 36 semester hours of library science. I think this would help to provide us with the influence Daniel mentioned: "By ignoring these two areas, [school and rural librarians] we lose the opportunity to exercise guidance and leadership."[26]

By taking appropriate action, we can hold the line against further erosion of our standards, and can establish, for ourselves and for others, exactly what our professional status is and how it is achieved. And in the process, we can achieve a sense of unity that we have not had before.

NOTES

1. Roy Stokes, "Master of What?" *Wilson Library Bulletin* 51 (December 1976): 331.

2. Bernard Vavrek, "Profession Needs New Entry Level," *American Libraries* (April 1982): 271.

3. Patricia W. Berger, "The New Federalism: How It Is Changing the Library Profession in the U.S." *The Bowker Annual of Library & Book Trade Information,* 28th ed. (New York: Bowker, 1983), p. 40.

4. Trevor N. Dupuy, *Ferment in College Libraries: The Impact of Information Technology* (Washington, DC: Communications Service Corporation, 1968), p. 28.

5. Ronald Bryson, "A Theory of Librarianship" (unpublished Ph.D. dissertation, College of Education, University of Kentucky), pp. 42-55.

6. Gardner Hanks and C. James Schmidt, "An Alternative Model of a Profession for Librarians," *College & Research Libraries* 36 (May 1975): 175-187.

7. Ibid., p. 181.

8. Ibid., p. 183.

9. Ibid.

10. Trevor N. Dupuy, *Ferment in College Libraries,* p. 28.

11. Ibid.

12. Gardner Hanks and C. James Schmidt, *College & Research Libraries* 36 (May 1975): 182.

13. Ibid., pp. 184-185.

14. Ibid., p. 183.

15. Ibid.

16. Karen A. Schmidt, "The Other Librarians: Undergraduate Library Science Programs and Their Graduates," *Journal of Education for Librarianship* 24 (Spring 1984): 231.

17. Ibid., p. 223.

18. Evelyn H. Daniel, "Expanding A.L.A. Accreditation," *Library Journal* (February 1, 1983): 178.

19. American Library Association, Standing Committee on Library Education, *Undergraduate Programs in Library Education* (Four-Year Schools), Chicago, A.L.A., 1980.

20. Evelyn H. Daniel, *Library Journal* (February 1, 1983): 178.

21. Herbert S. White, "Recent Developments in Library Education," *The Bowker Annual of Library & Book Trade Information,* 28th ed. (New York: Bowker, 1983), p. 259.

22. Ibid.

23. Ibid.

24. Patricia W. Berger, *The Bowker Annual of Library & Book Trade Information,* 28th ed. (New York: Bowker, 1983): pp. 36-41.

25. Evelyn H. Daniel, *Library Journal* (February 1, 1983): 178-179.

26. Ibid., p. 178.

12

Continuing Education Programs and Activities

Darlene E. Weingand

Education for professional librarians, a vital issue and a worthy topic for this book, encompasses a continuum of both possibilities and realities. In the real world, this education has moved through an evolutionary process in which the locale in which the requirements for entering the profession are obtained has shifted from the baccalaureate environment to the graduate school. Over time, the demands of the profession have correspondingly intensified until today, when the horizons of professional librarianship seem almost limitless.

In society, as well as in the information professions, the impact of change and technological development is staggering. The rapidity of movement of these two forces is steadily increasing, and maintaining professional currency is becoming more and more difficult. Based on observable changes in the information profession, this author estimates that the shelf life of the preservice MLS now stands at approximately five years—and the rate of societal change continually challenges that estimate. Occupational obsolescence is now a very real concern in all lines of work, but it is particularly critical in the information professions, for it is information and its modes of access which are accelerating at the fastest rate.

How, then, can the professional librarian effectively operate in such a shifting and ambiguous workplace? How can standards of excellence and service be maintained at the highest possible level? How can personal self-worth in the professional role be nurtured in the midst of this changing world? The seemingly simplistic—yet accurate—response is lifelong learning and continuing education, with the implication that such learning and education must indeed be continuous and nonstop. (An analogy: When the jetliner is in motion, the passengers must be in equal motion: if they choose to disembark enroute, they will perish.)

THE CONTINUUM OF PROFESSIONAL EDUCATION

The opening sentence of this chapter spoke of professional education as a continuum, and indeed it is one. Whereas preservice education initiates the continuum, continuing education of various types perpetuates it. Professional education must have a continuum of equal or greater length than the totality of the work life if the quality of that work life is to place between satisfactory and excellent on personal and/or organizational performance scales. When this continuum is either breached or inadequately maintained, performance slippage, stress and burnout become most prevalent.

Professional proficiency can burn out or become obsolete due to some combination of individual and situational changes. These changes can result from personal attitudes and experiences and through shifts in societal, career or organizational expectations.[1]

Obsolescence can be defined as less than optimal proficiency for current professional performance. An optimal level is usually based on implicit standards of effective practice as reflected in occupational expectations, demands and constraints expressed by opinion leaders in work settings, professional associations, educational institutions and regulatory organizations—the sum of which constitutes the current state of the art.[2] Any performance level not current with this state of the art can be deemed, at least in part, obsolete.

Proficiency upon completion of preservice education is presumed to be relatively sound, so obsolescence and burnout can be tied to what occurs during the librarian's professional life. It is a tall order for information professionals to avoid objective obsolescence and subjective burnout and to remain sufficiently competent to be accountable in their positions and enhance the joie de vivre of the professional life. Yet that is exactly what must take place if that aspect of human life is to flourish.[3]

For many years, popular belief held that the professional degree would suffice for the average length of the work life. This belief was probably not true then, and it is certainly a shortsighted and erroneous position to hold today. According to the assistant director of general library services at the University of Illinois at Urbana-Champaign, "The rate of change in information technology and its impact on libraries make it important for the recent graduate to realize that much of what was learned in professional school will soon be obsolescent."[4]

The reality of today (and through a series of projected tomorrows) is that continuing professional education is a necessity, a mandate for playing a professional role. As a necessity, continuing professional education assumes its rightful ownership as the majority stockholder on the continuum of professional education. It needs to be acknowledged that over a total work life continuing education will command more hours of involvement than the original preservice degree. With this perspective firmly in place, it is time to examine more closely the nature of continuing professional education and its place in professional development.

CONTINUING PROFESSIONAL EDUCATION: A SNAPSHOT

In addition to the now-acknowledged reality of continuing professional education, the continuum also contains a host of possibilities. These possibilities, which move along the professional education continuum, are directly related to perception of the professional role and educational formats.

In an effort to capture a glimpse of the professional role, it is useful to consider Houle's five characteristics of professionalization:[5]

1. Clarifying the defining function or functions: the mission
2. Mastery of theoretical knowledge: the information and theory that form the knowledge base

3. Capacity to solve problems: the application of theoretical knowledge and practical experiential wisdom
4. Use of practical knowledge: that body of knowledge that has grown out of the nature, history, scope and processes of practical application
5. Self-enhancement: new personal dimensions of knowledge, skill and sensitivity by the arduous study of topics not directly related to the occupation

Preservice education is primarily aimed at item 2, mastery of theoretical knowledge, and to some extent at item 1, clarifying the function. However, the remaining characteristics are dimensions of the merging of theory, practice and experience. The gap between preservice education and mature, optimal professionalism must be bridged by what can be defined as continuing professional education. Continuing education in library and information studies has the important mission of somehow coordinating the adult professional's various formal and informal learning experiences, accepting the assumption that the adult is a self-directed, self-motivated, problem-solving learner. Educational opportunities must be generated that assist librarians in enhancing the above-cited characteristics of professionalism and in nurturing personal growth and expanded expertise. This is no small task—but it is critical to individuals, organizations and the profession at large.

What are some of these educational opportunities? Formats can range from formal credit and noncredit classes to self-directed study. Other options include short courses and workshops, attendance at conferences, and teaching and writing. The concept of format can be further extended to include face-to-face instruction, video and audio courses (whether broadcast or pretaped), correspondence courses, and interactive telecommunications. Technological development will continue to foster new opportunities to respond to the needs engendered by corresponding change.

While it is clear that educational opportunities abound once the definition is expanded to include the full spectrum of formats, it must also be recognized that a much wider variety of options may be available in one geographical area than in another. The professional situated in some areas may have to be more creative in identifying nonformal methods of continuing professional education—frequently with the aid of that same technological impetus which is a prime mover in requiring that such education take place.

If the need for continuing professional education is accepted as a given, then the follow-up questions are: How much and how often? Frequency is an individual matter, but some states have passed legislation that establishes legal requirements. For example, the state of Wisconsin requires certification for directors of public libraries. Once certified, each level-one (MLS) library director must, at the end of every five-year period, present evidence of the completion of the equivalent of 15 continuing education points, or 150 contact hours of approved continuing education activities. Mathematically, this comes to 30 hours per year. One college-level course would meet this annual requirement—or four days of workshops, or a corresponding amount of more informal learning. The Wisconsin legislation is but one illustration, but it represents a sincere attempt to ascertain how much is enough to accomplish the goal of keeping current in the field.

There is much disagreement, however, in adult education circles across the nation as to whether various forms of mandated continuing education are desirable. Many theoreticians argue that adults should be responsible for their own learning and behavior and that mandatory continuing education flies in the face of this theoretical perspective. The opposing view states that mandatory continuing education, as a requirement of professional certification or licensing, supports the process by which the general public is restricted from the practice of a given trade, the provision of a given service or the use of a specific title.[6]

Mandatory continuing education is a national trend, promoted by consumer pressure, some professional associations (such as medicine and law) and legislation in some states, but the discussions over desirability continue. Considerable variation and inconsistency exist in requirements for continuing education, but the real issues are competence and accountability: how to somehow guarantee competent professional service.

Regardless of external requirements and pressures, the ultimate responsibility lies with the individual. Adults are self-directed, problem-solving human beings with a host of individual differences. The final decisions as to format and frequency are personal ones, but they must rest on both the desire for choice and the recognition of baseline responsibility.

What is the ideal scenario? If the self-directed view of the adult is accepted, then self-monitoring of competence, with the assistance of regular job evaluations and self-assessment, is the appropriate goal. One of the real benefits in self-assessment and personal goal-setting is the opportunity to examine a wider range of impinging factors than is normally considered by more structured evaluative agencies or procedures—and a range in which the implications are unique to the individual. Such self-assessment will include technical competence, but it will also factor in societal and technological change and personal life style and attitudes. This self-analysis should complement well the new movement toward competence assessment.

A NEW TREND: COMPETENCE ASSESSMENT AND DEVELOPMENT

The assessment of competence is appearing more and more in the literature as the drive for accountability intensifies. As the finite pot of available dollars is called upon to support an expanding universe of services, how those dollars are spent becomes an increasingly visible and popular issue.

Tied to both competence evaluation and accountability is the need for valid and reliable measurement. The ability to document the relationship between expenditures and effectiveness, whether that effectiveness be centered in overall library response to its community or in individual performance, is the critical factor in demonstrating whether or not the library/information agency is providing essential and relevant service. In times of decreasing resources, the perception of any agency's essential worth may well determine its ultimate survival—and certainly its ability to perform at any sort of reasonable level.

Several current studies have addressed the notion of individual competence. A two-part series in *Public Libraries* highlighted potential competencies of public library directors in terms of administrative, clinical and professional knowledge, skills and attitudes.[7] Building upon this beginning, a joint U.S.–Canadian study took place in 1983-84 which used the administrative competencies to assess public library directors in communities serving populations of over 100,000.[8] In addition, in 1982, the U.S. Department of Education commissioned a study of competencies in terms of library science education.[9] These studies indicate a growing concern with individual performance as related to the needs of a changing society.

However, that same changing society requires that competencies, once identified, be regarded as a snapshot in the course of time, for competencies that are absolutely basic to quality librarianship one day may be deemed of marginal necessity the next. The information professions must become and remain fluid in order to flow with the mainstream of societal change. The concept of fixed competencies would act as a dam to this vital flow and the forward progression would be slowed or halted.

Self-assessment is a valuable tool in the identification of appropriate competencies. Mechanisms such as self-assessment scales produced by Weingand[10] and the ALA Continuing Library Education Network and Exchange Round Table (CLENERT)[11] can be useful to individuals, as long as such scales are regarded as tools and not as prescriptive authorities.

Continuing professional education has a role to play in the identification of timely—and projected—competencies and the creation of learning experiences to produce those identified competencies. As the expectations of individual and organizational performance shift in response to perceived societal needs, the development of corresponding and appropriate educational activities must parallel these expectations.

This implies that providers of continuing professional education have a more complex charge than may have been envisioned. Such a charge would include the planning and development of learning opportunities; that is a basic assumption. However, beyond that assumption lies an implicit challenge to the effect that providers should be so in tune with the movements of society and the profession that they not only recognize but *anticipate* needs for professional development as they arise. This combination of stewardship and forecasting has its own problems for the providers, somewhat analogous to crossing a swamp without knowing where the stepping stones are located. The dilemma is predicated on the need for crossing the swamp of occupational obsolescence—without knowing where, or if, the stepping stones of student participation actually exist. It is all too possible that a continuing education provider who is truly in tune with present and projected needs may offer activities for which students are unwilling to commit time and money because they do not yet perceive the value. This is a perplexing part of the operations of the providers—but who are they?

WHO SHALL PROVIDE?

Continuing professional education is variously regarded as anywhere from a service to a source of revenue. This variation in provider approach results in registration fees that range from minimal to hundreds of dollars. Depending on the type of provider, the costs of the event may be absorbed in full or in part by the sponsor, or they may need to be recovered in full (including the indirect costs, such as overhead).

This variation also has a direct relationship to the content of the event. There is no question but that a workshop of a few hours prepared locally will have a different focus and level of sophistication from a course developed by an experienced full-time provider of continuing education. However, as the depth of instruction becomes more involved and complex—as it must if it is to keep pace with the dynamic of information manipulation and access—the actual cost of course development must be more realistically viewed by students. It is certain that the time of free and low-cost continuing education is phasing out; quality education has a price tag commensurate with the effort expended to produce it, and students must be willing to accept the higher fee if they wish to engage in high-quality continuing education.

There are a host of providers of continuing professional education on the market today; these include

- Colleges and universities, including library schools
- Professional associations
- Private corporations

- Private consultants
- Local library systems
- In-service by the employing library

Since so much externally provided continuing education does exist, the inherent problem of duplication and proliferation is a serious one. The parallel issue of quality control comes into play as programs do proliferate. To date, the prospective student has had to rely on word of mouth and the reputation of the provider as the criteria for anticipating the worth of a proposed continuing education event.

There is, however, one measure of quality control that has been available to students but underutilized. Originally founded in conjunction with CLENE (now CLENERT), the Voluntary Recognition System (VRS) of the National Council has attempted, through annual review of provider goals and objectives and program descriptions, to monitor the activities of providers who have sought certification by the CLENE-VRS. A logo was established so that approved providers could indicate their achievement on brochures and other publicity.

In the best of all possible worlds, where all continuing education providers offer high-quality events, how can the twin problems of duplication and proliferation be avoided? The solution to these problems comes from current marketing theory, which states that each organization needs to carve out its own market share—discover through market research what it can do that is unique and position itself in the market accordingly. This is not an easy task, but it is a necessary one . . . which leads quite nicely to the next topic.

WHO SHALL PAY?

In the Winter 1985 issue of the *Journal of Education for Library and Information Science,* the Continuing Education column was devoted to this knotty topic.[12] Possible contributors were targeted: the individual, in recognition of personal need and potential value; the organization, through released time and tuition reimbursement; the professional associations, through scholarships; and the state and national governments, through tax monies.

The analysis of such deliberations does not remove the question mark—but it does acknowledge the existence of a shared responsibility and a definite societal need. Society's need for competent professionals becomes more acute as the rate of change accelerates. The issue of paying for this competence is a catch-22—as economic austerity becomes more pronounced, the need for competence in information handling becomes more critical.

TODAY'S DILEMMA

The issues that have been discussed above—*Who shall provide?* . . . *Who shall pay?* . . . and *Quality control*—must be examined closely and seriously. The present configuration of professional library education, described in this chapter as a continuum incorporating both preservice and continuing education, is not universally viewed as a continuum. The responsibility for professional education beyond the initial degree is shared by a variety of providers with varying cost structures and levels of quality. No overall coordination or regulation is in place, except in scattered instances where states or associations require certification. There is a real need for the concept of the continuum, grounded in the academic library schools, to become a generalized understanding—if not a standard of the profession.

While there are no ready-made or easy solutions, creative thinking can be applied—with the understanding that the result may be outside the realm of accepted conservative boundaries. With that caveat in mind, let us consider one possible scenario, involving a revised educational system:

A PROPOSAL

WHEREAS the presently accepted model for educating professional librarians is the graduate library school, resulting in a master's degree from an ALA-accredited program; and

WHEREAS library schools traditionally see as their primary mission the educating of master's level students; and

WHEREAS some library schools also educate doctoral students and undergraduate students; and

WHEREAS the profession of medicine has developed a quite different model which has historically been proven successful; and

WHEREAS the information profession is potentially the most critical to societal development in the next several decades; and

WHEREAS the needs of society require competent information professionals; and

WHEREAS the educational tax dollar has been funneled primarily into K-12 education, secondarily into undergraduate education, and only marginally into continuing education (primarily through university extensions);

BE IT THEREFORE RESOLVED THAT

1. The education of information professionals will be restructured to approximate more closely the tested medical model, i.e.,

    a. Undergraduate preparatory education in information studies.

    b. A fifth year of study resulting in a master's degree.

    c. An internship year in which the beginning information professional is inducted into the profession, receiving close supervision for paid half-time work and support for continued professional study in the other half.

    d. A year of residence in which the new professional assumes primary responsibility for a position for which he or she is qualified, but under the continued supervision of an experienced professional.

    e. Continuance as a career professional with continuing education obligations required by law at five-year intervals.

    f. Opportunity to proceed with further education toward a specialist degree in a particular subject field or a Ph.D. or equivalent with research concentration.

2. Preservice library schools will be concerned and interactive with the field, with research directed toward the cutting edge of practice.

3. Library school faculty will be committed and competent in the field, with faculty to be drawn from both academe and clinical practice.

4. The funding for this lifelong commitment to professional education will be the shared responsibility of
    a. The individual, contributing whatever monies are required over and above the funds provided from other sources;
    b. The employing organization, through tuition reimbursement and released time from duties;
    c. The professional associations, through scholarships;
    d. The state, using federally designated funds and state subsidies to fund individuals equitably throughout the lifetime.

This proposal is a serious first attempt to stimulate a dynamic and fundamental structural change in both the educational preparation of library/information professionals and the funding patterns of library and information studies education. The importance of continuing professional education through the lifetime must be acknowledged in both form and function if society is to go boldly into the twenty-first century with an informed and information-rich population.

REPRISE: THE CONTINUUM

This chapter has encompassed both realities and possibilities in terms of both the present and the future. Continuing professional education is too closely associated with societal good to be allowed to drift aimlessly, without purpose or direction. The responsibility shared by individuals, organizations and governments is real, not hypothetical. There is a Chinese proverb that states: "If you want to plant for a year, plant rice; if you want to plant for a decade, plant a tree; if you want to plant for a lifetime, educate a man."

The challenge is indeed upon us. The continuum of education for professional librarians needs acknowledgment, support and the faith and energies of all of us. The gold ring on this carousel is worth reaching for!

NOTES

1. Darlene E. Weingand, *The Organic Public Library* (Littleton, CO: Libraries Unlimited, Inc., 1984), p. 77.

2. Alan B. Knox, "The Nature and Causes of Professional Obsolescence," in *The Evaluation of Continuing Education for Professionals: A Systems View,* edited by Preston P. LeBreton et al. (Seattle: University of Washington, 1979), p. 133.

3. Weingand, p. 77.

4. Paula D. Watson, quoted in "Launching a Successful Career in Academe: 32 Administrators and Professors Offer Advice," *The Chronicle of Higher Education* (September 4, 1985), pp. 42-44.

5. Cyril O. Houle, *Continuing Learning in the Professions* (San Francisco, CA: Jossey-Bass, 1980), pp. 35, 40-49.

6. Robert S. Donnelly, *Continuing Professional Education: An Appraisal* (A report for the Division of Continuing Education, University of Massachusetts at Amherst), n.d., p. 3.

7. Darlene E. Weingand, "Competencies for Public Librarians: A Beginning," *Public Libraries* 20 no. 4 (Winter 1981): 104-106 and "Librarians' Personal Continuing Education Planning," *Public Libraries* 21 no. 1 (Spring 1982): 13-16.

8. Darlene E. Weingand and Noel Ryan, "Managerial Competencies and Skills," *Journal of Library Administration* 6 no. 1 (Spring 1985): 23-44.

9. José-Marie Griffiths and Donald N. King, *New Directions in Library and Information Science Education* (White Plains, NY: Knowledge Industry Publications, 1986).

10. Darlene E. Weingand, *The Organic Public Library* (Littleton, CO: Libraries Unlimited, 1984), pp. 82-89.

11. Continuing Library Education Network and Exchange, "Self-Assessment and the Learning Contract: A Systematic and Personal Approach to Learning" (available from the CLENE Round Table, American Library Association).

12. Darlene E. Weingand, "Who Shall/Should Pay?" *Journal of Education for Library and Information Science* 25 no. 3 (Winter 1985): 223-225.

13

The View of the Student

Louise D. Schlesinger

Graduate library education today is in a state of turmoil at least equal to the turmoil that exists in the library field. As schools struggle to define basic competencies with which to equip their students for traditional library positions, they are simultaneously in the process of broadening the range of jobs to which their graduates may make legitimate claim. To current students entering a graduate library program, the ambiguity of professional parameters presents exciting and perhaps unimagined opportunities. To graduating library students, however, the chaos of the graduate library curriculum today is a source of frustration as they confront a job market which on the one hand offers positions for which they are only superficially prepared and on the other hand offers jobs that do not provide challenges commensurate with their educational attainment.

ENTRY-LEVEL JOB REQUIREMENTS

Library school students look to their schools to provide appropriate professional preparation. The definition of what is appropriate depends greatly upon what is considered professional. The issue is dramatically embodied in the heated debate over the MLS as the standard requirement for entry into the ranks of the profession. The federal government's Office of Personnel Management has aroused the wrath of the library community for explicitly suggesting that the MLS not be considered an absolute requirement for entry-level professional positions or in fact for any library positions with the government. Nevertheless, librarians themselves have implicitly challenged the MLS standard by their own practices.

For example, libraries, particularly public and school libraries, have been known to hire applicants who lack the MLS. Indeed, given the meager salaries that some of the smaller and more rural institutions can afford to offer for professional positions, it is a wonder that they attract *any* applicants who have completed master's level work. It is also true that some libraries have nonprofessional staff whose duties are indistinguishable from those of professionals.

At the other end of the spectrum, academic libraries are notorious for employing MLS degree-holders in jobs classified as nonprofessional. At the same time, they increasingly advertise for applicants who hold a second subject master's degree to fill entry level professional positions.

THE RESPONSE OF EDUCATORS

In response to the seemingly fuzzy idea of what separates professional librarians from nonprofessional staff, and possibly also to bolster their enrollments, library educators have served up a smorgasbord of degrees and programs. They have developed undergraduate library degrees, dual master's degrees, specialist certificates and doctorates in addition to the MLS. The situation becomes ever more complex as library schools attempt to broaden the opportunities of their graduates beyond the library profession to the information profession. The information profession is so new that its members end up being any who choose to think of themselves as part of it, and there are no agreed-upon standards for what constitutes appropriate preparation to join the ill-defined ranks of this body.

In short, the most serious problem with library education from the student's perspective really is the library community's indecisiveness about what constitutes an entry-level position for applicants holding the standard master's degree. How can the student make a rational choice to obtain a library master's degree when an entry-level position could be anything from the directorship of a small public library to a nonprofessional support staff position at a large research library? What incentive is there to work toward a master's degree if people with undergraduate library degrees can compete for the same pool of jobs? Indeed, how can library educators tailor their curricula to meet the needs of a profession that cannot agree upon what positions belong in the realm of technician and what belong in the realm of entry-level professional?

THE PROFESSIONAL AS MANAGER

One way to deal with the situation is to say that professional work by definition includes an administrative component. Thus, many library schools have added management courses to their curricula. My own experience indicates that such courses are a microcosm of the problem of library education in general: they touch upon a great many topics without sufficiently exploring any of them. To a large extent such courses consist of a survey of management theories and their application to personnel situations within the library. For example, library management courses breezily cover several methods of budgeting in a single week, while the planning process may receive two weeks' attention.

There is nothing wrong with the topics that are covered, but the coverage of management issues is incomplete. Library students' grasp of hard information, such as legal liability, legal constraints in personnel matters, the funding process, program evaluation, the tools of community analysis, etc., is impressionistic at best. Moreover, library students deal hardly at all with the larger picture of directing the library as a generic public organization or as part of a larger institution. It is just not possible to cover it all within the constraints of time.

As a result, students are graduating with only the most superficial ideas of the daily management of a library and even less knowledge of the outside forces that affect libraries. Since a recent survey of library employers indicates that there is inadequate support in the field for continuing education,[1] one must conclude that the future directors of libraries should receive a more substantial background in management while still in library school. It is highly questionable, however, that one or possibly two library management courses provide sufficient background for any student who has ambition to assume a responsible administrative position.

THE DUAL-DEGREE SOLUTION

Not surprisingly, library educators have turned to other professional schools to provide their students with a management background of more depth. According to the latest available survey by the Association for Library and Information Science Education (ALISE), seven of the 72 reporting ALA-accredited library schools had established a dual master's degree with the disciplines of business, management or public administration by the 1982-1983 academic year.[2] Twenty more joint degree programs with business administration, public administration or urban affairs were under consideration at the time.[3]

I had the opportunity to take advantage of one of these dual degree programs while in school. Its advantages are distinct, the most obvious being that in the extended program the student acquires a more sophisticated set of administrative skills. The budgetary process is not covered in one week; it is a full-semester course. The same is true for planning and program evaluation. In addition, a full-year course in statistical analysis is required. Personnel systems and labor relations are dealt with in separate courses. There is no need to make the list longer; the point is that students of other professional schools who are destined for equivalent administrative responsibilities acquire a vocabulary and understanding far beyond that of most library students.

Another benefit of library students taking classes in other professional schools is that they mix with their future counterparts in other public institutions or private industry. Not only does this give library students a new perspective on the role of the library within the larger context, but it also allows them to familiarize students of other professional schools with library-oriented concerns. Library schools could benefit from the overlap of interest among students. For example, several graduate students in public administration expressed to me the hope that they might find a course on information policy in the library school. They also sought out library students they knew to help them find information they needed in government publications for their research. They were interested in courses in systems analysis and database creation, too. Dual degree programs need not be a one-way street for library students into other programs.

THE DUAL-DEGREE DILEMMA

However, there is a danger lurking in these dual degree programs, too. It is one thing for a library student to pick up a second subject master's degree that has little or no job market value if considered by itself. The goal of getting a subject degree in the humanities or social sciences or even some of the hard sciences is to become a subject bibliographer in a research library. This may be a rational financial choice. When ARL directors were recently asked whether they would give preference in hiring to applicants with two graduate degrees, 70% of them responded in the affirmative and half of them said that they would probably pay more for people with dual credentials.[4]

On the other hand, library students who enter a joint program with another professional school may be co-opted by the latter. One reason for this threat is that, in general, compensation is higher for graduates of other professional schools. In 1984 the average salary offered to inexperienced library graduates was $17,408,[5] while the comparable salary offer for the inexperienced Master of Business Administration (MBA) graduate with a nontechnical undergraduate degree was $28,500.[6] The discrepancy in compensation may be less severe if discussion is limited to dual degree library graduates, especially those with MBAs or MPAs. Nevertheless, a gap remains that might tempt the dual professional degree candidate to consider the MLS the secondary degree of the pair.

It is highly unlikely that any MBA or MPA student is going to be tempted to enter the library field. Therefore, the library profession must rely upon MLS students to enter other professional programs to bring a higher level of administrative expertise into the field. Given these realities, it is clear that employers of librarians must address the issue of compensation for applicants possessing additional professional credentials before library schools rush ahead to set up more of these joint programs.

The profession might address the issue of low compensation by raising the level of responsibility at which it is going to accept this new breed of library graduate. It would be a mistake to consider all second master's degrees merely subject specialties of the academic librarian. Students who obtain degrees in administration have a second set of professional skills. Such graduates cannot be expected to be satisfied with packing away their management expertise for several years while they work their way through the librarian ranks. Nor can they be expected to jump into roles usually reserved for mature professionals who bring with them valuable experience.

From the perspective of the dual degree student, the library community needs to create middle management training positions modeled after those found in business and government. The failure of library employers to create these opportunities for students who have made an extraordinary commitment to bringing additional knowledge and skills to their first professional position results in a terrible waste of resources. Similarly, it is irresponsible for library educators to continue to direct their students into a no-man's-land where they are overqualified for the majority of entry-level positions and underqualified for everything else.

LIBRARIANS AS COMPUTER JOCKS

An equally critical question facing library education today is that of integrating computer technology into the curriculum. Several people have called for a substantial realignment of the graduate library curriculum to reflect the impact of computer technology. For example, Koenig surveyed corporate librarians and found that their ideal core curriculum would consist of five courses, two of which were online searching and programming.[7] This is not an opinion peculiar to corporate librarians, though, for representatives of the information industry and government, including the Library of Congress, have noted the shortage of individuals who can manipulate information and high technology.[8] In addition, school librarians are not untouched by the race to make ours a computer literate society, and no public librarian can have failed to notice that automation topics have become regular features of our premier professional journals. As for students, a cursory glance at job advertisements makes plain that one would be seriously handicapped in the job market without having taken at least one computer class. It is a hopeful sign that the voices of those who have no use for computers in storing and retrieving information have been silenced. In fact, the only evidence that this is not so comes from a recent study that found that employers considered a course in microcomputers as "not a major factor in a decision to hire" or, at most, as merely desirable.[9]

The study suggests that there appears to be no consensus yet in the field about whether high technology is essential or merely beneficial to librarianship. Perhaps this can be explained by the fact that there are many practicing librarians who have not used a computer or whose exposure to computers is limited to the age of cumbersome key punching and programming in complex languages. There is a sizable group of library students who share their distaste for the technology. However, there is a less reticent group of students, the kind that the profession says it most needs, who are demanding computer courses in the curriculum.

Library educators have responded to this demand because it is clear that when virtually every other school on campus is setting up microcomputer laboratories, the library school cannot continue to claim that their graduates are information professionals without computer skills. Thus, in a single year ALISE member library schools reported adding 34 new computer-related courses to their curricula, more new courses than in any other subject area.[10]

THE MYTH OF THE COMPUTERIZED CURRICULUM

It is one thing to add computer courses to the curriculum; it is quite another to make them worthwhile. One problem arises from lack of hardware. At a time when other professional schools are setting up laboratories with a dozen microcomputers linked in a local area network, the facilities provided by some library schools are laughable. Some schools have no hardware at all. One school, it is said, tried to teach online searching with only a book.

Other schools have computer labs that consist of "dumb" terminals hooked up to the campus mainframe computers. While this is better than nothing, it is unlikely that most graduates will have use for the primitive line editor word processing programs, unfriendly programming languages and unfathomable database software stored there. It is safe to say that students who encounter the frustration of trying to work in such an environment only have their worst impressions of computers confirmed.

Then there are the library schools that throw a couple of out-of-date microcomputers into an empty room and call it a microcomputer lab. In fact it is a junkyard of incompatible machines, all of which have limited capabilities. The uninitiated student who tries to use this kind of facility comes away with the impression that there is no rhyme or reason to the way computers work because each machine has a different set of commands for doing the same thing. Again, it is a frustrating experience.

Even if a library school has somehow gotten enough money together to set up a microcomputer lab with modern machinery, it is not necessarily true that the library student will find software equivalent to that being used by students in other professional schools. Running simple, limited programs on a computer capable of handling the latest software on the market is rather like training to be a race car driver in a Porsche with no gas.

Providing adequate hardware and software for library students to work with is as essential as it is expensive. If the library school cannot afford to do it, then it has an obligation either to set up cooperative arrangements with other schools on campus with similar interests or actively promote another department's courses which would benefit library students. No branch of librarianship is exempt from the need to have these skills. Everyone from the children's librarian to the archivist has an appropriate use for computers, and those in the smallest libraries with the least funding probably would benefit most from a practical understanding of how to apply the technology.

INTEGRATING COMPUTER TECHNOLOGY

In addition to the question of whether library schools are providing reasonable access to up-to-date hardware and software is the question of how the topic of computers is being included in the curriculum. Given the great number of new computer courses library schools are adding to their catalogs, it is a pretty sure bet that the technology is not being integrated into the curriculum at all. Instead, it is probably being separated into an information science track which timid students can largely choose to ignore.

Computers have applications in reference work, so computer technology should be taught in reference courses. Likewise, technical service departments in libraries have been completely transformed by automation, and the library curriculum should reflect that transformation. Computer applications should also be introduced at appropriate junctures in management classes. Forecasting and budgeting on electronic spreadsheets, as well as word processing, should be among the graduate's skills. Computer applications should be treated as part of the daily routine of all library positions.

Of course, there are automation technology courses for which separate status is desirable. Online searching comes to mind as does complex database development. No doubt there are other applications that a school might wish to explore in depth. There is, however, only one kind of worthwhile information science course for master's level students, and that is a hands-on computer applications course.

A hands-on course is one that actually involves using a computer, not merely talking about it hypothetically. It consists of doing online searching with a real vendor, creating a database with the latest software available, forecasting community needs with a spreadsheet, using a local area network, and acquiring a familiarity with the bibliographic utilities' capabilities. Students also need to understand the rudiments of microcomputer hardware so they can exploit their software to its fullest potential. It is ridiculous to waste time on topics like the history of automation.

"History" in computer terms means what the professor told you was a future development only last semester. Similarly, the attempt to lay a theoretical basis for the profession by studying information as a science is of limited use to those enrolled in the master's program.

Part of the problem is that library school faculties cannot or do not want to incorporate the topic of technology into their classes. The influence of computers, especially microcomputers, has spread so rapidly that it is not part of their experience. They are not comfortable with it, and so any topic beyond the most general use of OCLC is called "information science" and left to one or two faculty members to discuss. Instructors who are uncomfortable with computers impart piecemeal bits of information about using them, and wind up confusing and frustrating generations of students. Of course, this is not true in every school, but where this situation does exist, it cripples the curriculum.

Leaving aside their obligation to prepare those entering the library profession, library educators are scrambling to incorporate high technology into their curricula because computers have created a new market of nontraditional jobs for library graduates. Indeed, some library schools have become known for programs designed to meet the needs of this new market. Unfortunately, many schools are jumping on the bandwagon without proper facilities. Worse yet, the depth of knowledge about high technology among library school faculty appears to be too shallow to support an expanded curriculum. The disastrous result is a half-baked graduate degree that throws an inadequately prepared person into the market and does little to enhance the MLS as the degree of choice in the minds of those who hire.

THE ARRAY OF SOLUTIONS

In short, students are entering graduate library programs today that are awash in a sea of change. There are positive aspects to this turbulent atmosphere; there is creativity in the chaos. But the curriculum lacks cohesion and adds to a confusion of professional identity.

This is not news to educators. Indeed, several solutions to the situation have been proposed.[11] One of the more popular ideas is that of developing tracks by type of library because supposedly a different mix of expertise is required for positions in different library settings. In other words, a children's librarian track would place more emphasis on preparing the student to work with children than on preparing the student to store and retrieve information. The academic librarian would have different concerns than the public librarian because the academic library is part of a larger educational institution. Never mind that they both try to serve a clientele with the same stock in trade, information. The effect of this solution would be to reduce the actual core of knowledge that defines librarians as professionals. If setting were to define the profession to a greater extent than a substantial body of shared knowledge, then perhaps we ought to abolish graduate library schools and offer a couple of library certification courses to students enrolled in other fields.

Others call for an extended program of study, whether by offering undergraduate courses or by increasing the requirements of the graduate program. It is unlikely that any student will want to spend more time and money working toward the master's degree when it is unclear what distinction there will be in the future between the MLS and an undergraduate library degree. Moreover, it will be impossible for library educators to make a distinction between the content of undergraduate and graduate courses unless library employers make a distinction in job opportunities. The obvious distinction to be made is between those whose work can be classified as that of competent technicians and those whose responsibilities have less to do with library routines than with the administration of an organization. Perhaps this is the sort of tracking that graduate library schools ought to be considering.

In this scenario, the curriculum of the MLS would focus on budgeting, public relations, planning, information policy, statistical analysis, labor relations and personnel as well as advanced reference and technical services topics. The BLS would focus on what is generally considered the core of the MLS now. It is a pattern followed by other professional programs, and one worth consideration by library educators. The MBA, for instance, does not preclude one from rising through the ranks of an organization; rather, it exists to reeducate practitioners for the new responsibilities of higher level positions. It also provides a second port of entry for ambitious individuals.

Finally, it has been suggested that library schools should cease to identify themselves with the particular institution, the library, and instead should graduate information professionals—Masters of Information Science (MIS). This would be a challenge for library schools, but one for which they are ill prepared at present. It would require adding new areas of expertise to faculties already stretched thin in order to cover the content of present curricula. It would require sophisticated computer equipment and software at a time when library school budgets are strained. Moreover, the library school would have to compete with other schools that are moving quickly to control the MIS field even before it is defined.

THE NEED FOR ACTION

Library schools will probably retain their primary identity as the gatekeepers of the library profession rather than of some ill-defined information profession. Yet, if librarians are going to remain relevant as information providers, the curriculum must evolve in fact as well as in name. No spirited student wants to enroll in a musty program in preparation for a job in a field with diminishing potential. No librarian wants to see a brain drain of the brightest and most motivated students into nontraditional positions. Library educators and practitioners are going to have to work together to incorporate technological change into the education of librarians.

Furthermore, library educators should reconsider how they have attempted to meet the need for managers in libraries. The current practice of offering a management survey course or two is inadequate. On the other hand, the development of dual master's degrees with professional management schools may backfire. Library employers must work with educators to be sure that these students will have places in the library field.

Such is the opinion of a sole student. Although I cannot pretend to speak for all students, I am confident that the majority of my contemporaries would agree with these observations. My opinion must of necessity be shaped by personal experience, but I believe those experiences to be typical of any to be found in graduate library programs today.

It is unfortunate but natural that current students of library schools should feel somewhat let down by their educational experience. With glowing words about computers, changing roles for the librarian and new kinds of careers for those with an MLS, educators have let loose a flood of rising expectations. Unhappily, at this juncture, the curricula and facilities to prepare individuals to take on these roles are lagging far behind. Of even greater importance, though, is the fact that educators cannot begin to bring order to their domain without the help of the primary professionals they serve. Librarians themselves must decide what constitutes an appropriate entry position for the person with a graduate library degree, an undergraduate library degree and the dual professional degree before library schools can move forward in reshaping the curriculum.

NOTES

1. Herbert S. White and Marion Paris, "Employer Preferences and the Library Education Curriculum," *The Library Quarterly* 55 no. 1 (January 1985): 19-20.
2. Margaret Knox Goggin, "Curriculum," in *Library and Information Science Education Statistical Report, 1984,* (State College, PA: Association for Library and Information Science Education, 1984), pp. C9-C11.
3. Ibid., p. C41.
4. Maurice P. Marchant and Carolyn F. Wilson, "Developing Joint Graduate Programs for Librarians," *Journal of Education for Librarianship* 24, no. 1 (Summer 1983): 35.
5. Carol L. Learmont and Stephen Van Houten, "Placements and Salaries 1984: No Surprises," *Library Journal* 110, no. 16 (October 1, 1985): 65.
6. *CPC Salary Survey No. 3* (1985), p. 10. This figure was computed from an average monthly salary offer of $2,375 made for the period ending in July 1984.
7. Michael E.D. Koenig, "Education for Special Librarianship," *Special Libraries* 74, no. 2 (April 1983): 192.

8. John Berry, "New Threats to the MLS?" *Library Journal,* 110, no. 5 (March 15, 1985): 25.

9. White and Paris, p. 13.

10. F. William Summers, "Summary and Comparative Analysis," in *Library and Information Science Education Statistical Report, 1984,* p. SCA9.

11. See White and Paris, pp. 22-31.

14

Summary and Conclusions

Herbert S. White

In one sense this chapter is flawed before it even starts. As we noted in the introduction, an attempt to define optimal—or even minimal—preparation for entry into this profession is highly premature, no matter how many times federal agencies try to catch this bit of lightning in bottles built of perceived competencies. This book is only a beginning, an attempt to identify the issues that require articulation, discussion and ideally, at some point, solution. That process must include the establishment of parameters, since it is at least as important to decide what we do not want to consider talking about as it is to identify the issues for consideration. If we are not prepared to delimit, the process of prescribing what constitutes education and training can become endless, as a number of surveys that have merely asked individuals what they think others should do have already amply demonstrated. A list of "requirements" that takes no cognizance of economic, temporal and political constraints does little more than raise temperatures.

It must be noted that while we feel more or less comfortable in defining *librarianship,* we are far less comfortable in defining the information profession of which this is presumably an integral part. We have tried in this book to ask representatives of various segments of this profession to state their own personal perceptions. The editor was careful not to impose a common format of approach, and he did not ask the writers to poll their colleagues, although some undertook to survey their own literature intensively. These chapters therefore present the personal viewpoints of individuals who are members of their professional groups but are probably not representative of those groups. Representatives tend to depict an average or a consensus; these writers are too far in the vanguard for that. That must be borne in mind when individual authors write that general values and knowledge that can be acquired in a liberal arts college are more important than the specific training skills that can be acquired later. In the abstract they are undoubtedly correct and probably even their colleagues would agree. However, a policy of hiring a better educated but less thoroughly trained individual might cause a great deal of inconvenience for library managers and might make it necessary for them to confront management outside and above the library with the implications of that decision. In their willingness to do this, chapter authors in this book are probably not very typical.

Nevertheless, and despite this obvious risk, it was necessary to choose individuals who could see forests as well as trees and who could avoid the narrow self-seeking trivialization that characterizes so much of our literature. Examples of this attitude are evident in articles, conference papers, and letters and questionnaires addressed to library school administrators. These communications often complain about or demand to know the level of subject specialization provided in preparation for work with one specific type of material that deals with a particular clientele in a narrowly described library. That may be useful for someone looking for a first job, but is that the profession?

Our authors, I am grateful to say, did not stoop to that level of trivialization. As they addressed issues specific to their own parts of this profession (and this book considers it still one profession), they have done so in their own individual styles, but they have done so thoughtfully and even philosophically. They have provided useful material for further discussion, and it is of course part of the responsibility of this chapter to try to identify what some of these concerns are.

EDUCATORS AND PRACTITIONERS

As we have known all along, the issue involves an interaction between educators and employers. To the extent to which employers are themselves graduates of the educational programs from which they now recruit new hires, one can at least assume some mutuality of background and perhaps even some mutuality of overall interest. Almost all library educators are former library practitioners, because the process of moving through an educational program directly into a teaching post, which is so common in the humanities, is almost unheard of in the library field. Some are educators with recent and distinguished experience as practitioners, and part-time faculty members manage to keep a foot in each camp. Communication is not nearly as scarce as some would have us believe. Educators and practitioners belong to the same societies, and it is sometimes noted with irony that the process of evaluation and accreditation, presumably controlled by practitioners as members of the American Library Association, has in fact been "infiltrated" or "subverted" by educators who turn out to have prominent leadership roles in practitioner societies.

Nevertheless, there are clear differences in value systems between a library and a university, and both must be recognized and accommodated. Recent studies show that when a library school closes, there may be a lack of understanding on the part of the academic community of how library education contributes academic rigor and prestige to the university. At least part of this may be because too much attention is paid to the needs and preferences of librarian practitioners and not enough to those of the academic value system. In a recent theme talk at the January 1986 meeting of the Association for Library and Information Science Education (ALISE), Richard Budd suggests no less.[1]

In the discussion of accreditation at that meeting, the question was raised of what would happen if some, and particularly major, library educational institutions opted to ignore an accreditation process which they regarded as too prescriptive. This had particular interest in light of attempts by at least some professional societies to exert greater influence on the requirements for graduate degrees. The question was never answered at the meeting, but this writer has a prediction: Unless the practitioner and educator branches of this common profession can agree both on educational standards and on mechanisms for enforcing those standards, people outside our field, whose concern for economy may be greater than their concern for quality, will rip us to shreds.

There has been no shortage of communication between library educators and those library practitioners who often employ new graduates; they are also the primary recruiters of new candidates for the profession; and they are the alumni of the schools they now tend to criticize so harshly. Of course, friction between educational institutions and the alumni who fondly remember how much better things were in the good old days is not restricted to any one particular discipline. As Cyril Houle has written so charmingly:

> The voice of the aggrieved alumnus is always loud in the land and, no matter what the profession, the burden of complaint is the same. In the first five years after graduation, alumni say that they should have been taught more practical techniques. In the next five years, they say they should have been taught more basic theory. In the tenth to fifteenth years, they inform the faculty that they should have been taught more about administration or about their relations with their coworkers and subordinates. In the subsequent five years, they condemn the failure of their professors to put the profession in its larger historical, social, and economic contexts. After the twentieth year, they insist that they should have been given a broader orientation to all knowledge, scientific and humane. Sometime after that, they stop giving advice; the university has deteriorated so badly since they left that it is beyond hope.[2]

We often hear the argument that educators have lost touch with what is happening in real life, and the suggestion is often made that they return to the experience of working in a library to update their teaching methodologies. All of this assumes that a great deal has happened in the workplace of which educators are unaware, and it contradicts the perception that some educators have that in fact very little has changed in libraries, and certainly much less than would be suggested by some innovative course descriptions. Are practitioners ahead of teachers, or are teachers ahead of practitioners in the advocacy of dynamic improvement and change? Undoubtedly there is some truth in both suggestions, depending on the one hand on the innovative currency of the library director, and on the other on that of the teacher.

In all of this discussion, at least two things seem clear. One is that practitioners appear to have little interest in conducting research. They do very little research and much of the research they do can be considered application development rather than scientific inquiry. They do not insist that their budgets include a research component, even in academic libraries in which such a request would appear perfectly natural. The second point is that they have very little interest in the kind of research that is performed in library schools, either by faculty members or by doctoral students. As this writer has already noted, the recent conference to identify a research agenda for the library profession developed no proposals that could be considered to have a genuine research content, and it expressed no practitioner interest in examining the curriculum of library education programs.[3] It may be that there is less perceived need to investigate and more of a desire to get library educators to implement what they are told to do.

Whatever the quality of discourse between educators and practitioners and employers who are themselves librarians, there is no shortage of contact and communication. As Patricia Berger notes in her chapter, a far different condition exists when we deal with nonlibrarians who have the power and interest to shape our professional requirements. In the federal sector, it was our own professional error that allowed a vacuum to develop into which the Office of Management and Budget (OMB) and the Office of Personnel Management (OPM) were able to step and define professional qualifications and professional criteria for us. Of course, we all face similar problems when we deal with the school superintendents and principals, public library board members and city managers, and corporate personnel administrators who select and hire people whom they then call librarians. The effort to reach an agreement among the various parts of this profession should have at least one powerful motivation—survival.

COMMONALITIES AND DIVERGENCES

Are there then ways to determine, first, those general qualifications on which all can agree, and then those specific skills and knowledge that may be required by individual branches of the profession? Those are the questions with which a united profession must ultimately deal, and the main purpose of this book is to permit at least a preliminary identification of what commonalities and divergences there appear to be.

Importance of Technological and Management Skills

Two common threads can be perceived in all of the chapters: an emphasis on preparation in the use of technology and the need to develop management skills. It is interesting that these issues drew more common support than the so-called bread-and-butter library science courses of basic reference, cataloging and materials selection. Some respondents, and in particular those who represent larger libraries, even went so far as to suggest that these skills could be taught on the job. Other libraries, and in particular smaller ones, argued that students had to have some basic level of common training preparation.

Library Size as a Factor

The differentiation between the attitudes of large and small libraries as employers rather than between types of libraries, such as academic, public and special, was not expected and has not been addressed to any appreciable extent in earlier studies. Most of these have dealt with the attitudes of types of libraries, and only one study, by White and Paris, attempts to differentiate by size of library.[4]

Size of library, it appears, makes a significant difference in the attitude toward expected qualifications of new hires. Some of this comes from a perceived difference in the role of the library in serving its users. Library educators are already familiar with the argument that research libraries have requirements that differ from those of other academic libraries, and Evan Farber makes a strong case in his chapter in support of the librarian's expanded role in the teaching (as differentiated from the research) mission of the institution in college libraries. Recently library educators have begun to hear from junior college and community college librarians, who also argue that their missions and needs are different and that they require students with unique characteristics and educational preparation.

Responsibility for Training

However, much of the differentiation in large-versus-small hinges on the ability of the library to undertake posteducational in-house training programs. Both Sheila Creth and Donald Sager argue that large academic and public libraries should be prepared to mount training programs for new graduates designed not only to teach particular skills but also to acclimate new employees specifically to the needs of that particular library and its user community. Both Sara Laughlin and Elin Christianson point out that in small public and special libraries the resources for such training and, even more so, individuals to do the training may be limited or even nonexistent. Karen Niemeyer supports this observation. In school libraries and media centers in which the newly hired librarian may have less immediate contact with another librarian than with some other administrator, the responsibility for further training may be neither understood nor accepted. Laughlin argues that networks and consortia of small public libraries could take on some of this training responsibility, but she also acknowledges the difficulty of obtaining funding for such endeavors. Christianson's description of on-the-job training as a process of sink or swim applies not only to small special libraries; it applies to large general libraries as well.

This obviously raises a difficult and immediate issue for library education. If large academic and public libraries can agree with regard to what elements of job training can be left out of the master's curriculum because employers will take responsibility for it, then obviously the emphasis on general and theoretic education can be strengthened. But if training is now to be deemphasized, how will new hires be trained for libraries where there are no training facilities and no recognition of the need for training? It is a difficult issue, and it demands at least a clear and forceful statement on the part of professional associations that the person who has been hired is only an apprentice and not a fully qualified librarian and that further training (as well as education) must continue.

There will no doubt be difficulty in establishing let alone enforcing such a continuing learning process, particularly in an environment in which employers don't necessarily assume that a library degree, let alone a graduate library degree or an accredited graduate library degree, is required at all and in which professional associations have made no real attempts to mandate such a requirement. As Sager notes, public librarians at the national level have been unwilling to attempt to mandate anything at all when it comes to qualification requirements. Where any specifications have emerged, it has been at the state level, and with varying degrees of success and enforcement.

A mandated continued education and training experience is at this point only in the planning stage for medical librarians, and even here the association has until now backed away from attempts at enforcement to the extent to which it would ultimately involve some form of deprofessionalization or disbarment. Medical librarians, of course, have the model of medical education which they can emulate, and which their employers can at least recognize. Academic librarians would have a more difficult time, public librarians would have to seek enforcement at the state level and special librarians in industry would probably have extreme difficulty in demanding anything at all of their employers because it is not clear what the alternative threat would be. School librarians and media specialists would probably first face the prospect of wresting control over their specialization from the certification process now firmly ensconced in the education community. A variety of options ranging from persuasion to some form of enforcement appear in all of these settings, but none may ever be implemented. The situation may even get worse, or at least more confusing, as federal agencies attempt to substitute experience and equivalency without much of an attempt to define either, and as advocates within the profession argue for alternative preparation routes in the name of fairness or affirmative action.

UNDERGRADUATE VS. GRADUATE DEGREE PROGRAMS

There are, of course, complexities even within the educational mechanisms for the profession. There are relatively few graduates with unaccredited library science master's degrees, in large part because qualifying for such a degree entails by and large the same cost and effort as obtaining an accredited degree without offering the opportunity for employment in the academic and public libraries that require certification. Most individuals now stuck with such degrees either had no geographic choice or had never been told what limitations they would encounter. Undergraduate degrees are different. Ronald Bryson argues persuasively that not only have such degrees existed all along, but that graduates of such programs have found employment, particularly in school and small public libraries. Whether this is because these students are more specifically prepared for the needs of these libraries or because they can be hired more cheaply by employers who have little interest in evaluating a difference is obviously open to question. The difference between a library science graduate with a bachelor's degree and one with a master's degree is frequently in the eyes of the beholder, and certainly undergraduate degree holders argue with vehemence that they are as fully professional.

Ultimately, it is the employers who have to establish a distinction if indeed one is to be established. Although it is dangerous to oversimplify, it can be argued that undergraduate library degree holders may be better *trained* because in four years of schooling they have a greater opportunity to take more specific courses, but that they are presumably less well *educated* in the liberal arts background assumed to be desirable for professional librarians. They would certainly appear to lack the management and computer preparation being demanded by several of our chapter authors, although it is by no means certain that all accredited graduate programs provide this either. There is also some apparent contradiction between an emphasis on library education at the undergraduate level and the increased emphasis in academic and special libraries on subject degrees, particularly graduate subject degrees. People with undergraduate library degrees may find it difficult to get any sort of graduate degree, because graduate library education programs look at candidates with undergraduate library degrees with little enthusiasm, and some refuse to admit them at all or only on condition that they remedy their liberal arts deficiencies.

Joint Degree Programs

Library schools that grant both bachelor's and master's degrees in library science are relatively rare, and they are rarer still among schools with accredited MLS programs. Certainly where the two degrees coexist in the same institution the school faces the responsibility of explaining how the programs differ, particularly when undergraduate and graduate degree candidates are enrolled in the same course. But this problem does not appear to be of major proportions since students rarely move from an undergraduate to a graduate library degree, despite Bryson's claim that such a progression is not unreasonable. Most often holders of undergraduate degrees have their eyes on jobs that do not require graduate degrees, either from choice or necessity, and they rarely move either to graduate education in library science or to jobs that require a graduate degree.

Of far greater complexity is the growing tendency of schools with accredited library graduate degree programs to offer an undergraduate degree as well, most frequently in information science rather than library science. The trend is still too new to have established any characteristics, but some things are already apparent. The graduates of these programs, like those of unaccredited undergraduate library education programs, do not move on to graduate education, either in this program or in another. They move directly into jobs, and one of the attractions to educators in starting these programs is the fact that indeed there are such jobs. What sort of jobs? The only clear support for such levels of education comes from the information industry, as represented in this book by Herbert Brinberg.

Brinberg is a knowledgeable spokesman, but that industry is quite complex. He argues for an undergraduate degree in the preparation of information technicians. In the job duties for such technicians he includes many of the skills now imparted in graduate library education programs, including such tasks as cataloging and searching. Brinberg recommends an entirely different graduate-level program dealing with information concepts and policy and business principles and practices. This is somewhat similar to the argument for stronger graduate library educational preparation in areas of technology and management. At present, at least, the graduates of undergraduate programs in information science have shown no particular desire to seek graduate degrees, and certainly not graduate degrees in library/information science. They seek their bachelor's degrees to get jobs, and at least up to now they have been able to find them. Are they the kind of jobs *appropriately* filled by undergraduate degree holders? It is really a variant of the same question as applied to the holders of bachelor library degrees.

Relationship Between Degrees and Jobs

One thing appears certain. The profession is going to have to establish and enforce the criteria of what jobs require a graduate degree, what can be done with an undergraduate degree, and what can be done with some other kind of degree or no degree at all. It seems clear that employers will not make that distinction for us, particularly in view of the statement often repeated (at least by this writer) that users cannot be trusted to differentiate between a good library and a poor one, only between more or less expensive ones.

One possible scenario would involve different nomenclatures for institutions depending on the professional level of their staffing. Ideally, a library would be an institution headed by a graduate professional librarian with an accredited degree. In the nomenclature of the medical profession, we could use the term *clinic* or adopt the term *reading room* to denote something else on a lower level. It may be that the terms *librarian* and *library* have already become too generic to be saved, and this writer would feel a twinge of remorse at abandoning such a time-honored set of words, but we have failed to protect them. The term *information center* has been popular in the special library field for some time, and recently some public libraries have begun to adopt the term. The reader may or may not find the nomenclature attractive, but at least for the present it has the advantage of being clean and unspoiled, and we have allowed *library* and *librarian* to be so overused without protecting either that they may now prove to be beyond saving. College libraries, and to some extent school libraries, have shown some preference for the phrase *learning resources center*, but this writer does not regard that as any sort of image improvement. A resources center suggests a rather passive sort of relationship, perhaps even a stockroom or warehouse.

Another thing also appears certain. If the practitioner profession expects an upgrading in the educational programs that produce graduate-level employees, then it must also move to protect the investment that these individuals have made. That protection includes assurance that the jobs for which they prepared are indeed reserved for them, and that less well prepared applicants cannot have them. It is to some extent because we have tolerated and even encouraged this confusion in nomenclature by allowing our volunteer helpers to call themselves librarians that we now encounter the turf problems that Berger describes so accurately.

SUBJECT AND DUAL DEGREES

Other issues very obviously remain, and these can be perplexing. A number of the writers, but especially Elin Christianson in her description of special library needs, stressed the importance of subject degrees, sometimes advanced subject degrees, and that emphasis also appears important in large academic libraries. However, it is not clear what the sequence of these educational experiences is to be. In this writer's experience, the attraction to library education programs of individuals who already have some career experience in subject fields, following education at the bachelor's, master's, and even doctoral level, is not uncommon. Having seen many librarians who later sought law degrees for work in law libraries, we also see occasional candidates with law degrees who now desire a library education. At the same time, it is less likely that MBA graduates will flock to our library education programs, and here the present sequence of first library, then business is likely to remain. A number of schools have developed dual master's programs to allow students to pursue two advanced degrees simultaneously, with some advantage in scheduling and cost. Indiana probably is in the vanguard with nine such packages. While not hugely popular, such dual-degree programs attract a steady stream of applicants.

Louise Schlesinger, writing on behalf of students and herself a graduate of a dual-degree program, points out, however, that the exposure of library science students to the marketing activities of other, more financially rewarding disciplines may cost us some of our better recruits. She also notes the inconsistencies faced by students entering the job market. Some are placed in positions for which the expectation of specialized advanced preparation may not be realistic, while others are placed in assignments that could be performed by any clerk. She notes no direct relationship between the skills demanded and the skills utilized, and neither, from his own observation, does this writer.

UNDERGRADUATE PREPARATION AND BEYOND

The question of subject preparation inevitably brings us back to undergraduate preparation. To earn a graduate subject degree, one obviously must first have an undergraduate subject-specific degree. If that degree is in the humanities, the social sciences or some of the physical sciences—the traditional liberal arts fields—we agree with the widely held view that a good broadly based liberal arts education is the best preparation for librarianship. However, if the degree is in engineering, we must recognize that the pressures of the engineering curriculum still tend to shortchange what we call the liberal arts.

The limits on what can be accomplished in one year of graduate library and information science education may also tempt us to push some of the course work back into an undergraduate curriculum. Again, however, we do this at a price. Demanding specific undergraduate library science courses taken as part of some other bachelor's degree inevitably displaces other courses, and what those courses might be and how useful they might prove to be for librarians is, of course, problematical. Ultimately, taking this to its fullest extent we are led to the suggestion made by Bryson, that undergraduate library degrees serve both as standalone job preparation programs and as an introduction to graduate programs in the same discipline. This suggestion raises two immediate concerns. First, an undergraduate program in library science is not a liberal arts educational process, at least to the extent to which such students take library science courses in lieu of others. Library science courses, in particular at the undergraduate but even at the graduate level, are often more involved with issues of vocational preparation. The second concern involves the attitudes of graduate education programs. At present most of them look with disfavor on candidates who have specialized in librarianship as undergraduates, as they look askance at majors in music performance skills. They could indeed adjust the curriculum to accommodate such candidates and undoubtedly thereby provide more opportunities for genuine graduate level contact. But what would a school do if some of its students came from undergraduate library science programs, others from the more traditional liberal arts route and some even from law school? A curriculum that serves all of these expectations would be difficult if not impossible to devise.

For many reasons the suggestion that we add to the end rather than to the beginning of the graduate educational process is the cleaner and simpler approach. Darlene Weingand argues for a consistent and assured approach to this process in the proposal for the future in her chapter on continuing education. Attractive as her suggestion is, we are still left with uncertainty about guaranteeing its implementation. Can we leave this process to chance and to the recognition by both professionals and employers that this is a good thing that ought to be supported? Up to the present time only medical librarians have taken any concrete steps toward assured implementation, and even they have backed away from the ultimate of enforcement mechanisms with teeth in them. We now find that continuing education is being mandated for teachers and not just physicians, but that imposed requirement has not as yet spilled over into school librarianship or public librarianship. Neither Niemeyer nor Sager nor Laughlin suggests such a step, or even considers its political possibility. It is not unreasonable to expect that such a demand would be opposed not only by employers reluctant to spend the money, but also by some of the librarians who would have to take the courses or attend the workshops and seminars.

ROLE OF PRIOR EXPERIENCE AND INTERNSHIPS

Both library schools and their graduates face the insistence by some libraries that candidates have prior professional experience.

Carried to an extreme, such a requirement would be absurd because if everyone demanded prior experience there would be no place to obtain it. Some of the positions advertised do indeed appear to require prior experience for the individual expected to cope with the job description, and that raises further questions particularly in larger libraries, where it should be possible to differentiate quite clearly between junior and senior positions and the work performed in them. Other libraries prefer experienced candidates because they would rather pay higher salaries than take the time to train junior professionals. Finally, still others are not prepared to pay more but are willing to take advantage of a job market that may permit them to bring in experienced candidates without paying for that experience. This approach is found at least to some extent in special and large academic libraries.

One refreshing proposal emerges quite independently from the chapters written by Sheila Creth, Donald Sager and Erika Love. That proposal is for the establishment of paid post-MLS internships, as planned learning experiences, and indeed some major universities have begun to implement such programs. The internship can be modeled either on the original concept of the Library of Congress program, which involved a one-year training experience as the front end of a permanent job with assignments yet to be determined, or it can be based on the National Library of Medicine approach of making no commitments of employment beyond the one year of the internship. In either case, if internships became the rule rather than the exception, a much clearer distinction could be drawn between what should be learned in school and what should be learned on the first job.

Library schools could indeed concentrate on principles and concepts if specific skills adaptation became a recognized responsibility of the first employer, acting either independently or on behalf of the profession. Such arrangements are not unusual in professional education and training. Graduate chemists and accountants enter into positions in which their lack of initial productivity is accepted and expected, and the receipt of either an M.D. or a J.D. degree signifies only the start of a lengthy and laborious training program to achieve professional status.

In library education the receipt of a master's degree (and sometimes much less) implies instant preparation to do whatever needs to be done, and that public perception is of course highly injurious to our professional image. Serious logistical problems immediately suggest themselves, particularly in institutions in which the individual being hired is the sole professional librarian, and also in those even more common institutions in which the candidate is eagerly awaited because the organization is already understaffed and the backlog is crushing. However, mechanisms can be devised for internships or other forms of learning experience *if* the employer is prepared to accept both the cost and inconvenience of this process as a professional commitment. As Laughlin notes, even for small public libraries, networks and consortia can provide further education and training.

What is lacking is a willingness to deal with the issue on a general professional level. The fact that in this book representatives of three professional groups have independently embraced this concept is certainly a good start.

RECRUITMENT

Many of the chapter authors, and indeed independent surveys, call for more junior librarians with management competencies, but there appears to be a split between those who ask for so-called people skills and those who prefer competence in dealing with the specific tasks of managers—budgeting, reporting and forecasting. Creth points to other paradoxes that may be generic, although she seeks to establish them only for large academic libraries. In one sense we argue that we want innovators, entrepreneurs and risk takers, but there is also an increasing awareness in the management literature of the need for group participation and for team players. Entrepreneurs and innovators do not naturally gravitate to this profession, and if we wanted to attract more of them we would have to devise some recruitment strategies. This writer has observed that the graduates of the Indiana program who are outspoken, impatient and assertive (as management theory tells us junior professionals are supposed to be) may well run into significant difficulties in a library bureaucratic system in which the emphasis may be placed primarily on getting along and not making waves.

Other recruitment concerns may be specific to certain types of libraries. Certainly employers who are not prepared to search nationally and pay relocation expenses limit their options and probably have less right to complain. Writing about the needs of large urban public libraries, Sager stresses the desirability of attracting minority candidates, but they must be recruited to the educational process before they can be recruited to the hiring process, and here the most effective job can probably be done by the very libraries that serve large minority population centers and are therefore in a position to know potential candidates. Sager also notes outside pressures on the recruitment and evaluation process through civil service regulations. Veterans preference points may, for example, be perfectly acceptable as a societal goal, but they have little to do with the qualifications we seek in our field.

The question of who is really going to take responsibility for recruiting individuals into our profession remains unsolved. Library education programs are accused of not recruiting the "right kind" of candidates, and that charge may or may not have some validity. In a larger sense, however, library schools don't really have the opportunity to recruit, only to accept or reject. Recruitment is done by the profession, and by the image it projects. We must also bear in mind the concerns expressed by Nancy Van House.[5] There is an inevitable relationship between the candidates we are able to attract and retain, and the salaries we are prepared to offer. Unless this relationship is borne in mind, the risk noted by Schlesinger that exposure to subject degree programs can also cause us to lose some of our brightest candidates to those programs with higher starting salaries becomes even more grave. Ultimately, we must recognize that if we want bright and energetic students, other disciplines can recognize them and want them, too.

CONCLUSION

In conclusion, a number of issues suggest themselves as topics for further professional discussion, and these questions must be dealt with seriously before we try to tackle solutions and implementation mechanisms:

1. Can we even specify a common professional level of educational preparation or intellectual awareness that everyone who is

called a librarian should be able to demonstrate? I am not talking about specific skills or even competencies. The ability to remember Anglo-American filing rules or to dial up databases does not make a person a professional. Can we insure and protect this process against outsiders and interlopers who want the credit without doing the work? Is it perhaps already too late to save the term *librarian,* and should we abandon it to the volunteers and student assistants who have already laid claim to it?

2. Can we develop distinct specialization tracks that meet the needs of specialized constituencies as separate from and in addition to the requirements for basic professional competencies, whatever we decide to call the individual who demonstrates them? Do we develop these skills as part of the basic degree after paying some attention to a common core, and can we make all of this fit into one manageable program? Do we expect all specializations to be offered at all schools, or certain specializations at certain schools? If it is to be the latter, how do we establish national search pools so that only the individuals with the proper specializations and not just the nearest available candidates will be considered for available jobs? In other words, as with the basic degree, how do we protect the intellectual investment of the candidates? If courses in special librarianship and business databases are essential for work in an investment firm library, will all such libraries abide by the rule that they can consider only those candidates who have the specialized qualifications? Under such conditions, virtually all such searches become national searches. How will small public libraries searching for children's librarians, which rarely pay either interview or relocation expenses, feel about that?

The imposition of specialization tracks within the degree program causes this writer some further discomfort. Many students don't know about the various options available to them in the profession, and it seems unreasonable to demand that they choose at some point in their first semester. Other students, of course, are constrained by geographic factors, and this is particularly true for the increasing body of older students returning to school and to the work force after spending time as full-time homemakers. Many of these students would certainly prefer to keep their options as open as possible, and removing that opportunity is not something we should do lightly. Ideally, specialization would take place after completion of a generalized degree, and that is certainly possible if internships become more broadly accepted. But at least at present this concept conflicts directly with the demand of employers that newly hired graduates be immediately productive and useful.

3. Inevitably we will have to differentiate between and among the parameters of preprofessional experience (practice work with or without academic credit), degree education, job training, continuing education, continuing training and the potential role of internships. How can we make these differentiations more consistent? How can we make them more attractive to students, who invest their time and career potential? How can we sell the recognition of professional responsibility to nonlibrarian employers such as corporate personnel managers, school principals and public library boards?

4. Finally, what sort of people do we *really* want to join us in this profession? There are clear contradictions between the general public perception of librarians—introverted book lovers whom guidance counselors are happy to send us; the so-called people-oriented people we now believe we really prefer and need; and subject specialists to work in particular disciplines. That last concentration appears particularly important to special librarians, but even the Library of Congress makes it clear in its advertisements that in the recruitment of an Arabic cataloger a knowledge of Arabic is more crucial than a knowledge of cataloging. Furthermore, the insistence on subject concentration can be interpreted narrowly or broadly. Will a geology library insist on a degree in geology or petrochemistry? Or will it consider a macrobiologist because such an individual is at least familiar with the process of scientific inquiry and with methods of communication common to scientific disciplines? Is it possible that such a library might accept a nonscientist who has had the necessary library school courses to understand a scientific communication? At present there are barriers to such an appointment, and those barriers stem largely from the biases not of librarians but of scientific users, who prefer to be served by individuals whose academic preparation resembles their own.

We have a great deal to talk about and decide before we begin the prescriptive process of examining and approving specific curricula or developing checklists against which to measure specific candidates. Fortunately, as we noted earlier, in this field in particular educators and practitioners closely share a heritage and a professional identification. The process of communication does not face insurmountable barriers, only the need to rid ourselves of self-righteous preconceptions.

NOTES

1. John N. Berry, III, "Tension, Stress, and Debate: A Report on the January 1986 Conference of the Association for Library and Information Science Education," *Library Journal* 111(5) (March 15, 1986): 29-31.
2. Cyril O. Houle, "The Role of Continuing Education in Current Professional Development," *ALA Bulletin* 61 (March 1967): 263.
3. Herbert S. White, "The Research Agenda: No Panacea, but a First Step," *American Libraries* 13 (April 1982): 270-272.
4. Herbert S. White and Marion Paris, "Employer Preferences and the Library Education Curriculum," *The Library Quarterly* 55 (January 1985): 1-33.
5. Nancy A. Van House, "An Argument for Higher Salaries; MLS Delivers a Poor Payoff on Investment," *American Libraries* 16 (September 1985): 548-551.

Bibliography

Aaron, Shirley. *School Library Media Manual, 1984*. Littleton, CO: Libraries Unlimited, 1985.

Asheim, Lester. *Library, School Preparation for Academic and Research Librarianship; A Report Prepared for the Council on Library Resources*. Washington, DC: Council on Library Resources, 1983.

Association for Library and Information Science Education. *Library and Information Science Educational Statistical Report*. State College, PA: the Association, 1984.

Atkinson, William. "Home Work." *Personnel Journal* 64 (1985): 105-109.

Battin, Patricia. "Developing University and Research Library Professionals: A Director's Perspective." *American Libraries* 14 (1983): 22-25.

———. "The Electronic Library: A Vision for the Future." *EDUCOM Bulletin* 19 (1984): 12-24.

Bechtel, Joan M. "Rotation Day Reflections." *College & Research Libraries News* 46 (1985): 551-555.

Berger, Patricia W. "The New Federalism: How It Is Changing the Library Profession in the U.S." *The Bowker Annual of Library and Book Trade Information,* 28th ed. New York: Bowker, 1983.

Berry, John. "New Threats to the MLS?" *Library Journal* 110 (1985): 25.

———. "Tension, Stress, and Debate: A Report on the January 1986 Conference of the Association for Library and Information Science Education." *Library Journal* 111 (1986): 29-31.

Bishop, D. "Planning the New Medical School Library in Relation to Local and Regional Information Resources." *Bulletin of the Medical Library Association* 59 (1971): 292-295.

Blanchard, Kenneth, and Johnson, Spencer. *The One-Minute Manager.* New York: Morrow, 1982.

Bloomquist, Harold. "The Status and Needs of Medical School Libraries in the United States." *Journal of Medical Education* 38 (1963): 162.

Bolt, Nancy M., and Johnson, Corinne. *Options for Small Public Libraries in Massachusetts.* Chicago: American Library Association, 1985.

Borko, Harold. "Trends in Library and Information Science Education." *Journal of the Association for Information Science* 35 (1984): 185-193.

Branscomb, Harvie. *Teaching With Books, A Study of College Libraries.* Chicago: Association of American Colleges and American Library Association, 1940.

Bucher, Rue, and Stelling, Joan B. *Becoming Professional.* Beverly Hills, CA: Sage, 1977.

Budd, John. "The Education of Academic Librarians." *College & Research Libraries,* 45 (1984): 15-24.

Casey, Genevieve M. "Energy Information Specialist Program: A Feasibility Study." *Journal of Education for Librarianship* 24 (1983): 53-61.

Catholic University of America Graduate Department of Library Science. *Continuing Library and Information Science Educa-*

tion: Final Report to the National Commission on Libraries and Information Science. Washington, DC: U.S. Government Printing Office, 1974.

Colson, J.C. "Professional Ideas and Social Realities: Some Questions About the Education of Librarians." *Journal of Education for Librarianship* 21 (1980): 92.

Compaine, B.M., ed. *Understanding New Media: Trends and Issues in Electronic Distribution of Information.* Cambridge, MA: Ballinger Publishing Company, 1984.

Conant, R.W. *The Conant Report: A Study of the Education of Librarians.* Cambridge, MA: MIT Press, 1980.

Cronin, Blaise, and Martin, Irene, "Social Skills Training In Librarianship." *Journal of Librarianship* 15 (1983): 105.

Daniel, Evelyn H. "Accreditation." *Library Journal* (1985): 49-53.

De Gennaro, Richard. "Shifting Gears: Information Technology and the Academic Library." *Library Journal* 109 (1984): 1204-1209.

Dollard, Peter. "A Paradigm for College Libraries." In *College Librarianship,* edited by William Miller and D. Stephen Rockwood. Metuchen, NJ: Scarecrow Press, 1981.

Donohue, J.C. "Information Resources Management. Passing Fad or New Paradigm?" *Information Management Review* 1 (1985): 68.

Dupuy, Trevor N. *Ferment in College Libraries: The Impact of Information Technology.* Washington, DC: Communication Service Corporation, 1968.

Durrance, Joan. "Issues Forum—Creative Staff Development in Times of Economic Stress." *Public Libraries* 22 (1983): 118-120.

Eshelman, William R. "The Erosion of Library Education." *Library Journal* 108 (1983): 1309-1312.

Fry, M. Ray. "U.S. Department of Education Library Programs, 1984." In *The Bowker Annual of Library and Book Trade Information.* 30th ed. New York: R.R. Bowker, 1985.

Gerczak, Anthony. *Library Selection Project: Job Analysis Report: Phase I.* Sacramento, CA: Selection Consulting Center, 1977.

Giuliano, Vincent E. "The Mechanization of Office Work.' *Scientific American* 247 (1982): 149-164.

Gleaves, Edwin S. "Library Education: Issues for the Eighties." *Journal of Education for Librarianship* 22 (1982): 268.

Goggin, Margaret Knox. "Curriculum." In *Library and Information Science Education Statistical Report, 1984.* State College, PA: Association for Library and Information Science Education, 1984.

Griffiths, José-Marie. "Our Competencies Defined: A Progress Report and Sampling." *American Libraries* 15 (1984): 43-45.

Griffiths, José-Marie, and King, Donald N. *New Directions in Library and Information Science Education.* White Plains, NY: Knowledge Industry Publications, Inc., 1986.

Haycock, Ken. "Editorial—Hard Times . . .Hard Choices." *Emergency Librarian* 9 (1982): 5.

Hayes, Robert M. "Manpower Issues: Implications for Training and Retraining Librarians." *Bulletin of the Medical Library Association* 71 (1983): 427-432.

Heintze, Robert A. "The NCES Survey of Public Libraries, 1982." In *The Bowker Annual of Library and Book Trade Information,* 30th ed. New York: R. R. Bowker, 1985.

Hoadley, Irene B. "Reactions to 'Defining the Academic Librarian.'" *College and Reserach Libraries* 46 (1985): 469-471.

Holley, Edward G. "Defining the Academic Librarian." *College & Research Libraries* 46 (1985): 462-268.

Houle, Cyril. "The Role of Continuing Education in Current Professional Development." *ALA Bulletin* 63 (1967): 263.

Jaques Cattell Press, ed. *American Library Directory*. 38th ed. New York: R. R. Bowker, 1985.

Joint Committee of the Association of American Medical Colleges and the Medical Library Association. *Journal of Medical Education* 40 (1965): 1-72.

Kiesler, Sara. "The Hidden Messages in Computer Networks." *Harvard Business Review* 64 (1986) 46-60.

Koenig, Michael E.D. "Education for Special Librarianship." *Special Libraries* 74 (1983): 185-187.

Kortendick, James J. and Stone, Elizabeth W. "Education Needs of Federal Librarians." *Drexel Library Quarterly* 6 (1970): 264-278.

Lauer, Jonathan D. "Recruiting for the Profession." *College & Research Libraries News* 45 (1984): 388-390.

Loughridge, F. Frendan. "Against the Self-Image of the Trade: Some Arguments Against Computers in Libraries." *Assistant Librarian* 72 (1979): 114-116.

Love, Erika. "Research: The Third Dimension of Librarianship." *Bulletin of the Medical Library Association* 68 (1980): 1-5.

Lukenbill, W.B. "Clinical Education Experiences for Librarians: Implications for Public Libraries." *Public Libraries* 19 (1980): 61.

Lundin, Roy. "The Teacher-Librarian and Information Skills— An Across the Curriculum Approach." *Emergency Librarian* 11 (1983): 8-9.

Lyle, Guy R. *The Administration of the College Library,* 4th ed. New York: H.W. Wilson, 1974.

Malinconico, S. Michael. "People and Machines: Changing Relationships." *Library Journal* 108 (1983): 2222-2224.

Marchant, Maurice P., and Smith, Nathan M. "The Research Library Director's View of Library Education." *College and Research Libraries* 43 (1982): 437-444.

Marchant, Maurice P., and Wilson, Carolyn F. "Developing Joint Graduate Programs for Librarians." *Journal of Education for Librarianship* 24 (1983): 35.

Maurer, Charles. "Close Encounters of Diverse Kinds: A Management Panorama for the Director of the Smaller College Library." In *College Librarianship,* edited by William Miller and D. Stephen Rockwood. Metuchen, NJ: Scarecrow Press, 1981.

Miles, W.D. *A History of the National Library of Medicine.* Washington, DC: U.S. Government Printing Office, 1982.

Moffett, William A. "Reflections of a College Librarian: Looking for Life and Redemption This Side of ARL." *College & Research Libraries* 45 (1984): 338-349.

Moran, Barbara. *Academic Libraries: The Changing Knowledge Centers of Colleges and Universities. ASHE-ERIC Higher Education Research Report,* no. 8. Washington, DC: Association for the Study of Higher Education, 1984.

Naisbitt, John. *Megatrends: Ten New Directors Transforming Our Lives.* New York: Warner Books, Inc., 1984.

Olson, Edwin E. *Survey of Federal Libraries Fiscal Year 1972.* Prepared for the National Center for Education Statistics and the Federal Library Committee. Washington, DC: U.S. Government Printing Office, 1975.

Olson, Lowell. "New Modes for Continuing Education." *Bookmark* 41 (1983): 207-216.

Olson, Margrethe H., and Lucas, Jr., Henry C., "The Impact of Office Automation on the Organization: Some Implications for Research and Practice." *Communications of the ACM* 25 (1982): 838-847.

Peters, Thomas J. and Waterman, Jr., Robert H. *In Search of Excellence.* New York: Warner, 1982.

Pitts, Judy M. "A Creative Survey of Research Concerning Role Expectations of Library Media Specialists." *School Library Media Quarterly* 10 (1983): 166-167.

Pizer, Irwin H. "Looking Backward, 1984-1959: Twenty-five Years of Library Automation—A Personal View." *Bulletin of the Medical Library Association* 72 (1984): 335-348.

Porat, M.U. and Rubin, M.R. *The Information Economy: Definition Measurement,* 9 vols. Washington, DC: Government Printing Office, 1977.

Powell, Lawrence Clark. *A Passion for Books.* New York: World Publishing, 1958.

Powell, Ronald, and Creth, Sheila. "Knowledge Bases and Library Education." *College and Research Libraries* 47 (1986): 16-27.

Rayward, W. Boyd. "Academic Librarianship: The Role of Library Schools." In *Issues in Academic Librarianship, Views and Case Studies for the 1980s and 1990s,* edited by Peter

Spyers-Duran and Thomas W. Gann, Jr. Westport, CT: Greenwood Press, 1985.

———"Conflict Interdependency, Mediocrity; Librarians and Library Educators." *Library Journal* 108 (1983): 1313-1317.

Richardson, John. "Theory into Practice: W.W. Charters and the Development of Library Education." In *Reference Services and Library Education: Essays in Honor of Frances Neel Cheney.* Lexington, MA: Lexington Books, 1983.

Riggs, Donald E. "Leadership Is Imperative." *Journal of Education for Librarianship* 24 (1984): 208-211.

Roberts, Lynn. "Megatrends: Implications for Staff Development." *Colorado Libraries* 9 (1983): 8-11.

Robinson, Gleniece. "Management Development Programs in Large Public Libraries in the U.S." *Public Library Quarterly* 5 (1984): 27.

Roper, Fred W. "Special Programs in Medical Library Education, 1957-1971." *Bulletin of the Medical Library Association* 61 (1973): 387-395.

Rush, James E. "The Challenges of Educating Library and Information Science Professionals, 1985 and Beyond." *Technical Services Quarterly* 3 (1985/86): 102.

Schmidt, Dean. "Qualifications Sought by Employers of Health Sciences Librarians, 1977-1978." *Bulletin of the Medical Library Association* 68 (1980): 58-63.

Schmidt, Karen A. "The Other Librarians, Undergraduate Library Science Programs and Their Graduates." *Journal of Education for Librarianship* 24 (1984): 236.

Sewell, Winifred. "Study of Federal Library/Information Service Staffing as Affected by Classification and Qualification

Standards." Prepared for the Federal Library Committee. Washington, DC, 1978.

Shera, Jesse. *Foundations of Education for Librarianship.* New York: Becker & Hayes, 1972.

Smith, Nathan, Marchant, Maurice, and Nielson, Laura. "Education for Public and Academic Librarians: A View from the Top." *Journal of Education for Librarianship* 24 (1984): 233-245.

Stevens, Norman. "Centralization/Decentralization: New Views on an Old Issue." *Library Issues* 4 (1984).

Stokes, Roy. "Master of What?" *Wilson Library Bulletin* 51 (1976): 331.

Stone, Elizabeth. "Continuing Professional Education." In *ALA Yearbook,* 1983.

Stueart, Robert D. "The Education of Academic Librarians." In *Academic Librarianship: Yesterday, Today, and Tomorrow,* edited by Robert Stueart. New York: Neal-Schuman Publishers, 1982.

Todaro, Julie. "Public Librarianship in Library Education: What Are We Doing." *Public Libraries* 21 (1982): 159.

U.S. Civil Service Commission. "Position—Classification Standards, Librarian Series, GS-1410." Washington, DC, 1966.

U.S. Civil Service Commission. "Qualification Standards, Librarian Series, GS-1410." Washington, DC, 1968.

U.S. Intergovernmental Library Cooperation Project. "Toward a Federal Library and Information Services Network: A Proposal." Submitted to the National Commission on Library and Information Science and the Library of Congress. Washington, DC: U.S. Library of Congress, 1982.

U.S. National Center for Educational Statitics. Preliminary Report: Library General Information Survey, LIBGIS III: Public Libraries, 1977-78. Washington, DC: The Center, 1982.

U.S. Office of Management and Budget. "Performance of Commercial Activities." Circular no. A-76 (revised). Washington, DC (1983): 1.

Van House, Nancy A. "An Argument for Higher Salaries; MLS Delivers a Poor Payoff on Investment." *American Libraries* 16 (1985): 548-551.

Vavrek, Bernard. "Profession Needs New Entry Level." *American Libraries* (1982): 271.

Veaner, Allen B. "1985 to 1995: The Next Decade in Academic Librarianship, Part II." *College Research Libraries* 46 (1985): 295-308.

Wedgeworth, Robert, ed. *The ALA Yearbook of Library and Information Services,* vol. 10. Chicago: ALA, 1985.

Weingand, Darlene E. "Competencies for Public Librarians: A Beginning." *Public Libraries* 21 (1982): 159.

Weingand, Darlene E., and Ryan, Noel. "Managerial Competencies and Skills." *Journal of Library Administration* 6 (1985): 23-44.

White, Herbert S. "Continuing Education—Myth and Reality." *Indiana Libraries* 4 (1984): 138-145.

———. "Critical Years for Library Education." *American Libraries* 10 (1979): 468-470, 479-481.

———. "Defining Library Competencies." *American Libraries* 14 (1983): 618.

White, Herbert S., and Paris, Marion. "Employer Preferences and Library Education Curriculum." *The Library Quarterly* 55 (1985): 6-10.

Williamson, Charles C. *Training for Library Service. A Report Prepared for the Carnegie Corporation of New York.* New York and Boston: D.B. Updike, 1923.

Wilson, Pauline. "Impending Change in Library Education: Implications for Planning." *Journal of Education for Librarianship* 18 (1978): 159.

Winston, Stephanie. *The Organized Executive.* New York: Warner, 1983.

Zackert, Martha Jane K. *The Government Library: Simulation for the Study of Administration of a Special Library—The Federal Library Model,* 3 parts. Washington, DC: The Catholic University of America, Graduate Department of Library Science, 1971.

Zuboff, Shoshana. "New Worlds of Computer-Mediated Work." *Harvard Business Review* 60 (1982): 142-152.

Index

The Administration of the College Library, 62-63
ALA-accredited schools, 33, 41,44-45, 180
Allerton Invitational Conference on Education for Health Science Librarianship, 109-111, 118, 119
Allred, John, 84, 86
American Libraries, 39
American Library Association (ALA), 74, 176-177, 198
American Library Directory, 29, 38
Annual Statistics for Medical School Libraries in the United States and Canada for 1983/1984, 111
Asheim, Lester, 56
Atkinson, William, 12
Austin College, 51

Battin, Patricia, 4-6, 15, 18, 56-57, 60
Berger, Patricia, 255, 262
Bloomquist, Harold, 106, 117
Bolt, Nancy, 67, 70, 71
Borko, Harold, 56
Branscomb, Harvie, 58, 60
Brinberg, Herbert, 260
Bryson, Ronald, 259, 260
Bucher, Rue, 42
Budd, John, 56
Budd, Richard, 253

Bulletin of the Medical Library Association, 110

Casey, Genevieve M., 97
Charters, W.W., 74
Christianson, Elin, 257, 262
CLENERT (ALA Continuing Library Education Network and Exchange Round Table), 229, 231
Clutter's Last Stand, 132
College librarianship
 aspects of, 52-56
 preparation for, 56-61
 recruitment for, 61-63
College libraries
 characteristics of, 49-52
Colson, J.C., 38, 42
Committee on Accreditation (COA) 176-183, 186
Committee on Institutional Cooperation, 187
Conant, Ralph W., 34, 150-151
Continuing education. *See* Professional education
Cooper, John A.D., 148-149
Corporate librarianship
 education for, 91-94
 subject specialization for, 96-99
Corporate libraries
 and corporate dynamics, 94-96
 staff size, 90-91

Creth, Sheila, 15-16, 56, 257, 265, 266
Cronin Blaise, 39, 40

Dana, John Cotton, 74
Daniel, Evelyn H., 174, 215
Darling, Louise, 119
De Gennaro, Richard, 6, 8
Denver Public Library, 70
Dewey, Melvil, 173
Dickinson, C., 59-60
Dollard, Peter, 54-55, 57
Dupuy, Trevor N., 207
Durrance, Joan, 75

Eshelman, William R., 181

Federal government libraries
  and continuing education, 143-145
  future needs of, 149-151
  and standards, 141-143
Federal Interagency Field Libraries (FIFL), 148
Federal Library and Information Center Committee (FLICC), 147-148
Flexner, Abraham, 76
Futurist, 134

General Systems Theory, 208-209
Giuliano, Vincent E., 10-11
Gleaves, Edwin S., 34, 45-46
Graduate education programs
  accreditation of, 176-180
  distribution of, 181-183
  school closings, 183-190
  shift toward, 174
  strategies, 190-195
Guidelines for Medical School Libraries, 106

Hanks, Gardner, 208-209, 210, 211-212
Haycock, Ken, 129
Hoadley, Irene B., 15, 56
Holly, Edward G., 56
How to Put More Time in Your Life, 132
Houle, Cyril O., 225-226, 254
Hutchins, Robert Maynard, 187

Illinois State Library, 85
Indiana University, 83, 186
Information centers. *See* Federal government libraries
The Information Economy: Definition and Measurements, 155
Information industry
  definition, 155-161
  needs of, 161-163
  training for, 163-167
In Search of Excellence, 130-131
I Want to Change but I Don't Know How, 132

Johnson, Corinne, 67
Johnson, Lyndon, 106, 194-195
Journal of Education for Library and Information Science, 231
Journal of Librarianship, 39

King Research, 75
Koenig, Michael, 92, 242
Kortendick, James J., 144
Kronick, David A., 117, 118

Laughlin, Sara, 257-264, 266
Library profession
  commonalities and divergences within, 255-258
  and degrees, 258-264

experience and internships in, 264-266
interaction within, 252-255
and recruitment concerns, 266-267
Library Services and Construction Act (LSCA), 28
Library students
and computer technology, 242-246
curriculum possibilities, 246-248
and dual degrees, 240-242
entry-level job requirements, 237-240
Love, Erika, 265
Lukenbull, W.B., 42
Lundin, Roy, 128
Lyle, Guy R., 62-63

Maidment, Robert, 137
Malinconico, Michael, 11
Marchant, Maurice, 72
Martin, Irene, 39, 40
Matheson, Nina W., 148-149
Maurer, Charles, 53-54
Media centers. *See* School libraries, Media specialists
Media specialists
characteristics of, 125-137
Medical libraries
current and future needs of, 111-115
developments affecting, 105-111
problems of, 117-119
prospects for, 117-119
Medical Library Assistance Act (MLAA) of 1965, 106, 107, 108, 148
Medical Library Association, 109, 111

Miami University (OH) School of Business Administration Executive Development Program for Library Administration, 41
Moffett, William, 54, 55, 60, 62
Molz, R. Kathleen, 31
Moran, Barbara, 56

Naisbitt, John, 12-13, 70
National Center for Educational Statistics (NCES), 27-28, 34, 40-41
National Commission on Libraries and Information Science (NCLIS), 144-145
National Institutes of Health, 105
National Library of Medicine (NLM), 106-107, 108, 118
  Medical Subject Headings (MeSH), 108
  MEDLARS, 108-109
  MEDLINE, 108-109
  Regional Medical Library (RLM) network, 107
Nielson, Laura, 72
Niemeyer, Karen, 257, 264

Oberlin College, 51
Office of Management and Budget (OMB), 147-148
Office of Personnel Management (OPM), 145-147, 175, 216, 237-238
Olson, Lowell, 85-86
The One-Minute Manager, 131
The Organized Executive, 132

Paris, Marion, 91-92, 100, 256
Peters, Thomas J., 131
Porat, Mark U., 155, 156

Position-Classification Standards, 142-143
  See also Federal government libraries
Powell, Lawrence Clark, 61-62
Powell, Ronald, 15-16
Professional education
  and competence evaluation, 228-230
  continuum of, 224-225
  opportunities for, 225-228
  payment for, 231-232
  a proposal for, 232-234
  provision of, 230-231
Public Libraries, 41, 228
Public libraries, large
  future needs, 44-46
  personnel needs in, 28-29
  recruitment factors for, 29-37
Public librarians, large libraries
  educational expectations for, 37-44
Public librarians, small libraries
  education of, 74-86
Public libraries, small, 67-86
  emerging needs of, 71-72
  and political decentralization, 71
Public Library Association (PLA), 27, 31, 43

Qualification Standards, 141-142
  See also Federal government libraries

Rayward, W. Boyd, 56, 76, 185
Riggs, Donald, 78
Robbins-Carter, Jane B., 10
Roberts, Lynn, 69-70, 71, 72
Robinson, Gleniece, 41
Roper, Fred W., 115
Rush, James E., 38

Sager, Donald, 257, 258, 264, 265, 267
Saint John's College (MD), 49
Schlesinger, Louise, 262-263
Schmidt, C. James, 208-209, 210, 211-212
Schmidt, Karen A., 214
Schraml, Mary L., 11
School libraries, 123-138
Sewell, Winifred, 142-143, 146, 151
Shera, Jesse, 74, 76, 77, 78, 184
Smith College, 51
Smith, Nathan, 72, 73
Stelling, Joan, 42
Stephan, Sandy, 82
Stevens, Norman, 9
Stokes, Roy, 202
Stone, Elizabeth, 84, 144
Stone Hills Area Library Services Authority (ALSA), 74, 83, 86
Stueart, Robert, 56, 116

Teaching with Books, A Study of College Libraries, 58
Todaro, Julie, 45
Trezza, Alphonse, 145
Turock, Betty, 33-34, 45

Undergraduate library education
  and the bachelor's degree, 212-216
  and degree structure, 205-206
  and employment, 209
  and library development, 201-205
  and models of librarianship, 206-209
U.S. Department of Education, 229
University librarians
  education of, 17-19

recruitment of, 19-23
requirements for, 13-17
University of Maryland's College of Library and Information Service
  Library Administration Development Program, 41
University of Washington
  School of Librarianship, 108
University of Wisconsin
  Certificate of Professional Development in Library Management, 85
University research libraries
  impact of economics on, 6-7
  impact of technology on, 4-6
  organizational changes in, 9-13
  and university environment, 7-8

Van House, Nancy, 267
Vavrek, Bernard, 204
Veaner, Allen B., 5, 10, 15, 52, 56, 57
Voluntary Recognition System (VRS), 231

Waterman, Robert H., 131
Weingand, Darlene E., 41, 229, 264
Wheaton College, 62
White, Herbert, 56, 75, 82, 91-92 100, 215-216, 256
Williamson, C.C., 174, 175
Wilson, Louis R., 62-63
Wilson, Pauline, 38